**Stuka-Pilot Hans-Ulrich Rudel**

# His Life Story in Words and Photographs

GÜNTHER JUST

# Stuka-Pilot Hans-Ulrich Rudel

*Translated from the German by* David Johnston

**Schiffer Military History**
Atglen, PA

Translated from the German by David Johnston.

Printed in the United States of America.
ISBN: 0-88740-252-6

This book originally published under the title,
*Stuka-Oberst Hans Ulrich Rudel*,
by Motorbuch Verlag, Postfach 1370, 7000 Stuttgart 1,
© 1986. ISBN: 3-87943-390-9.

We are interested in hearing from authors with
book ideas on related subjects.

Published by Schiffer Publishing Ltd.
4880 Lower Valley Road
Atglen, PA 19310
Phone: (610) 593-1777
FAX: (610) 593-2002
E-mail: Schifferbk@aol.com.
Please write for a free catalog.
This book may be purchased from the publisher.
Please include $3.95 postage.
Try your bookstore first.

# CONTENTS

# FOREWORD

With 2,500 combat missions on the Eastern Front from 1941 to 1945 and his extraordinary, unique successes, Rudel is the outstanding combat pilot of all time. His personal battle exceeded human dimensions, becoming literally a strategic factor in the war.

In a war of mass, one of materiel, one man singlehandedly destroyed over 500 tanks and sank a battleship: Rudel's success has become legend.

The story of Rudel's achievements is that of a man who continually displayed the noblest human virtues in the midst of a terrible drama, a struggle for life and death.

Many extraordinary personalities rose to prominence from the nameless millions of the German army, navy and air force. Above all of these heroes stood Rudel, the Stuka pilot.

It was characteristic of this man that his unparalleled acts of heroism and his fame began at a time when the tide of the war had turned against German arms. The situation was already desperate by the time his star really began to shine.

What divine ordinance protected the life of this unique pilot? Perhaps this man, whose life was marked by the noblest soldierly and human virtues, readiness for service, modesty and comradeship, was spared as an example, not only for the youth of Germany, but for Europe. A film should be produced on Rudel's life — uninfluenced by political prejudice and tendentious propaganda — to complement this outstanding illustrated history.

The will of Rudel, which in time of war triumphed over the might of the machine, and in peace allowed him to overcome his wounds and handicaps — all this should be shown in a documentary film in order to prove, as this book does, that men of honour and principle still live in this world.

This necessary historical film on Rudel should be dedicated to the youth of the bloodied, shattered homelands of Europe, because they will all one day be citizens of a united Europe.

I congratulate the authors and publishers of this impressive documentary work on the legendary Stuka *Oberst* and his battles which remain unique in the history of warfare. Of Rudel I can only say what we in the Royal Air Force said of German fighter ace Walter Nowotny during the war:
What a pity that he hadn't worn our uniform!

Pierre Clostermann
France, early 1975

**Pierre Clostermann** With 33 confirmed air victories (14 flying Tempest fighters) and 420 combat missions, Pierre Clostermann was France's most successful fighter pilot of the Second World War. As a "Free French" pilot he went to a fighter training school in Wales in 1942, later joining 341 "Alsace" Squadron (radio call sign "Turban") and was awarded the Distinguished Flying Cross by British Aviation Minister Sir Archibald Sinclair. (Fighter pilots received this decoration after five victories and about 100 missions. The Bar to the DFC was awarded after 10 to 20 victories and the Distinguished Service Order was issued only to Squadron Leaders or Wing Commanders with 20 victories or 300 missions. The highest British decoration for bravery, the Victoria Cross, was awarded to only one fighter pilot during the war, Squadron Leader Nicholson.)

Pierre Clostermann was awarded his first Distinguished Flying Cross after 8 confirmed victories and nearly 300 missions; he received his second following 370 missions and 20 victories and the Distinguished Service Order after 420 missions and 33 victories, having commanded a squadron and later a wing.

After the war he wrote several books on his wartime experiences, including *The Big Show —Memories of a French Fighter Pilot in the RAF*, which was also printed in Germany.

Wartime enemies Rudel and Clostermann have maintained a close friendship since the end of the war of a type which could probably only develop between fellow pilots.

**Max Immelmann**

8

**Hans-Ulrich Rudel**

June 1916 — For nearly two years the bloody battles have raged on the western front of a European war which the history books would call the First World War. On June 18, six days before the massive British and French offensive on the Somme, the "Eagle of Lille", *Oberleutnant* Max Immelmann, *Jagdstaffel* leader and wearer of the *Pour le Mérite*, was killed when his aircraft crashed from an altitude of 2,000 meters following his 15th victory. The investigating committee of the German Sixth Army determined that the crash which had taken the life of the famous fighter pilot was the result of fire from his own machine gun striking the propeller of the light Fokker E-III, the motor tearing loose and collapsing the bracing wires which then led to the shearing off of the aircraft's wings.

Fourteen days later, on July 2, 1916, a minister's son saw his first light of a warring world in Konradswaldau, a village between Landeshut and Gottesberg in Silesia. Twenty-five years later he would achieve unique success as member of a Stuka Geschwader which bore the title of Immelmann and become the only soldier in history to be awarded the highest German decoration for valour. His name was Hans-Ulrich Rudel, a pilot revered by German soldiers during the Second World War as "the Eagle of the Eastern Front." The long awaited son and heir of Rev. Johannes Rudel and his wife Martha (nee Muckner), who weighed only five and three quarter pounds at birth, certainly gave no indication that he would one day overcome the most difficult trials as a soldier. If someone had suggested this to his two sisters Ingeborg and Johanna, who called the youngster "Uli", they would have laughed at him. He was a very delicate and nervous child and until he was twelve his mother had to hold his hand whenever there was a thunderstorm. His older sister scoffed, "there is nothing in the world which could frighten Uli enough to get him to go into the cellar alone." Rudel's mother mentioned this in 1950 in her introduction to his book *Trotzdem*. She wrote, "this mockery immediately went against Uli's honour and he began to harden and take part in many sports. Now his studies took a back seat to sports. His school report was not presented to his father for signature until summer vacation was over.

I once asked his teacher, "how is Uli at school?" He replied, "as a boy lovely, as a student terrible."

After the minister's son had conquered his fear — as is common with children — no tree was too high, no ski slope to steep, no brook too wide and no boy's prank too risky. "Uli" always wanted to prove to himself, to his sisters and to his schoolmates that, "one can do anything if one wants to." Later, in action, this will to maintain his self-control remained an ingredient of his personality. In hopeless situations he maintained, "only he who gives up on himself is lost!" "Uli" discovered that nature places physical limits on a person's will in 1924 as an eight year old in Seiferdau, where his father had been transferred. Here the future "Eagle of the Eastern Front" took to the air for the first time. Thirteen years later, his instructor would say to him and his classmates before their first solo, "staying up is nothing!."

Rudel made his first acquaintance with this element with the aid of his father's umbrella while his parents were away. Excited by stories of a flying display in Schweidnitz, "Uli" jumped from the second story of the rectory with the open umbrella. The umbrella collapsed and the youngster fell into a flower bed. This cushioned his fall somewhat, although he did suffer a broken leg.

In the course of the Second World War Rudel never made use of his parachute. This was probably unique in the *Luftwaffe* since he was shot down by Russian flak and infantry weapons over thirty times, although never by fighters, and was sometimes forced to land in very unfavourable terrain. During close support missions at low altitude there was little opportunity to abandon a damaged aircraft and take to one's parachute.

The broken leg resulting from the umbrella jump could not dampen Rudel's enthusiasm for flying. With his leg still in a cast he said, "Now I want to become a proper pilot!" This attitude was typical for him during the war and afterwards when, in spite of an artificial leg, he achieved excellent results in sporting competitions. During his school years, mainly in Schweidnitz, Sagan, Niesky, Gorlitz and Lauban, he was to be found more often on the ski slopes, at sports fields and on his motorcycle than at his books and studies. However, by last-minute cramming he was able to fill the gaps in his studies, matriculating at the secondary school in Lauban, Lower Silesia. His achievements on the sports field and his numerous successes at sporting meets at school and in the Hitler Youth allowed him to become a decathlete for whom a great, even "Olympic", future was predicted by trainers and gymnastics instructors.

Following matriculation Rudel hoped to become a civil pilot. However, the rectory budget crossed his career plans: his family could not afford the expensive training, as his sister was already studying medicine. He decided to become a sporting instructor. When Rudel one day heard of the formation of a new *Luftwaffe* he was determined: "I will become a pilot!" He volunteered for the *Luftwaffe* officer corps, taking the difficult entrance examinations in 1936 and receiving an acceptance pass for the air warfare school at Wildpark-Werder near Berlin.

Before beginning his training as an officer cadet and student pilot, Rudel did two months service in the *Reichsarbeitsdienst* (Reich Labour Service) and was employed with his labour battalion on the Neisse river control project near the well known Muskau mud baths in the Cottbus district. Rudel's basic infantry training began on 4 December 1936 at Wildpark-Werder; officer cadet and pilot training followed from June 1937. In June 1938, on completion of this training, he was posted from the Air Warfare School as an *Oberfähnrich* to I. *Gruppe* of *Stuka Geschwader 168* at Graz-Thalerhof in the Austrian province of Styria. It was there during dive bomber training that Rudel flew the Junkers Ju 87 for the first time; an aircraft which was to be inextricably linked with his name and success. Dive bomber training involved formation flying, battle formation practice, practice dive bombing attacks at angles up to 90 degrees with cement bombs, low altitude flying and air firing.

Rudel later related, "One could not say that I learned quickly, especially since the rest of the pilots in the unit were already flying well when I arrived. My progress was slow, too slow for my *Staffelkapitän*, who believed that I would never make it."

Here, as at the Air Warfare School, Rudel spent every spare minute at sports. On every free weekend he wandered through the magnificent countryside surrounding Graz and climbed every accessible mountain. He thought little of mess life which did little to improve his position as the cadet who was slow to get the hang of Stuka flying. His superiors said of him, "He doesn't smoke, drinks only milk, has no tales to tell about women and spends all of his free time at sports: Rudel is a strange bird!" When a message arrived one day at the Graz Stuka unit requesting the release of a *Leutnant* or *Oberfähnrich* for training for operational air reconnaissance, the *Staffelkapitän* saw an opportunity to get rid of the "strange bird" and slow learner. All of Rudel's efforts to have his transfer to the reconnaissance school at Hildesheim, Lower Saxony rescinded came to nothing. When his reconnaissance training began on December 1, 1938, Rudel received another disappointment. Because observers also served as aircraft commanders, they were not permitted to fly the aircraft. At the conclusion of his training as an observer, which included a basic aerial photography course, Rudel was promoted to *Leutnant* and posted on 1 January 1939 to *Fernaufklärungsgruppe 121* at Prenzlau. Shortly before the beginning of the Polish campaign, the *Gruppe* was transferred to Schneidemühl near the "Polish Corridor" which had separated Danzig and East Prussia from the Reich since the signing of the Treaty of Versailles (6/28/1919).

During the Polish campaign *Leutnant* Rudel flew his first mission as the observer and commander of a reconnaissance aircraft. During the flight the only shots he took were with a camera and no enemy fighters were encountered. In subsequent missions Polish fighters were met only rarely. These missions were not pleasure trips however; Polish anti-aircraft gunners made great efforts to bring down the German reconnaissance aircraft which were photographing bridges and rail junctions. Several missions were flown over the Brest Litovsk—Kovel—Luck rail line. The German High Command wanted to know where Polish troop movements were taking place and the dispositions of the Russians, who had moved into eastern Poland with no reaction from the French and British.

The Red Army occupied the territory in eastern Poland up to the river Bug as agreed in the German-Soviet Border and Friendship Treaty of 9/28/1939. The Blitzkrieg against Poland, which came to be known as the "Eighteen Day War", ended on September 18. Heroic Polish resistance continued in Warsaw until September 27; the fortress of Modlin capitulated several days later.

Leutnant Rudel and his reconnaissance unit transferred back to Prenzlau on November 10, and he was awarded the Iron Cross Second Class for his missions over Poland. In the meantime, Rudel endeavoured to secure a transfer to a Stuka unit. He was sent to Flying Training Regiment 43 at Vienna-Stammersdorf. Soon afterwards the Regiment, which trained *Luftwaffe* recruits, moved to Crailsheim where Rudel was serving as Regimental Adjutant when the Germans launched their western campaign. As they had already done in Poland, the Stukas served as flying artillery, preparing the way for the onrushing German Army. Rudel continued to submit requests for transfer. Finally, he bypassed official channels by calling the Personnel Department at the Air Ministry in Berlin. For whatever reason, perhaps to get some peace from their tormentor, Rudel's request for transfer was approved after the conclusion of the western campaign. (Cease-fire signed June 22, 1940, Compiegne forest near Paris) He was posted to his old Stuka unit from Graz, which was now stationed in northern

France near Caen, the capital city of the *departement* of Calvados. There one of the Staffel's officers endeavoured to pass on to Rudel the operational lessons which had been learned during the French campaign. However, in the limited time available he was unable to make up for what he had missed. He still could not master the Stuka. This plus the fact that this "strange bird" drank only milk even in France, while his superiors were sampling the famous Calvados in the mess, and that he spent every free moment at sports and declined to join the nightly expeditions through the night life of Caen, once again made him a conspicuous outsider.

On September 1, 1940, Rudel was promoted to *Oberleutnant*. When the *Stukagruppe* was transferred to the southeast theatre prior to the commencement of the Balkan campaign, the "strange bird" was sent to the Stuka Replacement *Gruppe* in Graz. There he was to be taught the subtleties of flying the Stuka which had so far eluded him. For a few days at the beginning of the Balkan campaign the airfield at Graz-Thalerhof was a base for the aircraft of *General der Flieger* von Richthofen's *VIII Fliegerkorps*. Rudel watched the bomb-laden Stukas take off on missions and once again he was not with them.

On a practice mission he suddenly sensed, "now I have got it; now I can make the machine do everything I want it to." From then on, no instructor could lose him in aerial manoeuvres; no flying trick or aerobatic manoeuvre could shake him off; his aircraft always remained close behind that of his instructor ahead. Most of his practice bombs now fell within the ten meter target circle and in air firing his bursts were rarely off the mark. Once he scored ninety of a possible one hundred.

Soon after Easter 1941, Rudel was posted to *I. Gruppe* of *Stukageschwader 2 Immelmann*, which was stationed at an airfield near Molar on the southern tip of the Greek peninsula of Peloponnes. He was happy that at last he was to see action as a Stuka pilot. The conquest of the Greek-British island of Crete began on May 20, 1941 with the dropping of German paratroops. The Stukas of *I. Gruppe Immelmann* flew regular sorties against the island and units of the British fleet operating in the waters around Crete. Rudel watched the aircraft take off. Chance and the prejudice of the commanding officer and his adjutant stood between him and his first mission. The *Gruppe* Adjutant was by chance his Stuka instructor from Caen, who thought little of Rudel's flying ability. In response to his question, "What are you doing here? Have you learned so much already?", Rudel replied, "I am now completely the master of my aircraft." The adjutant said, "I will present your case to the commanding officer." When *Oberleutnant* Rudel reported to the CO he was greeted with the words, "We know each other already." Rudel denied this. "Of course we know each other, because my adjutant certainly knows you. I even know you so well that for the time being you will not be allowed to fly with my *Gruppe*."

In his book *Trotzdem*, Rudel wrote of the feelings which stirred in him: ". . . Often the fires of rebellion blazed high within me. Discipline! Discipline! Control yourself; only thus can you become something. You must have understanding for all, even for the mistakes of your superiors. Only thus can you become a better commander and show understanding to your subordinates. Control yourself; your time is yet to come when you will really be worth something. Never lose your self-confidence." And the time for the man who later would have no higher award for bravery left to win, came; soon he would show the results he was capable of achieving in action.

By June 1, 1941, Crete was in German hands. Soon afterwards Rudel had to deliver a Ju 87 to the aircraft production facility at Cottbus for repairs. There, in the early hours of the morning, he heard over the radio of Germany's attack on Russia. On the same day he flew a repaired aircraft to Insterburg in East Prussia and from there a half hour flight southeast to the air base at Raczki. *I. Gruppe* had just transferred there from Crete. The commander attached him to *1. Staffel*, which was led by *Oberleutnant* Ewald Janssen (Knight's Cross 10/31/1944).

Janssen was also an outsider with the *Gruppe* staff and allowed Rudel to fly with him as his wingman on the next mission. His first sortie against the enemy was directed against Soviet troop and armor concentrations in the area of Grodno and Njemen and in the Wolkowysk region. As Technical Officer, Rudel worked between sorties and in the evening with the head of maintenance to ensure that the aircraft were ready for operations. Sleep was seldom on the schedule for the Technical Officer and the ground crews.

During the first missions in Russia it became apparent to Rudel and his comrades that the Russians had assembled powerful troop and tank forces in the frontier area and had constructed a network of front-line airfields, some of which were not yet complete. The Stuka crews had the impression that they had surprised the Russians as they were moving up into positions in the west.

The *Immelmann* Stukas successfully supported units of the Army and the *Waffen-SS*, attacking targets ahead of the advance. In many sectors of the front the Soviets used every means at their disposal, including flak, anti-aircraft machine guns, rifles and even pistols in attempts to bring down the dreaded Stukas which were dive bombing their positions. Many a black smoke cloud marked the spot where a Stuka crew had met a flier's death in the crash of their machine. At this time losses to enemy fighters were slight as any of the maneuverable "Ratas" which appeared over the front lines quickly fell victim to the Messerschmitt Bf 109s of the *Luftwaffe*.

In the summer of 1941, Rudel was transferred to *III. Gruppe* to assume the duties of *Gruppe* Technical Officer. On August 6, *Hauptmann* Steen arrived as the unit's new commanding officer. Rudel was soon flying missions as his number two. On July 18, Steen had been awarded the Iron Cross First Class and the Mission Clasp in Gold. In October he received the distinction of an Honour Goblet for particular accomplishments in the air war.

*III. Gruppe* was often active against enemy troop concentrations on the Smolensk-Dniepr-Moscow road and supporting Army Group North as it advanced towards Leningrad. At this time Rudel and Scharnowski, his unflappable East Prussian gunner, were able to celebrate their first "flier's birthday." On 8/18/1941, they returned from a mission against the Chudovo station on the important Moscow-Leningrad supply route with the remains of two birch trees embedded in the wings of their aircraft. Following a dive through cumulo-nimbus clouds in poor visibility, Rudel was able to pull out at the very last minute. The commanding officer, *Hauptmann* Steen, forecast a short life for this crazy fellow who dropped his bombs late in order to be sure of hitting his target.

On August 29, 1941, the *Gruppe* transferred to Tyrkovo south of Luga. From there Rudel flew numerous missions in support of the German Sixteenth and Eighteenth Armies which were advancing northwards. Following successful attacks by the Stukas on bunkers and field positions, the infantry divisions, among them the East Prussian 121st Infantry Division, whose divisional insignia was the cross of the Teutonic Knights and an eagle, succeeded in breaching the first of Leningrad's defensive lines. Sluzk, Pushkin and Krasnogvardeysk were taken in the assault. Rudel and his comrades launched very successful attacks in support of the 118th Infantry Division leading up to the assault on Araposki. The taking by storm of the Duderhofer Heights on 10-11 September in the sector south of Krasnoje Selo was likewise effectively supported by Rudel and his *Gruppe*. Rudel destroyed several bunkers with direct hits.

The Soviet Baltic Fleet with the battleships "Marat" and "October Revolution" as well as several heavy cruisers, including the "Kirov" and "Maxim Gorki", occasionally intervened in the land fighting from the Gulf of Finland. In particular the two battleships with their long-ranging guns had caused the German troops a great deal of trouble. As a result of these Soviet bombardments the *Immelmann Stukageschwader* received orders to eliminate this floating artillery.

During an attack on September 21, Rudel succeeded in scoring a hit on "Marat" with a 500 kg. bomb, the battleship thereupon retiring to the port of Kronstadt for repairs. Better results were expected from the 1,000 kilogram bombs whose arrival at the *Geschwader* had been inexplicably delayed.

Examination of aerial photographs confirmed what Rudel and his comrades had suspected: around the harbour and surrounding coastline the Russians had massed over 1,000 anti-aircraft guns of all calibers. After the crews had made their first acquaintance with this dangerous "hedgehog" on September 22, the "flak hell" over Kronstadt was the number one topic of discussion. On September 23, the armorers were finally able to load the 1,000 kg. bombs onto the aircraft.

As the Stukas took off from the airfield and climbed into a clear sky, the one thought in Rudel's mind was to put his 1,000 kg. bomb squarely on the armored deck of "his" "Marat", which he had damaged in the earlier attack. The flak defence of Kronstadt greeted the approaching crews with such a concentration of fire that the exploding heavy, medium and light shells created regular cloud banks. Never before had Rudel and his comrades had to penetrate such an intense flak barrage. As the Stukas approached the harbour, doing their "flak dance" of evasive manoeuvres, the battleship "Marat" and the other warships opened fire, adding to the anti-aircraft barrage. As the Soviets were not aiming at specific aircraft, but putting up barrage fire, the standard evasive manoeuvres appeared quite useless to Rudel and Steen. They made no evasive turns but concentrated on the "Marat."

Rudel, flying close behind Steen's aircraft, saw him lower his dive brakes, which reduced the speed of the aircraft and increased the chances of obtaining a hit. Rudel also lowered his dive brakes, but, as he did so, noticed that Steen's aircraft was diving faster and pulling away from him. Rudel retracted his dive brakes; he assumed that Steen had not employed his dive brakes in order to get down on the target as quickly as possible. But Rudel was mistaken, for now he rapidly overhauled his commander's aircraft. In front of him he could see the shocked face of *Ofw*. Lehmann, Steen's well-tried gunner, who expected to be rammed at any moment. Rudel forced his Ju 87 into a 90 degree dive and passed beneath the Steen's aircraft, missing it by a hair's breadth. The "Marat" grew ever larger in his bombsight. When the center of the battleship filled his sight he released his bomb, and at the same instant began pulling back on the control column with all his strength. His altitude was only 300 meters. The thought, "would that be enough?", shot through his mind. What was more, it now occurred to him that in the pre-mission briefing *Hauptmann* Steen had warned that if the 1,000 kg. bomb was dropped below one thousand meters one's own aircraft would be endangered by the effects of the explosion. With both hands on the control column Rudel pulled out so hard that for the first time as a Stuka pilot he began to black out and was unable to see for a few seconds. Scarcely had the haze before his eyes disappeared when he heard the voice of his gunner; "*Herr Oberleutnant*, the ship is blowing up!" Rudel, who was flying at only three to four meters above the water, turned slightly to be able to see the smoke cloud which was rising slowly four to five hundred meters into the air. The bomb had apparently struck the "Marat's" magazine. Congratulations poured in from all sides over the radio. *Geschwaderkommodore* Dinort was heard to say, "Allow me to offer my congratulations."

When asked by a PK reporter of his feelings at that moment Rudel said, "It was as if I looked into the eyes of thousands of grateful infantrymen." Now the long-range guns of the Marat would endanger them no longer.

Flying at low altitude, Rudel succeeded in escaping the harbour area. Two enemy fighters which were closing to attack were shot down in error by Russian flak. A third Russian fighter which closed and fired on Rudel's aircraft but missed was shot down into the water by a Bf 109. Rudel's trusty East Prussian gunner had held his fire so as not to risk hitting the German fighter, which was sitting behind the Russian in firing position.

The 23,600 tonne "Marat" had been named after Jean Paul Marat, one of the radical leaders of the French revolution who was murdered in his bath by loyalists. The ship had been armed with twelve 30.5 cm. guns, sixteen 12 cm. guns, six 7.6 cm. flak and numerous other anti-aircraft weapons.

On September 23, *III. Gruppe* took off once more for the "flak hell" over Kronstadt. The target was the cruiser "Kirov" which lay tied up not far from the blown-up "Marat." Rudel was unable to accompany the *Gruppe* on this mission, because shortly before takeoff he had to hand over his aircraft to the commanding officer whose aircraft was unserviceable following an accident while taxiing on the rain-soaked airfield. Justifying his order to Rudel, Steen said, "I always want to be present when we're going against a strongly-defended target." Rudel was not very happy about the order but he understood Steen's motives. An hour-and-a-half later the *Gruppe* returned from Kronstadt. Rudel saw immediately that his aircraft, the one with the green spinner, was missing. The crews reported that they had seen how the aircraft's elevators had been damaged by flak, rendering a pull-up from its dive impossible. Realising this, *Hauptmann* Steen had steered the aircraft towards the "Kirov" with aileron and rudder, plunging into the water beside the cruiser with the 1,000 kg. bomb still attached. The resulting explosion severely damaged the "Kirov." It had been Steen's 301st mission. The grief felt over the loss of the *Gruppe*'s commanding officer, *Hauptmann* Steen, and Rudel's gunner Scharnowski was great, and over-shadowed the joy over Rudel's successful duel with the battleship "Marat."

Until October 1, the *Gruppe* flew several more missions against the Soviet Baltic Fleet. Rudel's new gunner was *Gefreiter* Erwin Hentschel. Rudel succeeded in sinking a cruiser and a destroyer, but all attempts to sink the second battleship "October Revolution" were unsuccessful. The ship was damaged on several occasions and took a direct hit from a 1,000 kg. bomb which turned out to be a dud. The remaining bombs of this calibre dropped on the mission also failed to explode. This case of sabotage was never completely cleared up. It was thought with some certainty that the fuses had been tampered with at the production level.

Following the missions over the Gulf of Finland which had brought a measure of relief to the fighting units, Rudel and *III. Gruppe* were transferred to Volkhov near Leningrad in the central sector to support the drive on Moscow. *Hauptmann* Pressler, a veteran Stuka pilot from another *Geschwader*, now took over command of *III. Gruppe*.

The terrible Siberian cold of the winter of 1941/42 — sometimes -40 to -54 degrees — caused more casualties to the German troops than did enemy fire. It also decreased considerably the operational readiness of the *Luftwaffe*. The achievements of the ground personnel, including those of the *Immelmann Geschwader*, who continued to work day and night during the winter months of this and following winters were most admirable and greatly appreciated by the air crews. The pilots had to contend with treacherous ice or snow-covered airfields during takeoffs and landings through fog and snow. They needed all of their piloting skills during the missions to assist the ground forces hard hit by cold in their defensive battles against the overpowering strength of the attacking Siberian elite units.

When the weather did not permit operations to be flown, Rudel used the opportunity to play hockey with comrades if a frozen surface was available. Rudel needed sports to keep in top condition.

Approximately ninety days after flying his first Stuka mission, he made his 500th flight against the enemy and, in December 1941, received the German Cross in Gold. At the beginning of January 1942, *General der Flieger* von Richthofen (*VIII Fliegerkorps*) arrived in his *Fieseler "Storch"* and presented Rudel with the Knight's Cross in the name of the *Führer* and Supreme Commander of the Armed Forces. The award citation listed Rudel's successes against ships at

Kronstadt, direct hits on important bridges, supply routes, artillery positions and tanks.

Among others during the hard winter of 1941/42, Rudel flew successful missions to the headwaters of the Volga-Duna-Dniepr near the Valdai heights, in the Demyansk-Cholm area, the battle zone west of Rshev and to the Olinin and Sytschjewka rail lines. On January 18, 1942, the airfield at Dugino near Sytschjewka — about 60 km. south of Rshev — was attacked by Soviet troops just before dawn. *Oberleutnant* Kresken, chief of the staff company, put together a fighting unit from *III. Gruppe*'s ground personnel and led them in the defence against the attack at the airfield perimeter. At first light, Rudel and his comrades joined the fight, taking off and smashing the enemy tanks and escorting infantry which belonged to an elite Siberian division. The airfield was held until January 21 when a unit from the *Waffen-SS* Division *Das Reich* arrived, clearing up the threatening situation and securing the Gshatsk-Rshev sector. On several occasions during the war, airfields occupied by the *Immelmann Geschwader* were attacked by Soviet troops which had suddenly broken through the front.

●

The year 1942 began with an unpleasant surprise for *Oberleutnant* Rudel. He was ordered home on leave and posted to the Stuka Replacement *Staffel* at Graz-Thalerhof. Rudel used his leave, the first part of which he spent with his parents in Alt-Kohlfurt, to get married. Then he and his young bride took a skiing vacation in the Tirol. In the peaceful world of the mountains the strain of continuous Stuka missions disappeared. With typical energy Rudel took command of the Stuka Replacement *Staffel* in Graz and began the task of passing his front-line experience to the young pilots. Often he smiled as he remembered his own training with this *Staffel* when he simply could not master the art of flying a Stuka.

Those who knew Rudel anticipated that he would not be

able to bear for long being far away from the action of a front-line unit. When he learned that the Replacement *Staffel* of another Stuka unit had been transferred to Russia, he pushed with success to have his *Staffel* moved to the Eastern Front.

With gliders in tow bringing their technical equipment and personnel, the aircraft of the Graz Replacement *Staffel* flew to the Crimean peninsula where training continued from the airfield at Sarabus. As several crews were ready for front-line action, and their chief could not endure the ban on operational flying when every Stuka was needed to support the German summer offensive in the south, Rudel telephoned the commanding *Luftwaffe* General in the Caucasus and offered his *Staffel* for action. His offer was gratefully accepted. The *Staffel* flew over Kerch to an airfield near the Maikop oil fields north of the Caucasus. Together with another Stuka unit, Rudel's *Staffel* supported the German Seventeenth Army's drive toward the Black Sea port of Tuapse. By mid-September Novorossiysk had been taken but Tuapse was never reached.

Rudel and his Replacement *Staffel* flew numerous missions over the complicated, difficult terrain of the Caucasus. They were directed to their targets by radio by a air liaison officer accompanying the ground forces. Among their targets was a Russian armored train which was sealed up in a mountain tunnel by Stuka bombs. Other targets included harbour installations at Tuapse, airfields near Gelendschik and vessels on the Black Sea. There followed missions over the Terek front and again in the Tuapse area where Rudel flew his 650th mission. On a visit to the Stuka command post, General Pflugbeil, commanding the *Luftwaffe* units in the southern sector, noticed that Rudel's face was lemon yellow. On orders from the General, Rudel gave up his *Staffel* and flew to a military hospital at Rostov on the Don. When the head doctor wanted to put him on the next hospital train for Germany for further treatment, Rudel released himself from hospital. He flew a Ju 87 to the airfield at Karpovka, approximately 40 km. west of Stalingrad, which by chance had been at the main-

23

tenance depot at Rostov awaiting delivery to the *Immelmann Geschwader*. There he reported himself to the commander as "discharged as cured." Rudel, whose face was still bright yellow, maintained that discharge papers were to follow. He took command of *1. Staffel* of *I. Gruppe, Stukageschwader 2*, with which he had flown his first mission in Russia. It took all of his strength to endure the next several weeks of operations but finally the jaundice cleared up.

Troops of the German Sixth Army and Fourth Panzer Army had taken 90% of the city of Stalingrad despite fanatical resistance by the Soviets. Rudel and his comrades flew mission after mission against targets within the city. They had with them aerial photographs which clearly showed every street car, every bunker, and every factory which the Soviets had converted into a fortress. Other targets for the Stukas were Russian positions on the steep bank of the Volga and the area north of the city where the front ran nearly at right angles from the Volga to the Don. Several missions were flown in the vicinity of Beketovka, which was defended by heavy and accurate flak. From prisoners' statements the men of the *Immelmann Geschwader* learned that the flak crews consisted of women and girls. Before every mission into this area the crews would say, "today we're going through the ladies' flak", and it was not intended as a disparaging remark. The women at the anti-aircraft guns knew well how to fill the sky with "iron", so that every "rendezvous" with them left a respectful impression. While returning from an attack on the Russian bridgehead near Kletsskaya on the west bank of the Don on November 19, 1942, the Stuka crews were eyewitnesses to the beginning of tragedy. Entire units of Rumanian troops were fleeing, leaving behind their guns and equipment in their well-built positions. In his book *Operation Barbarossa*, Paul Carell described it thus: "Catastrophe was already looming by noon on the 19th. Whole divisions from the Rumanian front, above all the 13th, 14th and 9th Infantry Divisions, broke and fled to the rear in panic. The Soviets pushed after them towards the west to the

Chir and then to the south and southwest. It became clear that they wanted to break into the German Sixth Army's rear . . ."

By November 22, the German troops were surrounded in Stalingrad. A promising relief attempt got to within thirty km. of the pocket but the main force had to be pulled back to avert the threat to the entire southern front caused by the Italians' failure near Bogoduchov. The surrounded Sixth Army rejected Soviet demands that it surrender. Of this Field Marshall von Manstein said after the war, "This refusal was undoubtedly necessary, as the Sixth Army was still tying down over 60 Russian units whose release from Stalingrad to other fronts could have meant disaster for Army Group A."

Rudel and his comrades of the *Immelmann Geschwader* flew missions in support of the heroic defence of the pocket until the last possible moment. First, as bombs, ammunition and fuel became scarce they transferred to Oblivskaya, about 170 km. west of Stalingrad. One special Stuka unit, commanded by *Oberleutnant* Jungclausen, remained to operate from within the pocket. They flew under the most difficult operating conditions until the stocks of bombs and fuel were used up and then flew out to Oblivskaya.

Without adequate deliveries of munitions and rations, holding out in the bitterest cold and suffering heavy losses, the surrounded Sixth Army fought on to the bitter end. On February 2, 1943, 120,000 men, including 5,000 officers and Army officials, as well as 45,000 wounded, went into Soviet captivity. In the first week alone, 50,000 soldiers died in the prison camp at Beketovka on the Volga. By conservative estimates, no more than 6,000 of the prisoners taken at Stalingrad survived Russian captivity.

•

On February 10, 1943, Rudel, who often flew ten, fifteen or even seventeen missions a day, flew his 1,000th. This mission was flown against the Soviet 57th Army which had torn open a gap eighty kilometers wide in the front near Isjum.

One thousand missions meant one thousand trials in the face of the enemy and oneself. The physical and mental stresses on a Stuka pilot supporting the ground forces can scarcely be imagined by a non-flier; diving through bursting flak and tracer against the assigned target, withstanding the tremendous pressure of the pull-up, enduring concentrated defensive fire in low altitude flight a few hundred meters above the ground, seeing one's comrades die as their aircraft become fireballs or smash into the ground, grappling with superior numbers of enemy fighters — and all the while forced to make lightning quick decisions on which depend the lives of the other crews and the success of the mission. Multiply this by 2,530 times and one can conceive the unique accomplishments as a pilot and leader which Hans-Ulrich Rudel had achieved by the end of the war. His accomplishments were unique among all pilots of the warring nations.

●

Following his 1,001st mission, Rudel, despite his efforts to remain with his *Staffel*, was ordered to take fourteen days home leave which he spent skiing on the Arlberg at St. Anton in the Tirol. Rudel subsequently went to a special unit under *Hauptmann* Stepp which was located at Rechlin/Mecklenburg and Bryansk/Desna. This unit was testing the Ju 87 in the anti-tank role armed with two 3.7 cm. cannon carried beneath the wings. Flying such unwieldy and unmanoeuvrable "cannon birds", Rudel went on to destroy more than 519 Russian tanks by the end of the war. Rudel and the anti-tank trials unit flew to the airfield at Kerch which was being used by the *Immelmann Geschwader*, which was flying missions against the Kuban bridgehead near Krymskaya. The "cannon birds" soon proved themselves in action over the mouth of the Kuban river on the Sea of Azov. In several days of operations the test *Staffel* destroyed a large number of Russian landing craft with 3.7 cm.

high-explosive ammunition. Of these, *Oberleutnant* Rudel alone accounted for over seventy. These successful low level attacks with the Stukas' 3.7 cm. cannon were photographed by automatic cameras and featured in German newsreels.

On April 1, 1943, Rudel was promoted to *Hauptmann* and his seniority was backdated to 1/4/1942 for bravery in the face of the enemy. Effective April 14, 1943, he was awarded the Oak Leaves to the Knight's Cross, becoming the 229th German serviceman to receive the decoration. Rudel and twelve others received their decorations at the Reich Chancellery from Adolf Hitler, *Führer* and Supreme Commander of the Armed Forces.

At his request Rudel was soon transferred back to the *Immelmann Geschwader*. He took with him one of the "cannon birds" which he flew between regular Stuka missions when Soviet tanks were reported to have broken through. Additional anti-tank machines soon arrived which were operated independently by *10. Staffel*, which remained under Rudel's operational control. During the German offensive against the Kursk salient in July, Rudel succeeded in destroying twelve Russian tanks in one day's flying despite heavy ground fire. When he looked at his flak and bullet riddled aircraft in the evening following his last sortie, Rudel said to his ground crew chief consolingly, "the service life of such machines will always be limited . . ."

On one of the next missions Rudel was again able to celebrate a "fliers birthday"; a tank which he had hit blew up just as he flew overhead at an altitude of approximately ten meters. As a result of flying through the explosion, the aircraft's green camouflage finish was scorched in places and the "cannon bird" was holed in numerous locations by steel fragments.

In August and September *III. Gruppe* flew missions from the airfield at Konotop (Orel-North) in the Orel area. To the south Rudel destroyed the Kromy bridge (40 km. southwest of Orel) with a direct hit by a 500 kg. bomb. A tank which by chance was on the bridge was also destroyed. Several days later, 60 km.

northwest of Orel, west of Bolkov, Rudel was again incredibly lucky; his aircraft was hit in the motor by flak and he received facial injuries from shrapnel. With a dead engine he succeeded in making a forced landing in the German front lines. Scarcely had he and his gunner returned to the airfield near Orel when they took off in another machine for the same area where they had been shot down earlier.

On September 18, Rudel's friend from the Graz replacement *Staffel, Major* and holder of the Oak Leaves Walter Kraus, commander of *III. Gruppe*, was killed in a night bombing raid on Orel airfield. The tragic death of his friend and close comrade hit Rudel hard. The loss of this successful Stuka pilot and outstanding and well-liked commander was a painful loss for the *Immelmann Geschwader*. Rudel now had to give up his *1. Staffel* as he had been given command of *III. Gruppe*.

●

The *Immelmann Geschwader*'s crews and ground personnel knew that the Russians had launched a counterattack or had achieved a local breakthrough with tanks whenever they were required to transfer bases at short notice. They moved to wherever they were needed between the Gulf of Finland and the Black Sea. The pilot's log books reflected this; the difficult-to-remember names of the Russian towns changed almost daily. By the late autumn of 1943 Rudel had flown his 1,500th mission and had destroyed a total of 60 tanks. By the end of November his tally of tanks destroyed had climbed to over 100. On November 25, Rudel became the 42nd soldier of the Reich to be awarded the Knight's Cross with Oak Leaves and Swords. He received the decoration from Hitler in his headquarters in East Prussia. On the same day, *Feldwebel* Erwin Hentschel, Rudel's well-proven gunner (at that time 1,000 missions and several enemy aircraft shot down), received the Knight's Cross.

●

Over the southern sector of the front near Kirovograd, where the Soviets had launched an attack with superior forces, the weather was so poor on many flying days that even experienced Stuka pilots needed plenty of luck in order to bring their machines back through the "pea soup" in one piece. Returning with another aircraft from an early morning reconnaissance, Rudel and *Leutnant* Fickel had to force land in German territory due to fast-forming fog. Despite poor visibility — only 30-40 meters — they both landed safely. Rudel and his gunner Hentschel taxied almost thirty kilometers along a road to the vicinity of the airfield at Pevomaissk. There they could go no farther due to a low overpass. After the visibility had improved he took off from the road and flew back to his base. This was undoubtedly a world record for taxiing an aircraft. If so, it was made under difficult circumstances as the road was heavily travelled by army vehicles. The soldiers must have been amazed at the sight of this "Stuka on foot."

•

On March 1, 1944, Hans-Ulrich Rudel was promoted to *Major* and his seniority backdated to 1/10/1942.

In mid-March the Russians had thrown several bridges across the Dnestr unhindered by the *Immelmann Geschwader*, which was grounded by another period of bad weather. On March 20, when weather conditions again permitted operations, Rudel and his *Gruppe* flew seven sorties into the areas around Nikolayev and north of Balta, approximately 80 km. west of the river Bug. The eighth mission was against the Dnestr bridge near Jampol which was destroyed despite heavy flak and twenty intercepting Russian fighters. One machine had to force-land in enemy territory on the enemy-held side of the Dnestr with engine damage. Rudel, who had already saved six crews from Russian captivity or death, wanted to rescue this one as well. He landed safely but was unable to take off again. The wheels of his aircraft had sunk into the soft earth. Fleeing from pursuing Red Army soldiers, Rudel and two comrades were able to swim the swollen Dnestr in water barely above the freezing mark. However, his faithful gunner, Knight's Cross holder *Oberfeldwebel* Erwin Hentschel, sank in the icy flood. Rudel's rescue attempt was unsuccessful. Soon afterwards, he and his two comrades were taken prisoner by Russian soldiers. Rudel succeeded in effecting a daring escape and, despite being wounded in the shoulder by gunfire, reached the safety of the German lines. Only two days after his exhausting escape across fifty kilometers of enemy-held territory he was in the air again. Because of his injured feet Rudel had to be carried to his aircraft by his ground crew chief. The success of the missions flown by Rudel in the days following his fantastic escape was reflected in the OKW's reports. On 27 March the *Wehrmacht* communique stated: "Powerful German ground attack air forces have intervened in the fighting between the Dnestr and Pruth. They have destroyed numerous enemy tanks and a large number of motor- and horse-drawn vehicles. In the course of these attacks Major Rudel destroyed another nine enemy tanks. In more than 1,800 missions he has destroyed 202 enemy tanks . . ."

On March 29, 1944 Rudel became the tenth German soldier to be awarded the Knight's Cross with Oak Leaves, Swords and Diamonds. He received the decoration, the highest existing at that time, from Adolf Hitler at the Berghof near Berchtesgaden. Due to his injured feet, Rudel met the Führer wearing his fur-lined flying boots. It was the only time that an officer reported to the Supreme Commander in such irregular dress.

On June 3, 1944, three days after his 2,000th mission, the *Wehrmacht* communique stated: ". . . Major Rudel, who has been awarded the highest German decoration for bravery, flew his 2,000th mission against the enemy on the Eastern Front."

On the occasion of his 2,000th mission, which took place in the combat sector near Jassy, Rumania, the Commander-in-Chief of the *Luftwaffe*, Hermann Göring, awarded Rudel the Pilots Badge in Gold with Diamonds and the Mission Clasp in Gold with Diamonds. Until the end of the war Rudel was the only recipient of these decorations.

On August 6, 1944, Rudel was again mentioned in the *Wehrmacht* communique: "... 27 more tanks were destroyed by ground attack fliers. Of these Major Rudel alone destroyed 11 and scored his 300th enemy tank destroyed with cannon fire."

Only eight days later his total would reach 320 tanks destroyed.

●

From Rumania, Rudel's "Stuka fire brigade" transferred to the central sector, then to East Prussia and Courland. He and his comrades prevented several breakthroughs by enemy tanks, including one near Ergli on the Courland front on August 19. During that mission Rudel and his gunner Dr. Gadermann were forced to crash-land as a result of flak damage. Their aircraft was totally destroyed, Rudel was wounded in the leg and Dr. Gadermann suffered several broken ribs. However, this did not prevent them from immediately taking off on the next mission into the same area where they had been hit earlier and successfully attacking flak positions and vehicle columns.

From Courland, Rudel's "front fire brigade" was transferred first to Rumania and then to Hungary where it supported the heroic defence of encircled Budapest by units of the *Waffen-SS*.

In the late summer of 1944, Rudel, who had been promoted to *Oberstleutnant* on September 1, took command of *SG 2 Immelmann*. His successor as leader of *III. Gruppe* was Knight's Cross holder *Hauptmann* Lau.

During a successful tank-hunting mission, Rudel was wounded in the thigh but made a successful emergency landing at a fighter base near Budapest. After an operation in a military hospital, Rudel was taken to a sanatorium at Hevis on the Platensee (Lake Balaton) with the leg in a cast. He immediately asked the chief physician when he would be able to fly again. "If all goes well", went the answer, "you will be able to stand in six weeks." The doctor did not know Rudel. He had no intentions of lying in bed while his comrades in the ground forces were engaged in desperate defensive battles and his "Immelmänner" were risking their lives daily. After a few days he packed his bags and disappeared with one of the men from his unit who had come to visit him. He flew the next mission —with his leg in a cast!

In December his aircraft was again hit by flak resulting in another forced landing. Passing soldiers lifted him from the aircraft and returned him to his unit in their vehicle. He was back in time to lead the next sortie.

On January 1, 1945, Rudel became the first and only German soldier to be awarded the highest German decoration for bravery, the Knight's Cross with Golden Oak Leaves, Swords and Diamonds. He received the decoration at *Führer* Head-quarters West at Taunus in the presence of the commanders of all branches of the armed forces as well as *Generalfeldmarschall* Keitel, *Generaloberst* Jodl and several Eastern Front generals. At the same time he was promoted to *Oberst*. Rudel's joy turned to dejection when Hitler said to him, "You have done enough flying. You and your experience must remain alive as an example for German youth." The high-ranking officers held their breath as Rudel answered, "My *Führer*, I cannot accept this decoration and promotion if I am no longer permitted to fly with my *Geschwader*."

Hitler suddenly smiled, "Very well then, fly. But be careful, the German people need you." Afterwards, Rudel spent an hour-and-a-half in conversation with the Supreme Commander and was astonished by Hitler's knowledge in the field of armaments technology. Subsequently he flew back to his *Geschwader* in Hungary.

On January 16, 1945, Rudel became the sole foreigner to receive Hungary's highest decoration, the Golden Medal for Bravery, which was awarded only seven times in total.

●

On January 12, the Russians launched their great offensive from the Baranov bridgehead on the Vistula, driving deep into the central sector of the front with powerful forces and reaching Rudel's home of Silesia. He immediately requested authorization from *Fliegerkorps* to transfer with *II.* and *III. Gruppen* to Silesia. Operating from Udetfeld, an air base near Tarnowitz, Rudel's pilots flew many successful missions, mainly over the industrial region of Upper Silesia. At this time the ban on Rudel's operational flying was reinstated from *Führer* Headquarters but he ignored the order. "They can't forbid me to fly when Russian tanks are driving around on German soil." His tank kills were now credited to the *Geschwader* so that the High Command would not notice that he was still flying missions. There followed a brief transfer to Märkisch-Friedland in Pomerania and then to Furstenwalde/Oder with missions over the Frankfurt/Oder — Kustrin area. East of Frankfurt, Rudel and his *Immelmänner* were able to rescue an army unit surrounded and hard pressed by Soviet armored forces. On leaving the battle the Stuka crews saw the relieved troops wave and throw their helmets in the air for joy.

Then came February 8, 1945 — a day in the life of the legendary Stuka pilot which he would never forget — Rudel remembered every detail of that day . . .

Near Lebus, north of Frankfurt on the Oder, only about 80 km. from Berlin, Russian tanks had succeeded in reaching the west bank of the Oder by way of a pontoon bridge. While Stuka bombers attacked the bridge through dense flak, Rudel and *10. Panzerstaffel* went after the T-34 and "Stalin" tanks. Rudel left four tanks in flames but was hit by flak and was forced to change aircraft for the next mission. On the next attack Rudel was accompanied by his gunner, Knight's Cross holder Dr. Gadermann, the only *Luftwaffe* doctor to fly more than 800 missions and score several air victories as a gunner.

Rudel had already flown four missions and destroyed twelve tanks. Following several unsuccessful attempts, he finished off the thirteenth, a "Stalin", with his last round of ammunition.

At that moment his aircraft took a direct hit from a 4 cm. anti-aircraft round which nearly severed his lower right leg. Despite cruel pain and great loss of blood, he summoned all of his willpower and force-landed in friendly territory. Dr. Gadermann applied a tourniquet to the leg above the wound and prevented him from bleeding to death. When Rudel awoke from the anaesthetic at the *Waffen-SS* hospital near Seelow he learned from the doctor that he had been wounded in the left leg above his cast and that they had been forced to amputate his lower right leg. For the avid sportsman this was a crushing blow.

On orders from the Commander-in-Chief of the *Luftwaffe,* Rudel was transferred to the military hospital in Berlin's Zoo flak bunker. There the attending physician's opinion was, "You are finished with flying." He underestimated Rudel's fighting will to get back into action. Only six weeks later he was again in the air leading his *Geschwader* despite the great pain from his still only partially healed stump. After nearly every mission his crew chief had to remove traces of blood from the aircraft. *Hauptmann* Niermann, a war correspondent who had been recommended for the Knight's Cross, accompanied Rudel on these missions as his gunner.

Until the last day of the war the crews and ground personnel of the *Immelmann Geschwader* did out their duty as soldiers. Through their missions, Rudel and his comrades preserved the lives and freedom of countless soldiers and refugees. They have the Stuka crews to thank that they did not fall victim to the brutal invaders. On May 8, 1945, in the city of Niemes in the Sudetenland, Rudel and his comrades of *II. Gruppe* received the report of the surrender of the German armed forces. A short time later the *Immelmänner* were assembled. Their commanding officer walked slowly up to his men. His temporary prosthesis pressed painfully against his unhealed stump. *Oberst* Rudel scarcely noticed the pain; he was too stirred up inside by the report of the surrender. An officer presented the assembled unit. "Comrades", began Rudel; he hesitated, thinking of *I. Gruppe* in Austria and *III. Gruppe* at Kletzan airfield north of Prague; would he ever see them again? Rudel continued, "after we have lost so many comrades, after so much German blood has been shed at the front and at home, incomprehensible fate has denied us victory. The achievements of our soldiers and our entire people have been incomparably great. The war is lost . . . I thank you for the loyalty with which you have served the homeland in the *Geschwader* . . ."

For the last time Rudel strode to the front and gave each man his hand — no one spoke a word. His men understood the silent handshake. As he laboriously walked away on his temporary prosthesis, the command rang out: "eyes right!" It was a salute to him as a commander, a warrior and a comrade.

●

*Oberst* Rudel wanted to lead the ground column from the airfield at Kummer through Czechoslovakia to the American units in the west. The *Gruppe* commander would fly with the aircraft back to the homeland.

He wrote in his book *Trotzdem*: "When the General heard that I wished to lead the ground column, he ordered that I not fly, on account of my wound, and that Fridolin lead the ground column. . . After the column was gone, those who did not wish to wait for my departure flew off; for many it may have been possible to escape captivity if they landed somewhere in the vicinity of their homes. For me that was never in question; rather, I wished to land at an American base as I required immediate medical attention for my leg . . ."

●

Accompanied by his gunner, the PK correspondent *Hauptmann* Niermann, Rudel's aircraft and several others of the *Geschwader* landed at an American-occupied airfield at Kitzingen near Würzburg. There most of the Stuka crews were "relieved" of their watches, fountain pens and decorations. Rudel and his comrades protested in vain. While the other Stuka crewmen were taken to a nearby prisoner-of-war camp, the Americans took *Oberst* Rudel — without providing any medical attention for his very painful stump — and *Hauptmann* Niermann via Erlangen and Wiesbaden to prison camps in England and then France. After many weeks and after overcoming numerous difficulties, Rudel finally obtained a transfer to a German military hospital. Niermann was released in the British occupation zone. Rudel came to Fürth in Bavaria where German doctors provided exemplary care for his amputation wound. Following his release in mid-April 1946, he was active in Coesfeld, Westphalia as a teamster. With his excellent artificial leg, which had been constructed by Master Streide, an exceptionally-gifted builder of prostheses in Kufstein, Tirol, he took part in many skiing competitions and brought home numerous trophies. And he competed not only in events for the handicapped, but also against "healthy" competition. Together with his friends Bauer, a recipient of the Oak Leaves, and *Hauptmann* Niermann, he made the adventurous trip from Zillertal across the mountains to South Tirol, from there to Rome and then in June 1948 to Cordoba in Argentina where, like several other prominent German pilots, he became active as a consultant to the Argentine aviation industry.

In his free time Rudel's program consisted of swimming, tennis, riding, discus and javelin throwing, skiing and mountain climbing. When the weather was poor he wrote down his war experiences which were published under the title *Trotzdem*. The book was translated into many languages and total publication abroad reached more than a million copies. In 1949 he took part in the world skiing championships at Bariloche as the only disabled veteran and, despite his prosthesis, competed in the top class. In the same year he climbed the Aconcagua in the Argentine Andes, at 7,020 meters the highest peak in the Americas, but poor weather forced him to turn back just short of the summit. Undoubtedly his greatest alpine accomplishment was in 1953, when the one-legged athlete became the first man to climb the 6,920-meter-high Llullay-Yacu, an extinct volcano in the Andes. In order to carry out a close inspection of the Inca ruins concealed beneath the summit, he and his comrades made a second expedition in which photographer Erwin Neubert fell to his death. Not until the third expedition a year later was Neubert's body recovered and buried in a mountain grave on Llullay-Yacu as his parents had requested.

Rudel and his mountaineering comrades were received by Argentina's President, General Peron, and the newspapers and illustrated magazines of North- and South America gave extensive coverage to the event. In this context it was a matter of course that the foreign press cited the legendary Stuka officer's accomplishments and numerous decorations while the licensed press in the occupation zones concealed Rudel's successes.

At the conclusion of his contract with the Argentine government, Rudel returned to Germany. There, too, he won numerous ski and tennis competitions as well as disabled championships, so that the cupboard in his magnificently-situated "vacation refuge" on the Stimmersee in Kufstein, Tirol could scarcely contain all of his trophies. A place of honour was reserved for the cup which he had received from the West German skiing association as its most successful skier.

The successful career of the disabled sportsman who after the war still neither drank nor smoked, was suddenly interrupted at the age of 54: on April 26, 1970, Hans-Ulrich Rudel, for whom life without sports was unthinkable, suffered a stroke brought on by high blood pressure during training for a skiing event in Hochfugen, Austria. The skill of his doctors - and not least his own iron will, true to his fighting motto "only he is lost, who gives up on himself" — were to be thanked that he was able to endure the grave consequences. Although he would never again play tennis, he made such significant progress through daily conditioning that he was able to swim, hike and drive again and even to take down his beloved "boards" and ski. Anyone who saw Rudel's fighting spirit in action was firmly convinced that Rudel, who as an industry consultant makes frequent strenuous trips abroad, would one day ski down the white slopes on his prosthesis as in the old days, which meant all the world to him.

●

In 2,530 missions, the Stuka *Oberst*, who was respected by friend and foe alike, destroyed, among other targets, over 519 Russian tanks (approximately 5 Soviet tank corps!), a battleship, a cruiser, a destroyer, 70 landing craft, more than 800 motorized and horse-drawn vehicles, over 150 artillery, anti-tank and flak positions, as well as numerous important bridges, supply lines and bunkers. He scored nine confirmed air victories (7 Soviet fighters, 2 IL-2), was shot down over thirty times by ground fire, was wounded five times, saved six crews who had crash-landed in enemy territory and was the only German soldier to receive his country's highest decoration for valour, the Golden Oak Leaves with Swords and Diamonds to the Knight's Cross of the Iron Cross. His 2,530 combat missions and other accomplishments made him the most successful combat pilot in history.

*Generalfeldmarschall* Ferdinand Schorner said of him, "Rudel is worth an entire division!" Stalin placed a bounty of 100,000 rubles on Rudel's head, and a highly-decorated disabled Russian captain wrote in a letter which found its way to Kufstein, "It may well be that Rudel is the greatest pilot known to history! I would like to meet him and shake his hand. He is an admirable man!"

Pierre Clostermann, who became France's most successful fighter pilot at age 24 with 33 victories, 420 missions and numerous French and English decorations (including the "Distinguished Service Order", Britain's second highest decoration), wrote in the foreword to this volume, "It is characteristic of this man, that his unsurpassable acts of heroism and his fame began at a time when the fortunes of war had already begun to turn from German arms . . . I can only say of him with the greatest respect what we in the Royal Air Force said of the German fighter ace Walter Nowotny during the war:

"What a pity that he hadn't worn our uniform!"

Next to the respect of his own people, can there be any greater recognition for a soldier who did his duty, for the "Eagle of the Eastern Front", the "bravest of the brave", than that of a courageous former enemy?

Günther Just

SIGNIFICANT DATES
IN THE LIFE
AND CAREER OF

# HANS-ULRICH
RUDEL

| | |
|---|---|
| 7/2/1916 | Born in Konradswaldau, Landeshut district, Silesia; father Protestant minister; sisters Ingeborg and Johanna; elementary and high school to matriculation; as a student already an outstanding athlete. |
| 1936 | Passed entrance tests as *Luftwaffe* officer candidate; two months service in Reich Labour Service; employed in Neisse river control project near Muskau, Cottbus district. |
| 12/4/1936 | Entered the *Luftwaffe*; basic training at Wildpark-Werder near Berlin. |
| June 1937 | School of Air Warfare Berlin-Werder; beginning of flight training. |
| June 1938 | To *I./Stuka-Geschwader 168* at Graz, Styriaas an officer cadet for dive-bomber training. |
| 12/1/1938 | Transfer to reconnaissance school at Hildesheim; observer training. |
| 1/1/1939 | Promoted to *Leutnant*. |
| 6/1/1939 | Posted to *Fernaufklärungsgruppe 121* at Prenzlau, in the Neubrandenburg/Uckermark district as an observer. |
| Sept. 1939 | Reconnaissance missions over Poland; Iron Cross 2nd Class on 11/10/39; transfer back to Prenzlau, fruitless attempts to transfer back to Stukas. |
| 3/2/1940 | Flight Training Regiment 43 at Vienna-Stammersdorf and, soon after, transfer to Crailsheim, Wurttemberg; service as regimental adjutant; transfer efforts successful; return to old Stukaunit (*I./St.Geschw. 168*) which is based at Caen in France. |
| 9/1/1940 | Promoted to *Oberleutnant*. |
| April 1941 | To *I. Gruppe, Stuka-Geschwader Immelmann* in Greece. |
| 6/22/1941 | Beginning of Russian campaign; first Stuka mission with *I./St.Geschw.2 Immelmann*. |
| 7/18/1941 | Awarded Iron Cross 1st Class, Mission Clasp in Gold. |
| 9/23/1941 | Destroys Soviet battleship "Marat" in Kronstadt harbour with a direct hit; on next missions sinks a cruiser and a destroyer. |
| 10/20/1941 | Honour Goblet for outstanding success in the air war. |
| 12/8/1941 | Awarded the German Cross in Gold. |
| 1/6/1942 | Awarded the Knight's Cross of the Iron Cross |
| 8/15/1942 | Becomes a *Staffelkapitän* in *III./St.Geschw. 2 Immelmann*. |
| 9/24/1942 | 500th mission |
| Autumn 1942 | Commander of Stuka Replacement *Staffel*Graz-Thalerhof; takes *Staffel* to southern sector of Eastern Front. |
| Early Nov. | Hospital in Rostov |
| 2/10/1943 | 1,000th mission, southern sector Eastern Front near Isjum. |
| 4/1/1943 | *Hauptmann* (seniority back dated to 4/1/1942 because of conspicuous bravery in the face of the enemy) |
| Early 1943 | Sinks 70 landing craft in Kuban bridgehead while flying early Ju 87G "cannon machine" (two 3.7 cm. cannon) |
| 4/14/1943 | 229th soldier of the *Wehrmacht* to receive Oak Leaves to the Knight's Cross of the Iron Cross. |
| 7/19/1943 | Leader of *III./St.Geschw. 2 "Immelmann"*. |
| 8/12/1943 | 1,300th combat mission |
| 9/18/1943 | Officially commissioned to carry out duties of commander of *III./St.Geschw. 2*. |
| 10/9/1943 | 1,500th combat mission, his gunner *Ofw.* Hentschel's 1,200th, Ukraine combat zone. |
| 10/18/1943 | *Stuka-Geschwader 2* retitled *Schlachtgeschwader 2 Immelmann* (SG 2). |

| | |
|---|---|
| End Oct.1943 | 100th tank destroyed with Ju 87G, Kirovograd combat zone. |
| 11/23/1943 | Seven Soviet tanks destroyed in southern sector. |
| 11/25/1943 | Knight's Cross with Oak Leaves and Swords (becomes the 42nd soldier of the *Wehrmacht* to receive the decoration.) |
| 2/22/1944 | Named *Gruppe* Commander *III./SG 2 Immelmann*. |
| 3/1/1944 | Promoted to *Major* (seniority back dated to 10/1/1942 due to highest decorations for bravery.) |
| 3/21/1944 | Attack on Dnestr bridgehead near Jampol; landing in enemy territory to rescue downed crew; taken prisoner by Soviet troops; escapes Soviets, wounded in shoulder, flight of 50 km. to German lines; Knight's Cross holder *Ofw*. Hentschel drowned in Dnestr. At the time Hentschel had the second highest number of combat missions in the *Luftwaffe*. |
| 3/22/1944 | Return to *III. Gruppe*. |
| 3/25/1944 | 1,800th combat mission. |
| 3/26/1944 | Destroys 17 tanks with cannon fire. |
| 3/27/1944 | Mentioned in *Wehrmacht* communique: ". . .Major Rudel, a *Gruppe* Commander in a *Schlachtgeschwader*, destroyed seventeen Soviet tanks in one day on the southern sector of the Eastern Front." |
| 3/28/1944 | Mentioned in *Wehrmacht* communique: ". . .Powerful German close-support air forces have intervened in the fighting between the Dnestr and Pruth rivers, destroying numerous enemy tanks and a large number of motorized and horse-drawn vehicles. In the fighting *Major* Rudel knocked-out nine more enemy tanks. He has now destroyed 202 enemy tanks in more than 1,800 combat missions. . ." |
| 3/29/1944 | Oak Leaves with Swords and Diamonds (10th soldier of the *Wehrmacht*, at that time still the highest German decoration). |
| 3/29/1944 | Teletype message from the Commander-in-Chief of the *Luftwaffe, Reichsmarschall* Hermann Göring: "My dear Rudel! You, my bravest and best *Schlachtflieger*, were today awarded the highest decoration for bravery by the Führer. With deepest joy I congratulate youon the award of the Diamonds to the Oak Leaves ofthe Knight's Cross of the Iron Cross. This decoration is awarded only to soldiers whose deeds will be entered into the history of the German people. What you, filled with a fanatical will to fight and borne by a self-sacrificial comradeship, have achieved as an individual soldier and unit leader on the Eastern Front is truly admirable. No one was happier than I to receive the report of your rescue from enemy territory. My *Luftwaffe* is proud to know that you are in its ranks. Yours, Göring" |
| 3/30/1944 | Mentioned in *Wehrmacht* communique: ". . .The Führer has named *Major* Rudel, a *Gruppe* Commander in a *Schlachtgeschwader*, as the tenth soldier of the *Wehrmacht* to be awarded the Oak Leaves with Swords and Diamonds to the Knight's Cross of the Iron Cross." |
| 6/1/1944 | 2,000th combat mission in the Stanca combat zone near Jassy, Rumania. |
| 6/3/1944 | Mentioned in *Wehrmacht* communique: ". . .Major* Rudel, who has been decorated with the highest German award for bravery, flew for the 2,000th time against the enemy on the Eastern Front." On the occasion of his 2,000th mission Rudel was awarded the Pilot Badge in Gold with Diamonds and the Mission Clasp in Gold with Diamonds and 2,000 Pendant by the Commander-in-Chief of the *Luftwaffe*. |
| 8/6/1944 | Mentioned in *Wehrmacht* communique: ". . .27 more tanks were destroyed |

| | |
|---|---|
| | by close-support aircraft. Of these, *Major* Rudel alone accounted for 11, achieving his 300th tank kill with cannon." |
| Mid-Aug. | Destroys 320th tank, Courland front. |
| 8/19/1944 | Shot down by flak near Ergli (Courland); wounded in leg; forced landing on German territory. |
| 9/1/1944 | Promoted to *Oberstleutnant* |
| 10/1/1944 | Takes command of *SG 2 Immelmann*. |
| 11/17/1944 | Wounded by ground fire in Hungary (upper right thigh); emergency landing at fighter base near Budapest; "escape" from hospital; flies missions with leg in a cast. |
| 12/23/1944 | 2,400th combat mission, 463rd tank kill. |
| 1/1/1945 | Becomes only German soldier to receive highest decoration for bravery: the Golden Oak Leaves with Swords and Diamonds to the Knight's Cross of the Iron Cross and is simultaneously promoted to *Oberst*. (Award date on Golden Oak Leaves certificate 12/29/1944). |
| 1/16/1945 | Awarded the Golden Medal for Bravery, Hungary's highest decoration, in Odenburg. (The decoration was awarded a total of seven times, Rudel being the only foreigner so honoured.) |
| 2/8/1945 | Destroys 12 tanks near Lebus/Oder; while destroying the 13th, Rudel's aircraft is hit by Russian 4 cm. anti-aircraft fire and he is wounded in the right leg; crash landing, saved from bleeding to death by gunner, Dr. Gadermann; right leg amputated below the knee at *Waffen-SS* main dressing station near Seelow, 20 km. west of Kustrin; hospital in Berlin. |
| 2/10/1945 | Mentioned in *Wehrmacht* communique: ". . .In recent days *Oberst* Rudel destroyed eleven Soviet tanks to raise his total to 516 tanks." (Rudel actually destroyed 13 tanks on February 8, as confirmed by witnesses.) |
| Easter 1945 | Return to *Geschwader*; Rudel flies missions despite unhealed leg stump and flying ban. Further tank kills not reported but credited to *Geschwader* "account." War correspondent *Hptm*. Niermann flies as Rudel's gunner. |
| 5/8/1945 | Lands together with several other aircraft at Kitzingen airfield, taken prisoner by the Americans. By war's end Rudel had flown a total of 2,530 mission (a total far surpassing that of any other combat pilot in the world), destroyed more than 519 Soviet tanks, sunk 1 battleship, 1 cruiser, 1 destroyer and 70 landing craft, scored 9 confirmed air kills (7 Soviet fighters, 2 IL-2), destroyed over 800 vehicles, more than 150 artillery, anti-tank and flak positions, armored trains and destroyed numerous bridges and supply facilities. He was shot down over thirty times by flak and infantry weapons, wounded five times and rescued six downed crews from death or capture by the Soviets. In the post-war period he won numerous sporting events (tennis, swimming, skiing) despite his prosthesis, including competition against non-disabled opponents. |
| 12/31/1951 | Climbs the Aconcagua in Argentina, at 7,020 meters the highest peak in the Americas, but is forced to turn back by inclement weather approximately 50 meters below the summit. |
| 3/31/1953 | With Dr. Dangl and Dr. Morghen, Rudel becomes first to climb Llullay-Yacu in the Andes, the highest volcano on earth. During second expedition to Llullay-Yacu the team photographer Erwin Neubert is killed in a fall. Neubert's body is recovered by a third expedition and buried in a mountain grave. |

# COMMENTS AND OBSERVATIONS

"Our Hans-Ulrich was a very delicate, nervous child (at birth he weighed five-and-three-quarter pounds). Until he was twelve years old, I had to hold his hand when there was a storm. His older sister used to say, "There is nothing in life that could frighten Uli enough to get him to go into the cellar alone!" This mockery went against Uli's honour and he began to become harder and play a great deal of sports. As a result, however, his studies took a back seat and it was not until vacation was over that he presented his report to his father for signature. I once asked his teacher, "How is Uli in school?"; he replied, "As a boy, lovely; as a student, terrible!" Much could be said of his boyhood pranks, but I am happy that he was allowed to have a carefree childhood."

Rudel's mother, Martha Rudel, nee. Muckner (1950)

"He is lost, only who gives up on himself" — that is a saying which our son adopted totally as his own. And he still lives by it today.
    We — his parents and both of his sisters, but also countless others — were often anxious for him and prayed for him — but always we could only repeat, as he did, the words of Eduard Morike: "The beginning and the end are in his hands, place everything in him."

Johannes Rudel, Pastor at Sausenhofen near Gunzenhausen, Sept. 1950.

He doesn't smoke, drinks only milk, has no stories to tell about women and spends all of his free time playing sports: *Oberfähnrich* Rudel is a strange bird!"

Superior in Graz-Thalerhof, 1938

"He catches on slowly, a typical slow learner! Will he ever become a good Stuka pilot?"

*Staffelkapitän* of *1./Stuka-Geschw. 168*, Graz-Thalerhof, 1938

**45**

"Of course we know each other, because my adjutant certainly knows you! I know you so well that for the time being you will not be allowed to fly with my *Gruppe*."

*Gruppe* Commander *I./Stuka-Geschwader 2* to *Oblt*. Rudel in Greece, 1941

"He is the best man in my Staffel! But this crazy fellow will have a short life . . ."

*Hauptmann* Steen, *Staffelkapitän, 1. Stuka-Geschwader 2*, northern sector of the Russian Front in June 1941.

"That is *Hauptmann* Rudel: A passionate Stuka pilot, a fighter of iron indefatigableness. Therefore, one gift is more valuable to him than all others: the infantry, which the *Gruppe* had flown to protect and support, said by phone that the Soviet attack, which according to the statements of prisoners was planned as a major operation, was smashed by our Stuka bombs while still in its assembly areas. The gift of the infantry was its gratitude to the Stuka pilots."

War correspondent Müller-Marein, 1943, after Rudel's 1,500th mission.

"A Soviet shock division with far-reaching objectives was destroyed. A thrust deep into the rear of our own front was halted and beaten back. The armored core of the Soviet attack force was stopped essentially by a single man, *Major* Rudel — a soldier who, after the most severe physical and mental trials, wounded and with injured feet, climbed back into his aircraft after only one day of rest and in two missions raised his total of tanks destroyed to over 200. This achievement and its effect on the situation on the southern front cannot be overestimated. He leapt into the breach the Soviets had opened and

War correspondent Hein Ruck, 1944, following Rudel's escape across the Dnestr.

Infantryman's prayer on the Eastern Front when Russian tanks had broken through.

closed it. Anyone who had the opportunity to meet him would declare that he embodied the highest soldierly ideals."

". . . let Rudel come!"

War correspondent commentator on the "German Newsreel", 1944

"Unbelievable! In spite of the heaviest flak defence he knocked out the tanks "Rudel style'!"

*Generalfeldmarschall* Ferdinand Schörner, 1944/45

"Rudel alone is worth an entire division!"

Adolph Hitler, Supreme Commander of the *Wehrmacht*, *Führer* Headquarters West, January 1, 1945.

"You are the greatest and bravest soldier that the German people have or have ever had. I have decided to create a new decoration for bravery which now will be the highest of all, the Golden Oak Leaves with Swords and Diamonds to the Knight's Cross of the Iron Cross. I hereby award it to you and at the same time promote you to *Oberst*."

Nicolaus von Below, *Oberst* and *Luftwaffe* Adjutant to the Supreme Commander of the German *Wehrmacht* from 1936 until May 1, 1945. (excerpt from Rudel's book *Trotzdem*)

"It was not the desire for honours or the pressure for new decorations which always drove him back to the front so quickly; the driving forces behind this man were his sense of duty and his readiness for action, which he took for granted. He believed that an officer had a career in which he belonged not to himself but to his country and the subordinates entrusted to him, and that he should therefore be an example to his soldiers, even more so in war than in peacetime, without regard for himself or his life. With the same unselfishness and conception of duty he bravely represented these views to his superiors. I was present at many discussions with Hitler and I can state that on these occasions Rudel did not hold back but stated his opinions honestly and openly, because as an officer and soldier he could not do otherwise and he considered it his duty to his comrades at the front and to his country. His bravery there was as great as at the front and it earned him to a special degree the trust of his superiors. He thus created the real foundation for his success, because maximum results could only be achieved where there was mutual trust between superiors and subordinates. The old soldierly virtues of loyalty and obedience determined his entire life."

(Excerpt from *Das waren die deutschen Jagdflieger-Asse 1939-1945*, Motorbuch-Verlag, Stuttgart, Page 363)
Heinrich Bär, *Oberstleutnant*, Knight's cross with Oak Leaves and Swords, 220 air victories, answering a question by an American about Erich Hartmann (Diamonds, 352 air victories) and Hans-Ulrich Rudel.

"They are the two most fearless and courageous men that I know."

Russian pilot, highly decorated, several times wounded, in a letter from the Soviet Union, 1971.

"It may well be that Rudel is the greatest pilot that history has known! I would like to meet him and shake his hand. He is an admirable man."

Newsletter for members of the former fighter units, official organ of the German Fighter Pilots Association, June issue, 1972.

"Rudel's 2,530 combat missions alone are enough to place him in first place among the greatest pilots of all time. The highest German decoration for bravery in the Second World War stands as a superlative for his unique number of accomplishments."

"Alte Kameraden", independent magazine of German soldiers, organ of the *Traditionsverbände and Kameradenwerke*, No. 10, Oct. 1972, Stuttgart-1

"Friend and foe, especially his former enemies, spoke and speak of him only in superlatives; more meaningful may have been the sighs of relief from the infantrymen on the Eastern Front which were heard when the legendary Rudel machine appeared on the horizon and dived on the Russian tanks. The picture of Rudel the soldier is completed by the man in peacetime who, as an amputee sportsman, conquered a seven-thousand-meter-high mountain and won numerous sporting events."

"War reporter in action"
**Major Rudel escapes the Soviets**
(Extract from a PK article by Hein Ruck, published in several magazines in 1944/45)

". . . The joy felt by his *Gruppe* that he, their commander and leader in many air battles, was back with them again, can only be understood by someone who knows the meaning of such comradeship. They knew what it meant to see so many empty beds at night and to know that a comrade who yesterday was part of their happy group now rested silent in foreign ground. Though this knowledge of death had hardened them, they had considered the commander indestructible. All the greater was their shock and sadness when he failed to return from the last mission and a search later revealed two aircraft in enemy territory but no sign of their crews. But today he was back with them again. Everyone came up and shook his hand firmly. Everyone saw the severity of the ordeal he had come through, and the sadness in one heart became general sadness at the loss of his old gunner, *Oberfeldwebel* Hentschel, their comrade-in-arms with over 1,400 missions to his credit.

—

The commander's story sounded like one of the legends from the ancient past . . . only with the difference that this story came from naked reality. This was in the truest sense of the word, because Major Rudel was brought back to his base naked. Here is the experience as their commanding officer related it to them:

"I still remember that after shaking off the Russian fighters on the last mission I turned back toward enemy territory in order to ascertain what had become of the aircraft which had landed on the far side of the Dnestr. I roared eastward and soon located the aircraft, which was resting in a cornfield. As the area appeared to be suitable for a landing I descended and touched down smoothly close to the other aircraft. The crew were unhurt and in good spirits but their aircraft had been hit and would not fly again. So both men climbed aboard my aircraft and we prepared to take off. The engine roared, but the aircraft would not move from the spot. The undercarriage had dug deep into the soft earth and the machine was stuck fast. What to do? Everyone climbed out and we attempted to remove the wheel spats, which were acting as brakes. The knives we were using broke, but the spats stayed firmly in place. Nevertheless, we did not lose our courage. Somehow we would get the aircraft out. First we tried pulling the tail around and rocking the wings with the motor at full power. All in vain, the machine would not move. . . Once again I scanned the terrain from the pilot's seat and then I saw them approaching. Now there was only one thing to do: Drop everything and make off toward the west. To the west was the river and on the other side the possibility of safety in our own lines. We soon reached the river and, though the bank there was very steep, we had no time to look for a better spot. We had to go down the 80 meter bank on the seat of our pants. Fortunately there were some bushes growing on the bank and we could slow down our descent now and again.

At the bottom it was necessary to remove everything which would make swimming difficult. We took off our boots, shed our flying suits, jackets and vests, and soon we were standing there in our shirts and trousers. We took with us only our sweaters and pistols, everything else was left on the east bank. Cautiously, I tested the water. I quickly pulled my toes back. The water temperature was one or two degrees above freezing. But what could we do? We had to cross the 300-meter-wide river no matter how cold the water. So in we went and began to swim. At first it went quite well until the cold began to work its way into our bodies. Soon I could feel that my hands and feet were becoming stiff. Only by exerting all of my willpower was I able to continue swimming. Just short of the safety of the shore a powerful current once again grasped us in a spot where the Dnestr was particularly fast. But we overcame this as well. 500 meters below our entry point we reached the west bank. But there were only three of us. Hentschel, my loyal gunner, was missing. He was about 50 meters behind and battling desperately with the waves. When he cried for help I leapt back into the water to go to his aid. Before my eyes I saw him sink beneath the surface! . . . calling on all my strength, I barely reached the shore again and fell there exhausted. In a hiding place, we tried to regain our strength because, although it had taken all of our efforts to cross the river behind us, a journey on foot of between 40 and 50 kilometers through enemy occupied territory still lay ahead of us.

It was our hope that by moving in a southerly direction we would encounter Rumanian troops sooner than if we went west, so we headed off to the south . . . Following the compass we marched cross-country, avoiding every village because the bolsheviks would be there. As the sun dropped toward the horizon, four soldiers approached us from out of the sun. From their high fur hats I took them to be Rumanian. I therefore told my comrades to put away their pistols otherwise they might start a shootout with us. The soldiers approached us with rifles levelled. At a distance of 10 meters — they had approached us out of the sun — I realized that they were not wearing fur caps. We could not turn away, so it was just as well go up to them and see what was going on. So I went up to the first and, smiling, clapped him on the shoulder and said, "Dear Rumanian comrade, we are German fliers who have crash-landed. Take us back to your positions so that we may return to our unit!" He did not appear impressed with my friendly request; then, with the words *"Nix Rumanski!"*, he whipped the pistol from my pocket. Realizing that we had fallen into the hands of the Russians I made the lightning-quick decision to flee. With a ducking movement I leapt to the side because I knew they would begin firing. The bullets whistled past my ears as, bent low, I dodged, zigzagging like a hare. Suddenly there was a stabbing pain in my left shoulder and blood spurted out. I had been hit! "Just don't slow down", I told myself, and in best 1500 meter style I left my pursuers behind. A hillock ahead of me presented the opportunity to disappear on the other side. I thought to myself, that never had I been so thankful that I had participated in athletics since I was young. Everything which had been only fun and games in countless competitions now stood me in good stead in this the most serious hour of my life. I had raced with death, and I was the faster . . .

Soon the hillock lay between me and my pursuers. They could no longer see me and I breathed a little easier. But only for a second, because I suddenly saw another group of soldiers ahead of me to the left. They ran down the bank parallel to me in an attempt to cut me off. But I hoped to shake them off as well. Then I saw a rider approaching in the distance. This must be the end, because a horse could outrun an exhausted and wounded soldier. I therefore fell to the ground and began to dig with my hands, throwing dirt over myself. My pursuers continued on ahead until they discovered that the game they were harrying was gone. Again and again they came close to my hiding place. It was a great test of nerves.

The worst came when a deep growl signalled the approach of German aircraft. My *Gruppe* had come with all of its aircraft and two Fieseler *Storch* to search for us. They came down low and the *Storch* were near enough to grasp. But I had to lay there helplessly and dared not make myself noticeable. Rescue was so close but I could not stretch out my arm to save myself . . .

Several hours later an entire company arrived with dogs and horses. Perhaps they knew which rare bird they were hunting. My two comrades had already been overpowered as they were too exhausted by our previous exertions to escape. I lost all hope when I saw the new body of men arrive. Now they had to find me; I could not escape the sight of so many eyes. They approached ever nearer along the road. Now they were level with me. Go on a bit farther, I thought.

And they did. The Bolshevik officer marched them another 50 meters. Then he halted them and had them spread out. 50 meters from my hiding place, they searched with dogs and horses, meter by meter. Gradually they moved away from me. I was saved . . . In the growing darkness I stood up and for the first time rubbed my limbs. The wound in my left shoulder was still bleeding and I had nothing to bandage it with. There was nothing I could do; I had to continue on, always toward the west or the southwest. I could no longer read the compass. It had become a very dark night. My sole guide was the east wind. I had to keep it at my back, then I would reach my own lines somewhere. The undulating terrain presented many difficulties. In the hollows there was mud and water. I had to avoid bridges which meant climbing into chest-deep water and wading across. Often I was left standing from exhaustion. As I had flown eight missions that day, meals had been neglected; thus, I had not eaten since five o'clock in the morning. Just don't sit down, I thought, stay up and hobble on, because their was no longer any question of marching. My bare feet were sore and pained with every step. Again and again I tripped over obstructions, fell into holes or walked into trees. To the left and right I could see artillery fire. I couldn't go that way. I had to try to worm my way through the lines. Once again a village appeared before me. I was determined to find something to eat here no matter what. Carefully, I sneaked around until I was standing just to the side of a house I had made out in the darkness.

I had to summon my courage. If there were Bolsheviks inside I would disappear quickly into the darkness. No one answered my knock on the door. Then I broke a window. An old woman appeared and motioned me inside. I brushed past her and went into the warm room. She did not understand my gestures for something to eat. An old man lay on a wooden bed under the covers. She went over and lay down beside him. The warmth was too enticing; I went over and lay down on the wooden bed as well. In moments I was asleep. After about an hour I woke up. Once again the palaver started with the old couple for something to eat. Finally she brought an old piece of corn bread and some pickled cabbage leaves. Rarely have I enjoyed a meal so much. Satisfied, I lay down on the family bed again and went to sleep with the intention of waking an hour later. Almost to the minute I awoke from my sleep. The battle with the darkness began again; but it was my only protection so it was onwards, farther and farther to the west. Had the wind not veered as well? It was my guide . . . My feet were burning all the more. My wound pained and I was hungry and thirsty again. But I continued on toward the west. Strings of tracer from a 20 millimeter curled into the sky. Flares soared into the air. That must be the front. I would have to pass between the lines. As it became light I saw a village before me. It must be behind our lines. It was abandoned and I was unable to find anything to eat. Two hours later I met a column of Rumanian refugees. I joined up with them and they gave me some *Zwieback* to eat. It tasted wonderful. At about midday I saw a town ahead on the horizon. My companions said that it was in German hands. I walked toward it. At the edge of the town stood two infantrymen. I asked them who was in command here. Suspiciously they sized me up. "Who are you, then?" — "I am *Major* Rudel!" "Anyone could say that", one of them said, "You don't look like a *Major* to us." I pulled my Knight's Cross from my pocket and showed it to them. Still suspicious, they brought me to their commander. There things were set in motion but they couldn't hunt up a uniform which would fit me. So there was nothing else to do but huddle naked under a blanket and have them take me to the airfield. The luck which had accompanied me for so long remained true. An aircraft of my own unit was there and returned me to my base . . ."

The commander finished his story. Everyone had listened breathlessly. They could scarcely grasp that a man could endure so much and not lose his courage. They stood about in groups discussing the story they had just heard. There is no flying weather today and for once it is a day of rest. Tomorrow they will be over the enemy once more.

It's a day of rest for the commander as well. His wound is dressed. His painful feet rest from their 40 kilometer march. His teeth once again have something to work on. The blood pulses in a steady rhythm from his sports-hardened heart through his body. Sleep, plenty of sleep! — That is the cure. The sun comes up again. A new day dawns. It is flying weather, beautiful flying weather, and activity at the base is in full swing. The commander does not lay in the bed to which the doctor has confined him. He must get up, he must fly, he must strike back at the enemy. The account for three lost comrades must be settled, especially for one . . .

Fortunately, in his aircraft he does not have to move around, so his feet can rest. . . Major Rudel is flying again. The familiar voice rings over the microphone. This time the mission is not a tank hunt. Bombs hang beneath the fuselage. Enemy positions are the target. The target area is reached. But what is this? High dust clouds reveal a long column of tanks on the move. They must be stopped. Stopped at any cost, because German troops are still in position to the east and the Soviet tanks apparently want to force a breakthrough and roll up the front. Orders are issued. The *Schlachtflieger-Gruppe* forms up to attack. Soon there is wild confusion where there was an orderly column only moments ago. Accompanying flak units fire wildly. They don't shoot badly but the attacking Stukas dive on them like hawks with bombs and guns. The commander occupies himself with the armored spearhead.

But what does he see? The Russians have loaded drums of fuel on the tanks. Their objective was probably a distant one, only that could explain the presence of the extra fuel load. That would be their undoing.

Rudel took on tank after tank. Burning fuel ran out of the drums and wrapped the tanks in a sea of flame. Like giant torches they drove on through the dusk until they blew up one after the other. 17 tanks exploded. A single man had brought them to destruction that evening. The armored spearhead was smashed . . .

Two days after his escape he had achieved his greatest success as a tank hunter. He had destroyed nearly 200 tanks in his 1,800 missions, had sent a battleship and a cruiser to the bottom, destroyed hundreds of transport trains and columns, smashed to pieces cannon and enemy bunkers with bombs and machine guns.

. . . The next morning he is once again up early and off to battle. The doctor is powerless. "I must fly", says the commander, "otherwise I won't become healthy again!" Once again the target is the Soviet tanks . . .

. . . A Soviet shock division with far-reaching objectives was destroyed. A thrust deep into the rear of our own front was halted and beaten back. The armored core of their attack forced was stopped essentially by a single man, Major Rudel. A soldier who, after the most severe physical and mental trials, wounded and with injured feet, climbed back into his aircraft after one day of rest and in two missions raised his total of tanks destroyed to over 200. This achievement, and its effects on the situation on the southern front cannot be overestimated. He leapt into the breach the Soviets had opened and closed it. Anyone who had the opportunity to meet him will declare that he embodied all the highest soldierly ideals."

War correspondent Hein Ruck

# COMMEMORATIVE ADDRESS

*Commemorative address by Oberst Hans-Ulrich Rudel (Rtd.)* at the dedication of the memorial to the dead of *Stukageschwader Immelmann* at Burg Staufenberg on May 22, 1965:

Traveller, go to Sparta and tell them there that you have seen us here as the law commanded.

This inscription is found on a commemorative stone at the pass of Thermopylae in northern Greece. This spot is in remembrance of the men who defended the pass with their lives to the last man. A similar inscription to that from the ancient pass could be placed on the memorial for our fallen comrades, who also sacrificed their lives in fulfilling their oath and their belief in their fatherland — and quietly we again use those words from antiquity: "As the law commanded." For us of the *Immelmann Geschwader*, this memorial will always evoke memories of our fallen comrades on all fronts of the last war where our *Geschwader* was employed, be they aircrew or ground personnel. Also fixed in our memories are those who had to give up their lives to the revenge of the victors after the official end of hostilities, like Major Fridolin Becker. Also in our memories are those whose fate could not be explained and remain listed as missing.

This is a memorial to our fallen comrades because there is no greater fulfilment of duty than to risk one's life in action.

The bond of comradeship holds us all together. Only with that bond was it possible for us to travel this difficult path. For the loyalty you showed us, we thank you, you whom we wish to honour here today. And we fulfil that thanks with the erection of this memorial.

The outsider may not quite understand why our aircraft are included in the memorial — for many years this aircraft and its style of attack was a part of our lives and became a symbol for us and also for those whom we honour today. May our fatherland remain spared from further wars; we know that the comrades whom we honour today are united with us in this wish. May this memorial also be a legacy for our youth; that they may recognize that a generation sacrificed itself in fulfilling its duty to the fatherland and a free Europe. This fact is also an obligation for our youth; they must prove themselves worthy of this sacrifice and hold the nation's dead in high respect as every one of the earth's peoples honours its members who gave their lives in the struggle. May our youth never allow our dead comrades to be placed in the political firing line — because thus they would not do justice to their sacrifice, because our comrades gave their lives — like their predecessors in previous wars, and like the members of other peoples — in fulfilment of their duty and their oath, for their fatherland. This applies to all the soldiers of the world, and therefore also to the Germans and their allies. Former friends and enemies have now gone to their eternal peace — far from the noise of battle; they are now also eternal friends.

Fate decreed that our comrades precede us; we survived and remain behind. We wish always to prove ourselves worthy of their sacrifice, and we will never tolerate that their reputation be tarnished, because we know that as German soldiers they fought correctly and fairly. They were there not for honours and decorations, but to do their duty, and, therefore, we are still proud today to have been their comrades.

May our fatherland now be granted a peaceful future within the European family of peoples, so that your great sacrifice might bring us a more understandable, deeper purpose. Honour and peace to you!

# WHAT IS A STUKA?

The following is an excerpt from the book *Sturzkampfflugzeug* by H. Brausewaldt, published by Verlag Hermann Hillger KG., Berlin-Grunewald and Leipzig in 1941.

According to the official abbreviation, a Stuka is a *Sturzkampfflugzeug* (dive bomber), which, as its name indicates, attacks in diving flight. The Stuka is fast, powerful and maneuverable. The Ju 87 is sinle-engined and has a crew of two men and two or three machine guns. It needs no bomb-aimer since the pilot fills this role himself. It requires no complicated bomb sight because the pilot aims with the entire machine — like the fighter pilot. The Stuka pilot, therefore, does not drop bombs like our bombers do in level flight, but dives from a height of several thousand meters nearly vertically onto the target with a speed that can scarcely be reached by any other aircraft. Then, at the designated height, he releases his bomb which, nearly always, lands squarely on target. After the bomb is dropped, the Stuka pilot pulls up and escapes at low altitude.

The Stuka unit flies mostly at higher altitudes. Once over the target, the individual aircraft peel off into a dive which reaches the near vertical in the last thousand meters before bomb release. Accurate defensive fire against a diving Stuka is almost impossible. Those with the best chance are light anti-aircraft weapons at or near the target. But it is not pleasant to be at or near the target when a unit of Stukas attack. Words can scarcely describe such an attack. The scene is accompanied by the howl of motors in diving flight. Then, suddenly, a black dot separates itself from the aircraft. Quick as lightning it nears the target. Then the impact. The several-thousand-pound bomb strikes the point of impact with tremendous force. There is an ear-shattering crack, a flash of fire, a blast of air, and men, trees and even houses in the immediate impact area are simply swept away. A black cloud of smoke and dust climbs a hundred meters or more into the sky above the point of impact. Fragments of concrete, stone, earth, steel and iron are flung upward and to every side. Within the wide area where they strike all life is extinguished. Before the smoke and fire from the explosion have subsided, the second aircraft has already begun its attack to be followed by the remaining pairs or *Staffeln*. On the ground below hell has opened up. In the course of the war against the western powers, the Stukas have hit smaller and smaller targets. Such targets are called point targets. One can remember from the *Wehrmacht* communiques the warships and commercial vessels reported sunk, the decisive missions in Poland, Belgium and France, as well as on all the other fronts. The Stukas have now been employed against an entirely new type of target: against enemy tank forces. Many times the Stukas have attacked enemy tanks preparing for an attack or even in the midst of an attack and hit them hard. The demoralizing effects of this weapon cannot be overestimated. Several powerful fortifications in Belgium, which had withstood the heaviest artillery fire, capitulated after undergoing their first Stuka attack. Prisoners stated that there units that could not be held together as our Stukas approached and which fled wildly.

Now a brief word on the stresses which must be withstood by the Stuka aircraft and its crew. The aircraft's structure must be strongly-built in order to be equal to the stresses of diving flight and particularly the pull-up following the diving attack. The forces during pull-up are great, and it requires precision German work to provide the Stuka with the safety that it possesses. Our enemies have not — despite numerous attempts in this area — been able to field an equivalent design. The crews of the Stukas have to endure the rapid changes in air pressure during diving flight as well as the deceleration forces during pull-up. Only completely healthy men with sharp eyes and hard hearts are suitable as Stuka fliers. It is a gratifying indication of the readiness for action of our young soldiers that the rush to join this special arm is particularly great. Our Stukas are not only feared by the enemy and loved by our Army as true comrades in arms and pioneers, but are also thoroughly popular with the masses as evidenced by numerous statements.

In summarizing, the main advantages of the dive bomber are clear: absolute accuracy — even against the smallest target, and lightning-quick attacks and with them surprise, which scarcely allows the enemy time for an effective defence because the Stuka's attack is over in seconds. At the same time, because of its speed and adroitness, the Stuka is outstandingly suited to low-level attacks against ground targets.

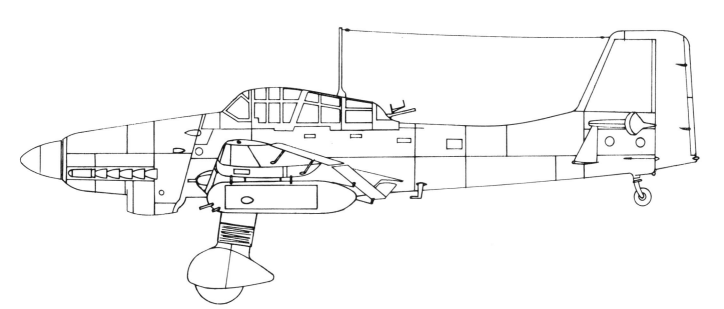

Illustrated is the Junkers Ju 87 D-1 dive bomber and ground attack aircraft. Crew: 2 men; Armament: 2 fixed 20 mm. cannon and a moveable 7.9 mm. machine gun; Bomb load: 1,800 kg.; Engine: one 1,300 HP Junkers Jumo 211JV motor; Wingspan: 13.80 meters; Length: 10.82 meters; Height: 3.84 meters; Maximum speed: 408 km/h at an altitude of 4,200 meters; Ceiling: 7,320 meters; Range: 1,000 km.

# THE EFFECTS OF DIVING FLIGHT ON THE CREW

Provided sufficient protection from the airstream, a man can endure any speed if airspeed and direction of movement remain unchanged — that is when no acceleration, deceleration or change of direction take place. But rapid changes of direction at high speed, for example during hard manoeuvring or pull-up, create a new force, the so-called centrifugal force, which is transmitted to the occupants of the aircraft and creates a series of effects which will be explored here briefly.

In free-fall an object will be pulled toward the center of the earth by gravity, accelerating at first. The rate of acceleration has been calculated at 9.81 meters/second/second; it is designated by the letter G. One G is the force which the body exerts as a result of gravity. At 4G, for example, a person will exert a force of four times his normal weight on his seat or the surface on which he is standing. By 5 or 6G the weight of blood is equivalent to that of iron. At this level there is a loss of consciousness if the force is acting in the direction head-to-foot.

Under the influence of gravity a body at rest presses upon its base, giving the body weight. Under the influence of centrifugal force, as in a turn or in a pull-up the gravitational force is multiplied, so that the occupants of the aircraft are pressed into their seats by a force equal to several times their own body weight. At this moment arms and legs become so heavy that movement and operation of controls and equipment may be impaired. If the pressure exerted by gravity exceeds the bearable limit the result is loss of visual impairment or even consciousness. Every Stuka pilot is familiar with the visual impairment associated with a pull-up from a dive; this is known in pilot's jargon as "seeing stars." It is therefore important for the pilot, as well as the aircraft designer, to know at which level and duration of centrifugal force these effects appear and to what degree these forces can be endured in modern fighters and dive-bombers. Experience has shown that standing personnel can endure centrifugal forces equal to four times the force of gravity, or four times their body weight, when they are prepared and distribute their weight equally on both legs. In unexpectedly sharp pull-ups or turns there is a danger of standing personnel falling to the side which, with the increased weight due to centrifugal force, can result in fractures of the lower leg and knee. Sitting personnel are subject to the following impairments as a result of the application of centrifugal force:

Forces greater than 5G can result in visual impairment in the form of the mentioned grey veil before the eyes to darkness and, finally, complete loss of vision. The subject remains conscious throughout these effects. In stronger forces of more than 6G, loss of vision is quickly followed by loss of consciousness. These effects are apparently brought about by a reduced supply of blood to the eyes and brain as a result of the blood's increased weight brought on by centrifugal force, the blood collecting in the body's lower extremities. If the visual impairment and mild loss of awareness persist for more than a few seconds, the possibility exists that the pilot will be unable to determine the altitude of his aircraft and become disoriented. Pilots who are susceptible to such effects are obviously unsuited to be fighter pilots. In general, loads brought about by centrifugal force which last only one to two seconds can be endured without ill effects up to 8 g. If the load is more than 5G and persists for more than five seconds, "blackout" will occur. In a normal sitting position a load of 5G can be endured at most for three to four seconds. Some pilots who are less susceptible to the effects of g can even endure 8 g for brief periods. It has been shown that slender people are less able to withstand high g forces than short, stocky individuals. In addition, a younger, not fully matured person is less able to stand the effects of g than a thirty- or forty-year-old.

The effects of G disappear as soon the forces are relieved. An empty stomach, lack of sleep, increased alcohol consumption, the inhalation of carbon-dioxide or the effects of high altitude can result in the earlier onset and longer durationof the effects of centrifugal force. Inverted manoeuvres must be flown precisely, as centrifugal force here acts in reverse, and an increased flow of blood to the brain and eyes must be expected. The results can be haemorrhaging of the conjunctive and persistent headache.

Tests have shown that the onset of visual impairment can be delayed to approximately 2G by the subject bending his upper body forwards with his face directed straight ahead and head held back. On average a person can endure several seconds at 6G without visual impairment under these conditions, as the heart does not have to pump the heavier blood as high as it would in a normal sitting position. This is especially true if the subject's abdomen is compressed, as this hinders the rush of blood to the lower extremities, delaying the loss of blood-flow to the eyes. The benefits are even greater if the subject is in a prone position.

From the preceding discussion it is clear that there are limits placed on the pilots of modern dive-bombers by the structural strength of their aircraft as well as the human organism. The absolute limit in both cases is 9G. A certain level of resistance to the effects of centrifugal force must be demanded of the pilot of any high performance aircraft. Ensuring that pilots are aware of this is the task of the flying instructor. Pilots should remain within these limits, as experimenting with higher G forces is dangerous and could lead to accidents.

The underwing dive brakes of a Ju 87 in the retracted position (left), and extended (right).

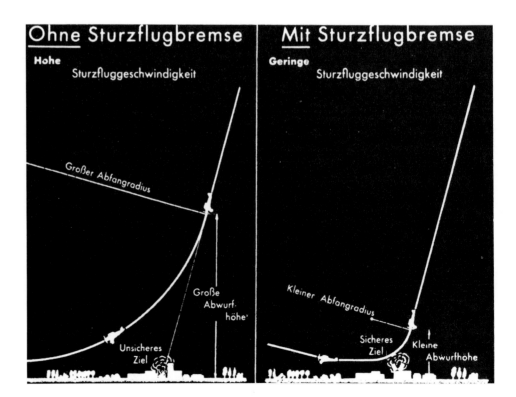

Ohne Sturzflugbremse — Hohe Sturzfluggeschwindigkeit

Mit Sturzflugbremse — Geringe Sturzfluggeschwindigkeit

Großer Abfangradius — Große Abwurfhöhe — Unsicheres Ziel

Kleiner Abfangradius — Sicheres Ziel — Kleine Abwurfhöhe

Two graphs depicting the dive and pull-out angles with the use of dive brakes, (right) and without (left).

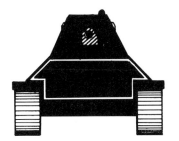 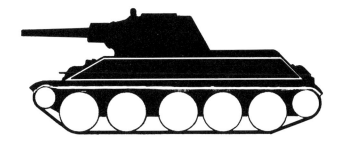 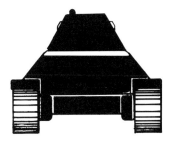

4 man crew
Length: 6.58 m. Width: 2.70 m.
Height: 2.39m.
Max. speed: 60 km./hr.
Armament: multipurpose 7.62 cm.

cannon, 2 — 7.62 mm. DT machine guns
Armor: Front: 45 mm. Side: 40-45 mm. Rear: 40 mm. Top: 16-45 mm.

KV-I heavy tank
44 tons, 5 man crew
Length: 6.8 m. Width: 3.33 m.
Height: 2.7 m.
Max. speed: 35 km./hr.
Armament: 7.62 cm. M-1940

multipurpose cannon 41.5 calibre, 3 -7.62 mm. DT machine guns
Armor: Front: 75 x 35 mm. Side: 75 x 77 mm. Rear: 75 mm. Top: 35-75 mm. + 35 mm.

KV-II heavy tank
53 tons, 6 man crew
Length: 6.8 m. Width: 3.3 m. Height: 3.67 m.

Max. speed: 25 km./hr.
Armament: 15.2 cm. M-1938/40 howitzer 20 calibre, 2 — 7.62 mm. DT machine guns

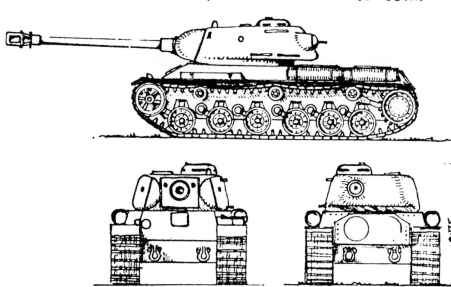

A four-view drawing of the Soviet JS II Stalin heavy tank. 48 tons. 4 man crew Armament: 12.2 cm. cannon 45 calibre with 38 rounds of ammunition 1 - 12.7 mm. anti-aircraft MG and 2 - 7.62 MG with a total of 2,500 rounds of ammunition Armor: Front: 105 mm./ sloped at 60 degrees Side:90 mm./ sloped at 80 degrees. Rear:60 mm./ sloped at 50 degrees Top:35 mm. 550 HP (diesel)Power-to-weight ratio 11.5 HP/ton. 35 km./hr. Range 250 km. on roads A heavily-armed and armored but cumbersome vehicle on the KV chassis. Low rate of fire. Similar JS I replaced in Soviet Army from 1947 by the JS III.

schw.Pz.Kpfw.
# JS II „Josef Stalin II"

Sowjet Union 1945
Ostblock

48 to          4 Mann

12·2 cm Kwk L/45   Vo 38 Schuss
1 Fla-MG 12·7mm ⎤
2 MG  7·62 mm  ⎦  2·500 Schuss
keine Patronenmunition f. Kwk !

Panzerung:
Front: 105 mm/60°
Seite : 90 mm/80•
Heck : 60 mm/50°
Decke  35 mm

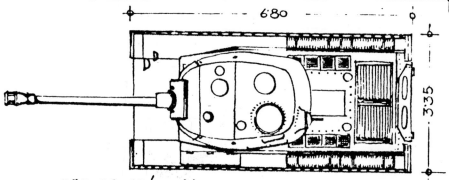

— 6·80 —          275 ·          335

550 PS (Diesel)     115 PS/to     35 Km/h
Fahrbereich 250 km auf Strasse

Stark bewaffnetes u. gepanzertes, aber schwerfälliges Fahrzeug auf KW-Fahrgestell. langsame feuerfolge. Ähnlich
JSI ( Fahrerfront wie bei KWI) im Sowj Heer ab 1947
ersetzt durch JS.III.

# HOME AND CHILDHOOD IN SILESIA

**Above:**
Konradswaldau, Rudel's birthplace in the Landeshut district. In the right center of the photo are the steeples of the Catholic and Protestant churches and in the background the snow-capped Riesengebirge.

**Bottom left:**
Silesian homeland. A view of the peaks of the Riesengebirge.

**Bottom right:**
Rudel's father Rev. Johannes Rudel with "Uli" in 1917; right his sister Johanna.

**Top left:**
The "son and heir" (left), at one-and-a-half years of age with his sisters in the rectory at Konradswaldau at the end of 1917.

**Top right:**
The family in the rectory garden Konradswaldau 1920; between his two sisters is the four year old "Uli."

Below: 1925 in Seiferdau, which is located between the Zobten and Schweidnitz.

Above: 1927 in the rectory garden at Nieder-Kosel/Oberlausitz from left: "Hanne", "Uli" and Ingeborg.

Bottom left: With his mother, Frau Martha Rudel, about 1927.

Bottom right: As a twelve year old in the rectory garden in Nieder-Kosel, Oberlausitz, 1928.

Above left:
Rudel's parents in 1929.

Above right:
With sister Johanna, who was known as "Hanne", and "Bella", the children's pet doberman bitch, in front of the Nieder-Kosel rectory in 1929.

Below: Paternal grandparents: teachers Hermann and Marie Rudel, Haynau near Liegnitz, 1931.

**Above:** Family portrait from his grandparents' golden anniversary in Haynau in 1931. Second row, far right: Rudel's parents with daughter "Hanne"; third row, right: Hans-Ulrich with sister Ingeborg.

**Bottom left:**
As a sixteen year old, "Uli" became a member of the German Lifesaving Society, receiving his membership in Breslau on 2/16/1932.

**Bottom right:**
"Uli" grew up on his skis. When there was snow to entice him onto the slopes his studies were often forgotten. The photo was taken in the Riesengebiege in 1932.

Above left:
Secondary school in Lauban (District Town in Lower Silesia) where he matriculated in 1936.

There was scarcely a sport in which Rudel did not excel. The photo shows him as a seventeen-year-old tennis player.

With his classmates in 1935 in front of the secondary school. In the first row, second from the right is Hans-Ulrich Rudel.

With sister Inge, who later
became a doctor, in the
rectory garden in Alt-
Kohlfurt, northeast of
Görlitz, in Silesia, about
1936.

66

"Uli" and his sister
Johanna in Alt-Kohlfurt,
about 1936.

Rowing on the Heidesee while on vacation. Alt-Kohlfurt, autumn 1936.

While still a schoolboy Rudel was already outstanding in the decathlon. This photograph of Rudel putting the shot was taken in 1936 on the sports field of Lauban's secondary school.

While hiking or on outings with the Hitler Youth most nights were spent in tents but occasionally in youth hostels. Depicted is a photocopy of Rudel's identity card from the Reich Federation of German Youth Hostels which was issued in March 1935.

**Rudel's father in robes, July 1939.**

**Rudel's parents while walking, 1944.**

**After the flight from the Silesian homeland, Reverend Rudel held office in Gunzenhausen, Bavaria, where he died on January 23, 1952. Rudel's mother passed away on May 8, 1960.**

---

Gott der Herr rief heute meinen lieben Mann, Herrn

## Pfarrer Johannes Rudel

nach qualvollem Leiden aus der Zeit in die Ewigkeit.

**Gunzenhausen**/Pflaumfeld,
den 23. Januar 1952.

In unsagbarem Leid:

**Martha Rudel und Kinder**

Beerdigung: Samstag, 26. Januar, 14 Uhr, in Pflaumfeld.

---

Am Geburtstag ihres Mannes, unseres Vaters, am Vorabend des Muttertages und wenige Tage vor Vollendung ihres 79. Geburtstages erlöste Gott unsere innig geliebte Mutter

## FRAU MARTHA RUDEL
### GEB. MUECKNER

von ihrem schweren Leiden.

In stiller Trauer:
INGEBORG, JOHANNA UND
HANS-ULRICH RUDEL

Dornhausen, 8. Mai 1960.

---

**Announcements of the passing of father (left) and mother (right) published by the family.**

# 1938-1940

Rudel as an officer cadet at the Air Warfare School in Wildpark-Werder near Berlin where, in 1937, he began his flying training. The photo shows Rudel in the cockpit of a Focke-Wulf Fw 44 *Stieglitz* before his first solo flight.

In June 1938, Rudel was transferred to *I. Gruppe* of *St.Geschw. 168* in Graz-Thalerhof for dive bomber pilot training. He soon became known to his superiors as a "strange bird" who drank only milk and spent his spare time on the sports field or in the mountains. This photo was taken during a rest stop on a weekend hike. Rudel is in the center between two comrades.

**Summer 1939:**

**During practice at the shot and discus at Prenzlau, Uckermark, where he trained as an observer with *Fernaufklärungsgruppe 121*.**

**Left:** *Leutnant* Rudel before a reconnaissance mission over Poland in September 1939.

**Right:** Back from the mission, the results of *Leutnant* Rudel's reconnaissance are entered on the situation map.

**Below:** Following the Polish campaign Rudel continues to have no success in his efforts to obtain a transfer to Stukas. He was transferred to Flight Training Regiment 143 at Vienna-Stammersdorf and later to Crailsheim, where he served as Regimental Adjutant and took part in numerous sporting events. This photo originated at a Battalion Sportfest at Vienna-Stammersdorf in 1940. In this "snapshot" the bar is at 1.60 metres.

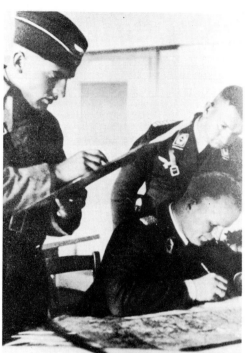

*Leutnant* Rudel with his victorious team following the "Across Vienna" relay race in 1940.

The Silesian decathlon championship on 10/6/1940. Rudel, seen here in the hurdles, second from right, placed 3rd in the decathlon.

Pole vaulting, at that time still with a bamboo pole.

Promoted to *Oberleutnant* on 10/1/1940, Rudel was transferred to the Stuka school at Graz, Steiermark. It would not be until the difficult sorties into the "Flak-hell of Kronstadt" that the strain of combat missions would leave its mark on the face of the young pilot-officer.

The Karl Ritter Ufa film *Stukas* was shot on one of the *Immelmann Geschwader*'s airfields in the Caen-Falaise area. Among the well-known actors taking part in the film were Carl Raddatz, Hannes Stelzer (later killed in action on 12/28/1944 in Hungary as a *Feldwebel* officer cadet and pilot with a night close-support unit), O.E. Hasse, Beppo Brehm, Albert Hehn, Georg Thomalla, Ernst v. Klipstein, Herbert Wilk, Karl John, Eduard v. Winterstein, Marina v. Dittmar, Ursula Deinert, Else Knott, Ethel Reschke, Lilli Schonborn.

A still from the film. The commander, who has been wounded in the right leg, is lifted from his machine by his comrades. The aircraft carries the emblem of the *Immelmann Geschwader*, the cross of the Teutonic Knights. This scene from the film was replayed in real life by Rudel when he was hit by Flak near Lebus on the Oder in 1945 and lost his lower right leg; a remarkable similarity between film and reality.

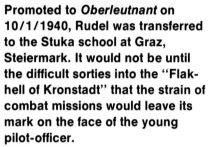

The producer of the film "Stukas", Prof. Karl Ritter. One of the "old eagles" (pilots licence No. 121 from 11/30/1911), he is seen here at age 85 with the famous test pilot and sport flier Hanna Reitsch in June 1974.

# EARLY 1941: GREECE

Early 1941 in Molai, Peloponnes: Rudel, eager to finally see action as a Stuka pilot, receives the greatest disappointment of his career with *I. Gruppe, St.Geschw. 2 Immelmann.* Prejudice on the part his superiors stood between him and his first mission. While his comrades were flying successful missions against the British fleet and supporting the battle on Crete, he remained tied to the ground. The photo from Molai is almost symbolic: A frustrated Stuka pilot in the midst of a "thorny environment."

76

The airfield at Molai, Greece: the aircraft wait to be armed with SD250 bombs (foreground) prior to takeoff for the island of Crete.

At dawn on June 22, 1941, the German campaign against the Soviet Union began on a front between the Arctic Ocean and the Black Sea. As part of *VIII. Fliegerkorps, I.* and *III. Gruppen* of *Stukageschwader 2 Immelmann* initially supported the attack operations of Army Group Center under *Generalfeldmarschall* von Bock. Beginning in August the two *Gruppen* operated over the northern sector of the front on the Gulf of Finland (including Leningrad and the Volkhov front) supporting *Generalfeldmarschall* Ritter von Leeb's Army Group.

*Oberleutnant* Rudel flew his first missions with 1. *Staffel*, where he served as the unit's technical officer. Operating from the airfield at Raczki (south of the Rominten heights), the unit's Stukas attacked Russian airfields, artillery and field positions, tank concentrations, bridges and important supply routes. By July 24, Rudel was able to enter his 100th mission in his log book. In the same month he received the Iron Cross First Class, the Mission Clasp in Gold and in September — after being transferred to *III. Gruppe* — the *Luftwaffe* Honour Goblet for particular success in the air war.

# THE RUSSIAN CAMPAIGN

Just before takeoff. Rudel's machine is in the foreground.

A *Kette* from *I./St.G. 2 Immelmann* overflies the front lines in
the central sector of the Eastern Front.

Peeling off into a diving attack.

**Above:** The German advance can continue. Infantrymen wave from their armored personnel carriers to one of the "infantrymen of the air", who answers by rocking his aircraft's wings.

**Left:** Only several hundred metres ahead of the leading German troops, Stuka bombs hammer enemy positions and tank concentrations.

**Right:** Happy infantrymen: "The Stukas are here."

A photograph of a typical Russian "road" in the summer of 1941. With the onset of the rainy season, the sandy "washboard" became a "mud road", making the delivery of supplies extremely difficult.

Returning from a mission.

80

This photograph, taken by a Stuka gunner, shows several hits in the aircraft's right wing from enemy machine gun fire.

Scarcely have the machines landed, when they are quickly refuelled . . .

. . . rearmed by the armorer . . .

81

. . . loaded with bombs and made ready to go by the crew chief.

An SD 250 is loaded beneath the fuselage and . . .

Left: . . . two 50 kg. bombs are hung beneath each wing.

Right: A gunner sets the pilot-activated automatic cine camera which is mounted in the aircraft's left wing.

The *Gruppe* takes off on another mission.

An armorer takes a nap between two explosive "eggs" while waiting for the aircraft to return.

On this occasion the target is enemy tanks in the Grodno area.

While the decoys remain intact, the T-34s, as shown in this PK photo, have been put "out of action."

Tank decoys — such as this one — were intended to attract the Stukas' bombs.

A KV-II destroyed by Stuka bombs.

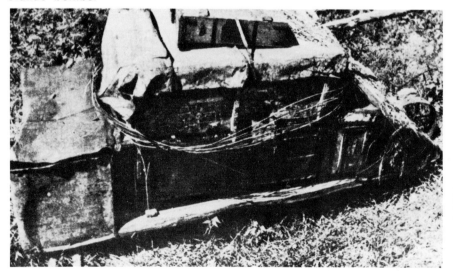

Bombing attack by *I./St.G.2* on June 28, 1941 against Novogrodek, between Grodno and Minsk. The town was an important traffic junction — five roads and a rail line crossed here — and was jammed with supplies. During the attack a munitions dump exploded high into the air.

The double-track rail line between Vitebsk and Smolensk was the target on several occasions for the *Immelmann* Stukas operating from the airfield at Slobodo.

The bridge near Vyasma on the Vyasma-Moscow highway was destroyed. The next attack was against the pontoon bridge and the Russian columns which were backed up there while attempting to escape encirclement by the German Army.

Takeoff from the airfield at Lepel (approx. 130 km. southwest of Vitebsk) on July 21, 1941: two direct hits on the bridge over the Chmost on the Minsk-Moscow highway 30 km. west of Jarzievo, northwest of Smolensk. The bombs tore up the roadway but failed to bring down the bridge.

Despite heavy anti-aircraft fire, the road and rail bridges spanning the Wop river approximately 50 km. northeast of Smolensk near Ulchovo were destroyed by several direct hits on July 22. First the road bridge (foreground), and then the rail bridge were attacked. Rudel's bomb scored a direct hit on the target.

Foreground: The two destroyed bridges over the Wop. Background: Several fires burning among the flak positions on the riverbank.

Supporting the German attack in the northern sector in September 1941, *I.* and *III. Gruppen* frequently attacked the important rail line between Leningrad and Moscow. The photo shows the "precision work" carried out on a mission on September 3 near Sluzk, southwest of Leningrad.

During this mission against the same rail line in the Leningrad-Lake Ilmen area, the tracks and rail embankment were torn to pieces by the bombs of Rudel and his comrades.

Forty kilometres south of Leningrad on the Leningrad-Luga line, southeast of Krasnogvardeysk, *Hauptmann* Steen and *Oberleutnant* Rudel score direct hits on an armored train which had intervened in the ground fighting. In spite of the heavy anti-aircraft fire, the train was destroyed.

When an aircraft returned with damage, it was parked in the dispersal area and camouflaged; after the day's missions had been completed, the technical personnel would make the necessary repairs.

With the loss of Libau, Riga, Port Baltic and Reval, the Soviet Baltic Fleet retired to its last remaining war port at Kronstadt, on the island of Kotlin west of Leningrad. From there, using their long-range naval guns, the battleships *Marat* and *October Revolution*, as well as several heavy cruisers and destroyers, provided fire support for the Soviet ground forces. Beginning on September 21, Rudel and his comrades of the *Immelmann Geschwader*, under the leadership of *Oberstleutnant* Oskar Dinort, flew almost daily sorties against the port of Kronstadt from Tyrkovo airfield (approx. 100 km. northwest of Lake Ilmen). Fighter escort was usually provided by *Jagdgeschwader 54*, commanded by *Major* Hannes Trautloft. Many crews, including the commander of *I. Gruppe*, *Hauptmann* Steen, and Rudel's gunner, *Unteroffizier* Scharnowski, failed to return from the "flak-hell" over Kronstadt.

# IN THE "FLAK-HELL" OF KRONSTADT

A Russian photograph of the battleship *Marat*, which took part in the land battle, giving the German units, in particular the 58th Infantry Division, a great deal of trouble. The 23,606-ton battleship had been launched in 1911 but was modernized during a major overhaul in 1931. The armament of the 181-metre-long *Marat* consisted of twelve 30.5 cm., sixteen 12 cm. and six 7.6 cm. (Flak) guns, sixteen 4 cm. flak and numerous light weapons. She was equipped with a catapult for launching aircraft, two heavy cranes for launching motor torpedo boats and carried a crew of 1,230 men.

The Russian destroyer *Opytnyj* on the river Neva during a night bombardment of German positions.

The 1,000 kg. bombs, which had been requisitioned long before, finally arrive at Tyrkovo.

Loading the "heavy artillery", as the 1,000 kg. bombs were referred to, manually, always meant hard work for the ground crews.

A German reconnaissance aircraft discovered that the *Marat*, which had suffered minor damage from Rudel's bomb on September 16, was now in the port of Kronstadt.

An enlargement from the same reconnaissance photograph of the *Marat*.

Shortly after 09.00: The *Immelmann Geschwader* en route to Kronstadt. The Soviet battleships *Marat* and *October Revolution* must be put out of action in order to relieve the pressure on German forces on the Leningrad front. The photograph shows four aircraft in flight above the clouds.

En route to the target.

93

Shortly after crossing the Baltic coast, Soviet heavy anti-aircraft guns put up a barrage. The numerous flak bursts are clearly visible above the clouds.

After a flight of approximately 50 minutes, the Stukas of the *Immelmann Geschwader* launched a mass attack on the naval port of Kronstadt. Following a direct hit by *Oberleutnant* Rudel, a giant cloud of smoke hides the battleship *Marat*.

Rudel's 1,000 kg. bomb tore off the bows of the 23,606-ton battleship. This reconnaissance photo, taken immediately after the attack, shows numerous Russian motor launches and tugs around the *Marat* engaged in rescue operations. The armored cruiser *Kirov*, attacked and heavily damaged the same day, may be seen tied up at dockside above the shattered *Marat*.

Hits by Rudel and his comrades on a large *Leningrad* class destroyer.

The badly-damaged destroyer was towed into the inner harbour of Kronstadt trailing a long oil slick across the surface of the water.

A few moments later: the *October Revolution*, which together with the *Marat* constituted the heaviest units of the Russian fleet, receives several hits which put her out of action for a considerable period of time.

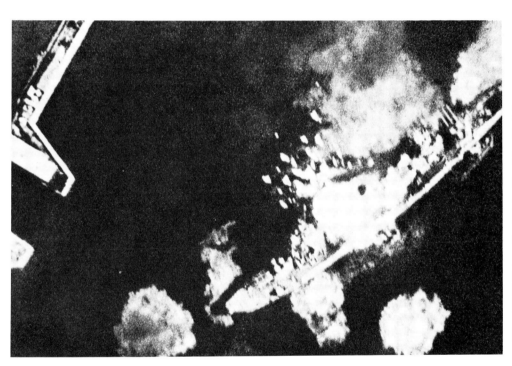

The 23,256-ton Soviet battleship *October Revolution* (armament similar to the *Marat*) under air attack by III. *Gruppe* of the *Immelmann Geschwader*.

The badly damaged *Leningrad* class destroyer is towed through the harbour entrance (1); a heavy cruiser of the *Kirov* class (2), and the as yet undamaged battleship *October Revolution*.

This so-called "flier's monument" proved to have fateful consequences. On returning from the successful strike against Kronstadt on September 23, the aircraft of the *Gruppe* commander, *Hauptmann* Ernst-Siegfried Steen, stood on its nose while taxiing across soft ground. Steen was forced to use Rudel's aircraft for the next mission. In order to save time, Rudel's gunner remained on board the aircraft while Steen's gunner, *Oberfeldwebel* Helmut Lehmann, stayed behind. Rudel's aircraft, with the commander and *Unteroffizier* Scharnowski aboard, was hit by flak. Unable to pull out of the dive, Steen steered the aircraft with its 1,000 kilogram bomb onto the target. The aircraft struck the water close beside the *Kirov*, exploding and causing severe damage. Steen was awarded the Knight's Cross posthumously. The mission into the "flak-hell" of Kronstadt, from which he and Rudel's gunner Scharnowski did not return, was Steen's 301st operational sortie. A mishap on a rain-soaked airfield proved fateful . . .

# AUTUMN
# 1941

The target is a Soviet troop concentration. On each of the aircraft's underwing bomb racks are two 50 kilo bombs with extended fuses, which were called "Dinort asparagus" after their inventor *Oberstleutnent* Dinort (commander of St.G. 2 in 1941). On impact the extended fuses caused the bomb to explode roughly a metre above the ground for maximum effect against personnel.

Shortly before a mission on the Volkhov front in the autumn of 1941. *Oblt.* Rudel checks the fit of both small throat-type microphones in his *FT-Haube.* (Helmet with built-in headset and throat-type microphones)

Stukas approaching Soviet troop assembly areas on the northern sector carry one 250 kilo bomb on the cradle beneath the fuselage and two 50 kilo bombs under each wing.

The troop assembly area is smashed, preventing a Soviet penetration of the German positions.

A machine of *III. Gruppe* is forced to make an emergency landing just on the German side of the lines with engine damage. A ditch stopped the rolling aircraft, the crew escaping uninjured.

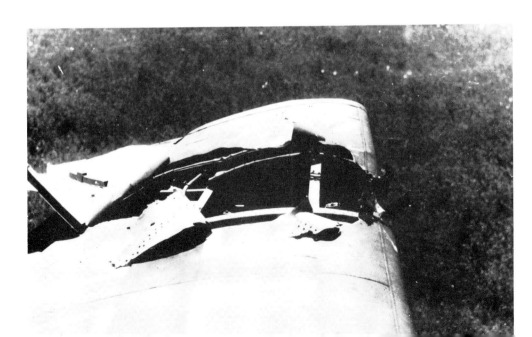

The crew of this Stuka was also very lucky: they returned safely to base with this large hole in the aircraft's left wing caused by anti-aircraft fire. (The photograph was taken during the return flight.)

The returning aircraft peel off over their base for a landing.

Left: During the muddy period in autumn and spring, most airfields in Russia looked like this Stuka base. The softened airfields placed great demands on the pilots during takeoff and landing and made the ground crew's task of servicing the aircraft much more difficult.

Right: The driver of this tank truck required all of his skill to get fuel to the aircraft.

# THE
# FIRST
# RUSSIAN
# WINTER
# 1941/42-
# ORDEAL
# IN THE
# ICE AND
# SNOW

The winter of 1941 arrived unexpectedly early, halting the German advance just short of Moscow. This marked the beginning of an extremely difficult ordeal for the German ground forces engaged in fierce defensive battles but also for the Stuka air and ground crews. The airfields had to be kept clear of snow, while engines refused to start in the icy cold and the ground crews were forced to endure temperatures of minus 20, 30 or even 40 degrees in order to have the Stukas of the *Immelmann Geschwader* ready for operations. Above left: Early in the morning, a member of the ground crew de-ices the windscreen of his Ju 87. Above right: The revolving propeller of a "snow sweeper" like this one could have kept the runways clear for takeoff and landing. Between the imaginative solution offered by a cartoonist in *Adler*, the *Luftwaffe*'s illustrated magazine, and cold reality, lay a difference as deep as the snows of Russia . . .

102

The technical personnel were forced to become masters of improvisation in order to keep aircraft engines, equipment and weapons functioning. Sometimes, even the motors of the refuelling equipment refused to start. Fortunately, in this case it has started at once.

In the Lake Ilmen district: a sentry with MG 15 on the airfield perimeter guarding against Russian low-level air attack.

Stukas ready for takeoff; each carries a bomb dispenser containing SD 2 fragmentation bombs beneath each wing.

*103*

This Ju 87D of the *Immelmann Geschwader* sports a white-spotted camouflage finish.

**Left:** An attack on the Kremlin in Cheryayeva, south of the Waldai heights. The walls of the citadel bristled with machine gun nests and anti-aircraft weapons.

**Right:** A photograph of bomb strikes in Cheryayeva, which served as an important supply base for the Soviets.

Near Chudovo on the Volkhov front, Rudel and his comrades successfully attack Russian positions and a truck and tank column at an intersection.

Rudel and his men have stopped another Soviet tank assault. The terrain is littered with burned-out tanks; in the foreground is a T-70.

From the airfield at Rjelbitzy to Staraya Russa was only a short flight. There the Stukas were able to smash a powerful Russian counterattack with bombs and guns. The white camouflage finish of this T-70 proved ineffective.

As the *Geschwader*'s Stukas fly off, clouds of black smoke hang over the battlefield as evidence of a successful attack.

A Stuka bomb was the undoing of this KV-1.

Rudel and the *Immelmann* Stukas fly back to base, pleased that they were able to assist their hard-pressed *Wehrmacht* comrades in the battle zone south of Lake Ilmen.

Over the airfield, the flights of Stukas peel off for a landing. A short time later they were in the air again, attacking Soviet artillery positions, supply routes and armor farther south near Demyansk. After changing airfields several times, attacks followed in the area of Kalinin and on the approaches to Moscow.

Left: Two aircraft in a diving attack.

Right: Rudel scores a direct hit on an armored train on the line just outside Moscow.

107

Attack against tanks on the central sector of the Eastern front.

On the return flight the Stukas often strafed targets of opportunity, such as motor transport. In this photo five personnel carriers sit shot-up and abandoned on the side of a road leading out of a Russian village.

On one of the next attacks, a Soviet fuel dump is hit and destroyed.

The aircraft return to base in low-level flight over the vast, open, snow-covered Russian countryside.

# JANUARY-FEBRUARY 1942

On January 15, 1942, *Oberleutnant* Rudel was awarded the Knight's Cross. The following is an excerpt from the award recommendation: " . . . displaying particular bravery, put the Soviet battleship *Marat* out of action with a direct hit, severely damaged the battleship *October Revolution*, sank a heavy cruiser and put another out of action. In missions against ground targets he has destroyed or seriously damaged 15 bridges, 23 batteries, 4 armored trains, and 17 tanks and assault guns."

110

On February 7, 1942, Air Fleet Chief *Generaloberst* von Dessloch visited the *Gruppe* at Dugino. There he presented the Knight's Cross to: (from left), *Gruppe* Commander *Hauptmann* Pressler, *Oberleutnant* Stepp (leader of *8. Staffel*), and *Oberleutnant* Kaiser (*Gruppe* Adjutant). In the background are (from left): *Leutnant* Graber (*Staffel* leader, Knight's Cross 6/19/42, KIA 1/30/43), *Oberleutnant* Dr. Otte (*Staffel* leader, Knight's Cross 4/5/42, Oak Leaves 3/24/44, KIA 5/20/44), medical officer Dr. Ernst Gadermann (Knight's Cross 8/19/44).

*III. Gruppe*'s three new wearers of the Knight's Cross with the flying personnel.

Becoming accustomed to conditions in Russia was all important; for the men of the *Immelmann Geschwader* this meant fetching water for cooking or washing from the primitive draw well near their "billets."

*III. Gruppe* (commander *Hauptmann* Pressler) moved to the forward airfield at Dugino, approximately 60 km. south of Rshev and 80 km. north of Vyasma. Occupying a key position on the Smolensk-Moscow highway, it was mentioned often in the Armed Forces communiques.
*Unteroffizier* Heinz Popp of the maintenance platoon noted in his pocket calender: 2/16 — night clear, minus 20 degrees; 2/20 - night to minus 40; 2/26 - snowstorm, minus 30 to 40 degrees! Despite the so-called "coffee warmers", which were fashioned from tent squares, temperatures inside during an engine change were still well below freezing.

Left: Many aircraft refused to start in the Siberian cold. The ground crews were always relieved when the propeller finally started to turn.

Right: For several days *III. Gruppe* flew missions against the Sytchevka-Rshev rail line (in photo), where the Soviets were trying to force a breakthrough.

The Soviets succeeded in breaking through the German lines. Shortly before dawn on January 18, 1942, they launched a surprise attack on Sytchevka and the airfield at Dugino-Djatlicha. *Oberleutnant* Kresken, chief of the Headquarters Company, was able to hold the airfield using ground personnel. With first light, Rudel and his comrades were able to support the defenders, making effective attacks on the attacking Russian forces with bombs and guns. Despite being unaccustomed to combat, the ground crews fought bravely. When it became light, they found heaps of dead Russians littering the ground in front of their snow dugouts. The Soviet troops were members of an elite Siberian division.

*Panje* sleighs were often indispensable as a means of transport during the severe Russian winter.

# WINTER-SUMMER 1942

The *Geschwader*'s three *Gruppen* were temporarily withdrawn from action to rest and reequip. Rudel received orders posting him to Graz in the Austrian province of Styria. There he took command of the Stuka Replacement *Staffel* and passed on his front-line experience to the young crews. As at all flying schools, there were serious accidents. One such flying accident claimed the lives of *Oberleutnant* Besser and *Oberfeldwebel* Posekardt. Knight's Cross holder *Leutnant* Jackel presents the assembled honour guard to *Oberleutnant* Rudel as their dead comrades are returned to the homeland.

The crew of this aircraft, which force-landed near Graz, escaped unhurt.

Rudel with his wife during a stop on an outing to Koflach. They had been married at Alt-Kohlfurt in Silesia while he was on leave. The church wedding was performed by Rudel's father.

During his short leave from the front, Rudel somewhat self-consciously receives the best wishes of the residents of Alt-Kohlfurt in front of his father's home. The townspeople even provided a serenade for the local hero.

During off-duty hours, Rudel played sports or went hiking in the mountains with members of his *Staffel*. This photo was taken by the cross on the summit of the Hochschwab in Styria, Austria.

On a free weekend — no flying due to poor weather — with a friend in front of a mountain cabin.

Rudel's efforts to return from Graz to the front finally succeed: he and his replacement *Staffel* are transferred to Sarabus, near Simferopol in the Crimea, then on to Kerch and a front line airfield near Maikop on the Caucasian front. From there the *Staffel* provided effective support for the advance toward Tuapse. Above: A striking photograph of a direct hit on a Soviet destroyer near Tuapse on the Black Sea, late summer 1942.

Precision work by the Stukas. A large fuel storage facility is destroyed at Mineralnyjewody in the Caucasus. The German pilots were able to destroy the target without resorting to carpet bombing which would have undoubtedly destroyed the entire city.

An operations conference, summer 1942: from right to left: the *Geschwader* commander *Major* Hozzel, *Gruppe* commander *Hauptmann* Dilley (*I./St.G. 2*), *Staffel* leader *Hauptmann* Lang (*1. Staffel*).

On the airfield at Tazinskaya following the 600th mission by *Hauptmann* Lang, leader of *1. Staffel* (center); on the left is his gunner *Feldwebel* Alois Berndl, right, crew chief *Feldwebel* Rothmann.

Above right: War correspondent *Feldwebel* Schalber (with oak leaf wreath) after his 300th mission as gunner for the commander of *I./St.G. 2*, *Hauptmann* Dilley (left).

*Generaloberst* Freiherr von Richthofen, the Chief of *Luftflotte 4*, visits the *Immelmann Geschwader*. From left: *Major* Hozzel, commander *St.G. 2*; von Richthofen; his adjutant; the *Geschwader* commander's adjutant, *Hauptmann* Pekrun.

# STALINGRAD
# MISSIONS
# 1942/43

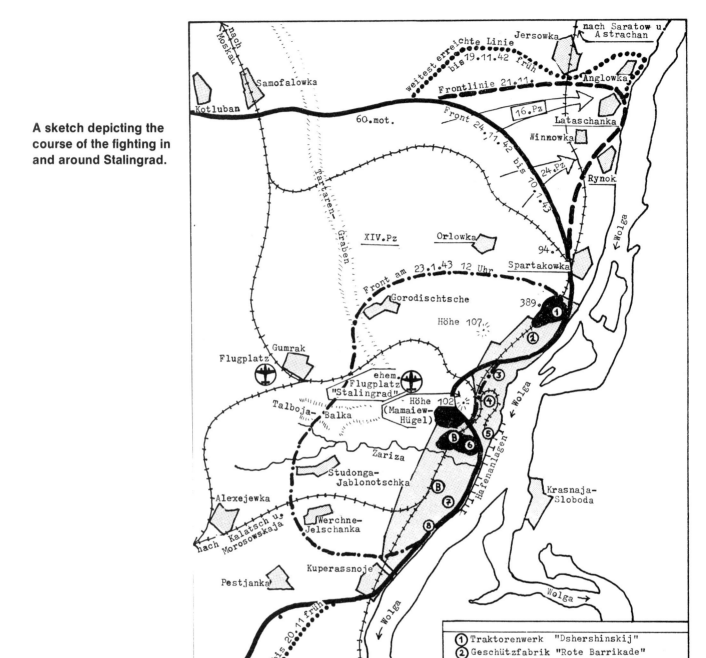

**A sketch depicting the course of the fighting in and around Stalingrad.**

nach Moskau

Samofalowka

Kotluban

weitest erreichte Linie bis 79.11.42 früh

Jersowka

nach Saratow u. Astrachan

Frontlinie 21.11.

Anglowka

60.mot.

Front 24.11.42 bis 10.1.43

16.Pz

Lataschanka

Ninnowka

24.Pz

Rynok

Tartaren-Graben

XIV.Pz

Orlowka

Wolga

94.

Spartakowka

Front am 23.1.43 12 Uhr

Gorodischtsche

389

①

Höhe 107

①

Gumrak

Flugplatz

ehem. Flugplatz "Stalingrad"

③

Talboja-Balka

Höhe 102 (Mamaiew-Hügel)

④

Wolga

⑤

Ⓑ

⑥

Zariza

Hafenanlagen

Studonga-Jablonotschka

Ⓑ

Krasnaja-Sloboda

Alexejewka

⑦

nach Kalatsch u. Morosowskaja

Werchne-Jelschanka

⑧

Kuperassnoje

Pestjanka

Wolga

Wolga →

weitest erreichte Linie bis 20.11 früh

Beketowka

nach Kotelnikowo

|  |  |
|---|---|
| ① | Traktorenwerk "Dshershinskij" |
| ② | Geschützfabrik "Rote Barrikade" |
| ③ | Metallurgisches Werk "Roter Oktober" |
| ④ | Chem.Fabrik im "Tennisschläger" |
| ⑤ | Raffinerie u.Treibstofflager |
| ⑥ | Roter Platz /Kraftwerk, Wasserwerk, Post |
| ⑦ | Getreidesilo u.Konservenfabrik |
| ⑧ | Sägewerk "Kubyschew |
| Ⓑ | Bahnhöfe Nord u.Süd |
| ⬛ | Letzte Kessel 26.1.~2.2.43 |

1  2  3  4  5                    10km

Key to table bottom right:
1. "Dzerzhinsky" tractor works
2. "Red Barricade" gun factory
3. "Red October" metallurgical works
4. Chemical plant in the "tennis racket"
5. Refinery and fuel storage facility
6. Red Square — power station, water works, post office
7. Grain silo and cannery
8. "Kubyshev" saw-mill
9. Rail stations north and south

Black areas. Last pockets 1/26 -2/2/43

On September 1, 1942, German forces reached the outskirts of Stalingrad. The *Immelmann Geschwader* supported the assault on this large industrialized city and regularly attacked targets within the town. Above left: This supply ship tied up on the bank of the Volga was hit by *5. Staffel* and destroyed.

Two tankers were shot up by *I. Gruppe* and left burning at a temporary oil terminus south of the besieged city.

Burned-out Soviet barracks, following an attack by *5. Staffel*.

When Rudel learned that his comrades were in action near Stalingrad, he left the hospital in Rostov, despite having jaundice, and flew missions over Stalingrad as leader of *1./St.G. 2*. Rudel also flew sorties over the Don basin as in this photograph, where a makeshift bridge over the river near Kalach has been destroyed.

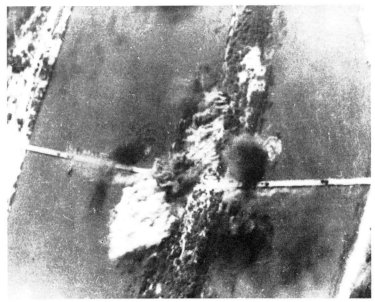

**The tenaciously-defended brickyard on the edge of the city was attacked successfully by *1. Staffel* on September 12.**

**A giant pall of smoke hangs over the city. On this occasion the Stukas' target was a large oil refinery.**

**An aerial photograph of the completely burned-out oil refinery.**

A view of the Stalingrad-North manufacturing plant and the northern rail loop prior to the Stukas' attack.

The same factory complex after the Stukas' attack.

123

The fiercely-defended, bitterly-contested grain silo, autumn 1942. This is one of the many photographs taken by war correspondent *Feldwebel* Josef Schalber who, by the end of the war, had flown on over 400 missions as an air-gunner, been awarded the German Cross in Gold and promoted to *Leutnant*.

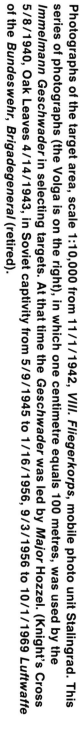

Photographs of the target area, scale 1:10,000 from 11/1/1942, VIII. Fliegerkorps, mobile photo unit Stalingrad. This series of photographs (the Volga is on the right), in which one centimetre equals 100 metres, was used by the Immelmann Geschwader in selecting targets. At that time the Geschwader was led by Major Hozzel. (Knight's Cross 5/8/1940, Oak Leaves 4/14/1943, in Soviet captivity from 5/9/1945 to 1/16/1956, 9/3/1956 to 10/1/1969 Luftwaffe of the Bundeswehr, Brigadegeneral (retired).

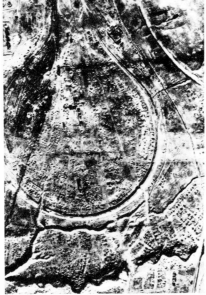

Left: Rudel and two companions over the city. Bomb bursts in the foreground, in the background a burning tanker on the Volga.

Right: An extract from a series of photographs (H.Q. AOK 6) from 11/3/1942. The reconnaissance photo shows the rail loop south of the "Red October" metallurgical works, which the Germans dubbed the "tennis racket."

The onset of the terrible cold at Stalingrad occurred in early November.

After an attack by *Immelmann Stukas* on Russian positions close to the grain silo.

One of the factories which the Soviets had turned into fortresses, under a hail of Stuka bombs.

An die im Raum
von STALINGRAD
eingekesselten deutschen
Offiziere und Soldaten!

**Deutsche Offiziere und Soldaten!**

Im Raum von Stalingrad haben die Truppen der Roten Armee den deutsch-rumänischen Truppen eine schwere Niederlage beigebracht! Allein in den ersten acht Tagen unserer Offensive habt Ihr 1320 Panzer, 1863 Geschütze, 4000 MG und mehr als 6000 Kraftfahrzeuge sowie 108 Lager mit Munition, Proviant und Winterausrüstung verloren. 63.000 deutsche und rumänische Soldaten und Offiziere haben sich gefangengegeben.

Eure Verbindungswege wurden durch die russischen Truppen abgeschnitten. Ihr seid von unseren Truppen eng umringt. Eure Lage ist aussichtslos und weiterer Widerstand sinnlos. Ihr würdet nur unnütze zahlreiche Opfer bringen müssen.

**GEBT EUCH GEFANGEN!**

Ein Soldat, der sich in einer aussichtslosen Lage gefangengibt, handelt nicht ehrlos, sondern vernünftig. Die Kriegsgeschichte kennt viele Beispiele, wo die tapfersten Soldaten und Offiziere die Waffen streckten, wenn weiterer Widerstand aussichtslos war.

Wer sich gefangengibt, ist nicht mehr unser Feind. Das Kommando der Roten Armee garantiert allen Soldaten und Offizieren, die sich gefangengeben, das Leben und völlige Sicherheit, ärztliche Behandlung der Verwundeten und Kranken, die Heimkehr nach Kriegsende. Eure Offiziere und Soldaten, die sich bereits gefangengegeben haben, sind wohlbehalten.

**GEBT EUCH GEFANGEN,
solange es nicht zu spät ist!**

Wer sich nicht gefangengibt, wird von unseren Truppen schonungslos niedergemacht. Ihr habt die Wahl: LEBEN oder "sinnloser TOD!"

Der Kommandeur der Stalingrader Front
Generaloberst JEROMENKO
Der Kommandeur der Donfront
Generalleutnant ROKOSSOWSKY

30. November 1942

Dieses Flugblatt gilt als Passierschein für eine unbegrenzte Zahl von deutschen Soldaten und Offizieren, die sich den russischen Truppen gefangengeben.

Эта листовка служит пропуском для неограниченного количества немецких солдат и офицеров при их сдаче в плен Красной Армии

Enemy propaganda: The Soviets dropped these leaflets in an attempt to induce the soldiers of Stalingrad to surrender. The few survivors from among the Germans taken prisoner at Stalingrad today regard the promises printed on the Soviet "passes" with the greatest contempt: "Whoever surrenders, is no longer our enemy. The command of the Red Army guarantees to all soldiers and officers who surrender, life and complete safety, medical attention for the sick and wounded and a return home after the war." Conservative estimates indicate that of the 120,000 German prisoners taken at Stalingrad, not 6,000 survived the Soviet "guarantee of life."

In the course of their winter offensive, the Soviets broke through on the southern sector of the front, crossed the north Donets and attempted to continue the advance, attacking with powerful forces between Slavyansk and Konstantinovka. *I. Gruppe,* in which Rudel led *1. Staffel,* was constantly in the air over that part of the threatened Don industrial region. The *Gruppe*'s targets lay only 40 km. northwest of the airfield at Gorlovka, north of Stalino. Once again, the men of the *Immelmann Geschwader* were fighting "on their own doorstep." It was at this time that Rudel flew his 1,000th mission, accompanied by his reliable gunner *Ofw.* Hentschel.

# THE 1000TH MISSION

# THE SIGNIFICANCE OF 1000 STUKA MISSIONS . . .

. . . on this subject a war correspondent later wrote in the *Luftwaffe* magazine *Der Adler*:

"Several photos from earlier in his life show the successful Stuka pilot as a proven athlete and skier. The photograph of him performing a somersault on snowshoes reveals daring and skill in the field of sports. - The significance of 1,000 Stuka missions can scarcely be described in words. The fact that such a tremendous individual accomplishment was achieved seems almost unreal. — The damage inflicted on the enemy from these 1,000 missions is likewise difficult to envisage. He often flew up to seven sorties per day and sometimes even more, as on the recent day when he was over the enemy seventeen (!) times . . ."

Immediately on landing from his 1,000th mission, Rudel receives a tumultuous welcome and congratulations from his comrades. On hand are a "good luck pig", a "chimney sweep" (left, partially concealed) and an honour goblet — filled with milk of course. Translator's note: In Germany the pig and chimney sweep are traditional good-luck symbols.

Gunner *Ofw.* Hentschel prepares to drink to the health of his *Staffel* leader and pilot with a sip of Rudel's favourite beverage.

The *Luftwaffe* magazine *Der Adler* described Rudel's 1,000 missions with these drawings and text.

1,000 combat missions equals a total flying distance of 300,000 km., or seven times around the earth at the equator. A tremendous flying accomplishment!

Approximately twenty tank cars of fuel would be consumed by a Ju 87 during 1,000 combat missions. If a truck were able to endure the journey, with that much fuel it would cover approximately 2.5 million kilometres.

Three freight cars of ammunition would be expended in 1,000 combat missions. That is a considerable quantity, but the tremendous results show that he knew how to put the ammunition to good use.

35 freight cars — 500,000 kg. of bombs . . . that many heavy bombs were dropped unerringly on their targets in 1,000 combat missions. They struck the enemy on his most sensitive locations. The losses inflicted on the enemy in men and materiel are difficult to visualize.

This photo was taken at the request of a PK correspondent: five Stuka officers — 3,500 missions! From right: *Oblt.* Thiede, *Oblt.* Rudel, *Hptm.* Dilley (commander *I. Gruppe*), *Oblt.* Jackel, *Hptm.* Mobus.

*Major* Hans von Herder (formerly a *Major* with the Staff of *St.G. 2 Immelmann*, now head of the rest home), ski instructor Toni Matt and *Hauptmann* Rudel. Following a fourteen day home leave, Rudel was posted to the anti-tank trials unit.

Despite his objections, Rudel was ordered to take home leave following his 1,000th mission. He spent his leave skiing at St. Anton on the Arlberg in Tirol. In the group photo from right: *Major* von Herder (founder and head of the *Schlachtflieger* rest home at St. Anton), Karlfried Nordmann, an officer and Oak Leaves wearer of *JG 51* "*Mölders*", also on leave, *Hauptmann* Rudel (promoted to *Hauptmann* with retroactive service date for outstanding bravery in the face of the enemy), his wife, *Major* Hitschold with wife, unidentified.

# THE CANNON BIRDS: THE FLYING ANTI-TANK GUNS

# Die »fliegende Pak«

## Ju 87 mit zwei 3,7 cm Flächen-kanonen als Panzerbrecher

Die großen Materialschlachten, die mit dem ganzen Aufwand moderner Kriegstechnik an der Ostfront ausgefochten werden, haben auf deutscher Seite zu der Entwicklung einer panzerbrechenden Bordkanone von 3,7 cm Durchmesser geführt, die, unter den beiden Tragflächen unseres altbewährten Stuka Junkers Ju 87 wie Bomben aufgehängt, bei der Bekämpfung von bestimmten Erdzielen eine im wahrsten Sinne des Wortes durchschlagende Wirkung erzielen. Vor allem hat sich die „fliegende Pak" als Panzerbrecher hervorragend bewährt. Mit ihr brachte allein der Brillantenträger Major Rudel über 200 Stahlkolosse zur Strecke

The Ju 87G: the "cannon bird", with which the most successful "tank cracker" of the Second World War achieved unique success. The soldiers of the Red Army dubbed Rudel's dreaded machine, "the Stuka with the long rods." Mounted under each wing was a 3.7 cm. cannon; the aircraft's dive brakes and bomb racks were deleted. With the two gondola-mounted weapons, each of which weighed 420 kg. (aircraft's all-up weight was ca. 17 tons), the aircraft was significantly slower than the other Stukas and required careful handling. The life expectancy of the crews and their "cannon birds" was not expected to be long. The aircraft's speed in horizontal flight averaged 260-270 km/hr; however, no Soviet flak crew or fighter pilot was able to "claim" the 100,000 ruble prize which Stalin placed on Rudel's head.

132

An armorer replaces the right cannon's six-round magazine. The special 3.7 cm. cannon shells featured tungsten cores. This special ammunition exploded after penetrating a tank's armor.

A "cannon bird" returning from a mission. Below: Rudel receives the Oak Leaves to the Knight's Cross at the Reich Chancellory, April 14, 1943. The photograph shows Hitler addressing the latest recipients of the Oak Leaves from the Army, *Waffen-SS* and *Luftwaffe*. *Obstlt.* Hozzel is 5th from the left, Rudel 8th from left.

The "cannon bird" trials unit under the command of *Hauptmann* Stepp tested the anti-tank Stukas at a proving ground near Bryansk. From there, Rudel flew with the unit to Kerch IV airfield in the Crimea. He tested the "cannon bird" with great success under operational conditions over the lagoons of the Kuban bridgehead. In early 1943, using standard ammunition without the tungsten cores, Rudel destroyed over 70 landing craft on the Sea of Azov between the bays of Temrjuk and Achtarsskij. His fellow pilots were also able to destroy numerous boats.

Bottom right: Two days later, Rudel once again took over command of *1. Staffel* at Kerch in the Crimea. *Hauptmann* Stepp was also posted from the trials unit back to the *Immelmann Geschwader*. Missions were flown daily against the Kuban bridgehead. Rudel's targets were often the in combat zone near Krymskaya where the Russians had placed large numbers of anti-aircraft guns. Sometimes the targets were Soviet supply ships operating along the coast; here a munitions ship receives a direct hit.

On July 2, 1943, Albert Speer, Reich Minister for Armaments and Munitions, arrived in Kerch and paid the *Geschwader* a visit. *Major* Dr. Ernst Kupfer, the *Geschwaderkommodore* (Knight's Cross 11/23/41, Oak Leaves 1/8/43, Swords posthumously 4/11/44), was celebrating his birthday and had just completed his 600th mission. Here he presents the officers of the *Geschwader* following Speer's arrival. From left: *Major* Dr. Kupfer, *Hauptmann* Krauss (KIA 7/17/43), *Hauptmann* Rudel, *Oberleutnant* Jackel.

Speer in discussion with the *Geschwaderkommodore Major* Dr. Kupfer (later *Oberstleutnant* and first *General der Schlachtflieger*) and *Hauptmann* Rudel (far right); left (partially concealed) *Hauptmann* Wutka, *Hauptmann* Krauss, *Oberleutnant* Jäckel.

From the cover of *Der Adler* from August 3, 1943: Speer (left) and *Major* Dr. Kupfer. The accompanying text states: "During an inspection tour of the Eastern Front, *Reichsminister* for Armaments and Munitions Speer paid a visit to the successful close support fliers. Wearer of the Oak Leaves *Major* Dr. Kupfer shows the minister several gifts which were presented to him by his comrades following his 600th mission."

The CO's birthday. During a break between missions the men enjoy coffee while their aircraft are fuelled, armed and made ready for action. On the left is the *Geschwaderkommodore, Major* Dr. Kupfer, following his 600th mission, which he flew on his 36th birthday. Dr. Kupfer was posted missing on November 6, 1943. On his left is *Major* Wolfgang Ewald, commander of *III. Gruppe* of *Jagdgeschwader 3* (Knight's Cross on 12/9/43 after 50 victories).

*Hauptmann* Rudel (right) in discussion with *Hauptmann* Wutka (Knight's Cross 11/30/42). Wutka was killed in action several days later.

Pre-mission briefing just before takeoff. Targets for the attack are the lagoons in the Kuban bridgehead (Sea of Azov). The crews have already donned their life jackets; Rudel (4th from left) has yet to put his on.

# Besuche bei den „Immelmännern"

Das Stukageschwader „Immelmann" hatte große Tage. Einmal weilte der Reichsminister für Bewaffnung und Munition Albert Speer zu Besuch unter den erfolgreichen Fliegern dieses bewährten Verbandes, Tage später konnte sich der japanische General Otani vom hohen fliegerischen Können und rücksichtslosen Einsatzwillen überzeugen.

**An excerpt from an article in *Die Wehrmacht* from 9/8/1943, titled "Visit with the *Immelmänner*.**

The following caption accompanied this photo when it appeared in an illustrated article in *Wehrmacht* several months later: "In front of the guest house ten expert eyes follow the *Staffel*'s fantastic ride through the clouds as it prepares to land."

136

"Several days later the commanding officer himself brought a Japanese visitor, General Otani, who was on a tour of the Eastern Front with other Japanese officers, to the air base."

Right: Major Dr. Kupfer. The article in the magazine of the *Wehrmacht* High Command included the note: "Photos by Ilse Steinhoff."

**General Otani signs the *Geschwader*'s guest book.**

Between missions, the crews of the *Immelmann Geschwader*'s *10. Panzer-Staffel*, which was under Rudel's command, receive instruction in tank recognition and combat tactics in the "cannon bird."

Using a model of a T-34, *Hauptmann* Rudel demonstrates the most favourable direction of attack and aiming points.

With a recognition chart in hand depicting Russian and American tanks in use on the Eastern Front, Rudel explains to his gunner *Ofw.* Hentschel (with model of Russian KV-II) the most important recognition features of current heavy and super-heavy tanks. Center is Rudel's aircraft mechanic at that time, *Obergefreiter* Wolfgang Slabbers. Slabbers flew numerous missions as a mechanic and gunner and later went on to flight school.

On July 4 the squadron was transferred from the Crimea to Kharkov and, in ceaseless action, supported "Operation Citadel", the great German pincer attack from north and south on the Russian frontal bulge near Kursk. During the course of the big attack, the largest tank battle in history took place. As was learned after the war, "Operation Citadel" was doomed to failure from the start! Through their espionage organization "Red Chapel", which had agents even in the highest command staffs, the Soviets had a detailed awareness of the operational plans from the Führer's headquarters so far in advance that they could prepare appropriately. In mid-July the Red Army made a counterattack and pushed the German army groups under von Kluge in the north and von Manstein in the south far back from their original positions.

# OPERATION "CITADEL"- JULY 1943

On July 5, the first day of the German offensive, Rudel and his *Geschwader* comrades took off on their first mission at 03.30. In the days that followed they supported the advancing German forces in the Belgorod area from morning until evening. The missions during the Battle of Kursk were difficult and costly. The Soviets had deployed massive concentrations of anti-aircraft weapons throughout the entire Kursk salient. Their in-depth defensive positions featured wide belts of mines, powerful anti-tank barriers and dug-in tanks. Often the Stuka bombers had to silence Soviet anti-aircraft guns before the *Panzer-Staffel* could attack. The motor of Rudel's "cannon bird" is started by hand crank.

Left center: A view of gunner Hentschel's position. Like all Stuka gunners, he sat with his back to his pilot, defending against fighter attack from behind with his MG 81 Z (twin-barrelled 7.9 mm. machine gun). Here he is seen loading a belt of ammunition.

Right center: A last wave for the faithful aircraft mechanics and armorers; without their efforts the missions would not have been possible. Rudel always acknowledged gratefully the accomplishments of the ground crews.

This *Staffel* will attack with bombs.

Rudel with his trusted gunner *Oberfeldwebel* Hentschel after a particularly successful mission.

Above left: A photo of the target area taken by the gunner, showing bomb bursts and exploding tanks.

Center: A successful Stuka attack as seen by *Panzergrenadiere* in the front lines.

Below: Effective attacks by Rudel on the first mission result in four Soviet tanks destroyed. They were put out of action "Rudel style." By the evening of this day he had destroyed a total of twelve tanks.

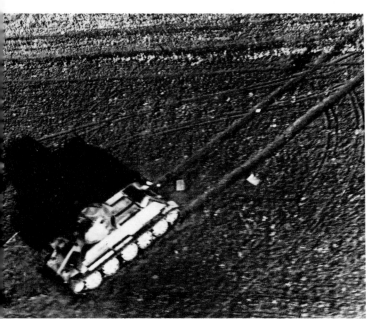

A T-34 tries desperately to escape from the "Stuka with the long rods." It was hit below the turret and immediately began to burn.

This T-34, which was dug in as part of the Soviets' extensive defensive positions in the Kursk salient, also fell victim to the Stukas.

Rudel's comrades also destroyed large numbers of Soviet tanks with bombs. This photograph by a gunner shows four tanks which have blown up.

Five Soviet tanks (above left) attempt to escape the Stukas. Neither sharp turns nor fleeing at full speed helps them: their tracks betray their position.

A rare photograph: one of the *Panzer-Staffel*'s "cannon birds" has been hit in the undercarriage by anti-aircraft fire; the pilot has jettisoned the damaged landing gear and is carrying out a belly-landing at his airfield.

This aircraft crashed on landing. One undercarriage leg had been shot away by flak; the other collapsed on landing.

Here, too, the Stuka crews were over the enemy from morning until night. Seven or more missions were not uncommon. The "infantrymen of the air", so valued by the German soldiers, en route to attack advancing Soviet armor near Alexandrovka.

The *Immelmänner* were often paid explosive visits by Soviet IL-2 or American-supplied "Boston" bombers. In this attack one Ju 87 (left) has been destroyed, but the bombs bursting to the right serve only to blast an open field.

From the middle of July, operating from Orel, the *Immelmänner* supported the Army units in the northern sector of the Kursk salient. The situation there was less favourable than in the south, where German forces had penetrated 40 kilometres into the Russian defences. During a mission over the northern sector, Rudel's aircraft was struck in the right wing by flak. He was able to carry out a smooth landing despite the badly-damaged wing: a tribute to the quality of the Junkers' construction and his flying skill.

Above right: During an attack in the area west of Bolkhov (60 km. north of Orel), where the anti-aircraft fire was unusually heavy, Rudel's aircraft was hit in the motor and he was struck in the face by shell fragments. His engine dead, he made a successful forced landing in the forward German lines. German infantry brought him back from the firing line, and two hours later an army vehicle delivered him back to his airfield. From the command post he first made his report on the action, including his observations of developments at the front. He then had himself "doctored" and led the next mission into the same combat zone. That mission saw the anti-aircraft positions which had been located earlier put out of action by the *Immelmänner*.

Walter Krauss, commander of *III. Gruppe*, was killed in a Soviet night bombing raid on the base at Orel on 17 July 1943. Krauss was awarded the Oak Leaves posthumously on 1/3/1944 and had been promoted to Major effective 7/1/1943. At the funeral, which was held at the large military cemetery at Orel, Rudel spoke the farewell for this universally popular and exemplary officer. He and Rudel had been friends since their time together in Graz with the replacement *Staffel*.

*Hauptmann* Rudel was forced to leave *1. Staffel* as he had been given command of *III. Gruppe*. On the morning of August 1, the *Gruppe* flew from Orel to Karachev, 20 km. south of Bryansk. During the flight the unit's aircraft attacked Russian units in the town of Shamyakino with bombs. A large number of Russian tanks had broken through the German front. All local close support units were placed under the command of Major D. Kupfer, commander of the *Immelmann Geschwader*, as "Battle Group Kupfer." Attacks by the battle group's aircraft halted the breakthrough; the Russian tanks were destroyed exclusively from the air. This photo was taken on one of the missions against the tanks.

Above right: A rare "shot" taken by the gunner's camera: a Stuka returns to base at very low altitude to avoid Soviet anti-aircraft defences. The shadows of both aircraft are visible on the ground below.

During another attack several tanks are destroyed. Three others tried to escape (left); a short time later they, too, were hit, began to burn and exploded.

A direct hit on an armored munitions carrier. On the left, several tanks have likewise been destroyed.

145

Below: When the situation in the area around Kharkov became critical, the *Geschwader* was transferred to Kharkov-South airfield. *III. Gruppe* flew its first mission from there at 04.45 on August 7. The *Immelmänner* found even more flak and fighters in the air over the North-Donets region south of Kharkov than they had in the north. Despite the provision of fighter escort, losses mounted. The dense flak often found its target as well. Despite the accompanying anti-aircraft defences, the long Russian truck columns — which consisted mostly of new American vehicles — still proved "easy meat" for the Stukas. The Russians usually moved up their reinforcements under cover of darkness.

Rudel and his *Gruppe* carried out successful attacks on the bridges near Krasny and Tschugujew.

August 12: *Hauptmann* Rudel, commander of *III. Gruppe*, after landing at Kharkov-South from his 1,300th mission. This was also gunner *Ofw.* Hentschel's 1,000th mission.

The commander's driver has decorated the staff car with garlands and a congratulatory sign. With horn honking, he drove both lucky fliers to the command post.

# AUTUMN
# 1943

## Im Kampfraum von Saporoshje harte, erfolgreiche Abwehrkämpfe

### In drei Tagen 209 Panzer und 155 Flugzeuge vernichtet

Aus dem Führerhauptquartier, 29. September.

Das Oberkommando der Wehrmacht gibt bekannt:

Am Kubanbrückenkopf blieben starke Aufklärungsvorstöße der Sowjets erfolglos.

Im Kampfraum von Saporoshje standen unsere Truppen auch gestern in schweren, aber erfolgreichen Abwehrkämpfen. Vorübergehend verlorengegangenes Gelände wurde durch Gegenangriffe zurückerobert. Neue Versuche des Feindes, an einigen Stellen des mittleren Dnjepr auf dem westlichen Flußufer Boden zu gewinnen, scheiterten.

Im mittleren Frontabschnitt griffen die Sowjets trotz Wetterverschlechterung weiter an. Zäher Widerstand unserer Truppen und energische Gegenangriffe brachten die feindlichen Angriffe zum Stehen. Einzelne Einbrüche wurden abgeriegelt.

In der Zeit vom 26. bis 28. September wurden an der Ostfront 209 Sowjetpanzer und 155 Flugzeuge vernichtet. Deutsche Flakartillerie schoß von sechs Sowjetbombern, die den rumänischen Hafen Konstantza anzugreifen versuchten, vier ab.

Anhaltender Regen verhinderte an der süditalienischen Front größere Kampfhandlungen. Die eigenen Bewegungen nahmen trotz starker Wegeschwierigkeiten den vorgesehenen Verlauf.

In der vergangenen Nacht überflogen einzelne feindliche Flugzeuge das westliche Reichsgebiet. Durch Abwurf einiger Bomben entstand nur unwesentlicher Gebäudeschaden.

Die Zahl der bei den feindlichen Luftangriffen am 27. September und in der Nacht vom 27. zum 28. September abgeschossenen Flugzeuge hat sich auf 65 erhöht.

## Der dritte Tag der Abwehrschlacht von Saporoshje

Berlin, 29. September.

Im Kampfgebiet von Saporoshje berennen die Bolschewisten nunmehr den dritten Tag mit starken, von zahlreichen Batterien und Schlachtfliegerstaffeln unterstützten Infanterie- und Panzerverbänden unsere Stellungen. Die Angriffe begannen im Morgengrauen unter Ausnutzung des Frühnebels und dauerten den ganzen Tag an. Besonders stark waren die Vorstöße südöstlich Saporoshje, wo der Feind außer mehreren Schützendivisionen noch 30 bis 40 Panzer einsetzte. Nachdem aber schwere Waffen die Panzerkeile durch Abschuß von 16 Panzern zerschlagen hatten, brachen auch die feindlichen Schützenwellen im deutschen Feuer zusammen. Östlich Saporoshje wurden bei der Abwehr weiterer Panzerangriffe noch 14 Sowjetpanzer vernichtet. Wo es dem Feind durch Zusammenballung seiner Kräfte vorübergehend gelang, Geländevorteile zu gewinnen, gingen unsere Truppen zu schwungvollen Gegenstößen über und stellten die ursprüngliche Lage wieder her. Dabei brachten sie an einer Stelle 110 Gefangene ein und erbeuteten zwei Geschütze sowie zahlreiche schwere und leichte Infanteriewaffen. Starke Luftwaffenverbände griffen immer wieder in die Kämpfe ein, zersprengten feindliche Angriffskeile und störten durch Bombenabwürfe den feindlichen Nachschub. Auch der dritte Tag der Schlacht bei Saporoshje befestigte damit von neuem den bisherigen Abwehrerfolg der deutschen Truppen.

Am mittleren Dnjepr versuchten die Bolschewisten wiederum, unter Ausnutzung der Flußinsel an unübersichtlichen Stellen den Strom zu überschreiten. In harten Kämpfen wurden die feindlichen Landestellen abgeriegelt und in Gegenangriffen bereinigt oder versengt. Auch hier fanden die Luftwaffenverbände lohnende Aufgaben.

Im mittleren Abschnitt der Ostfront standen unsere Truppen trotz der gegen Mittag einsetzenden starken Regenfälle weiterhin in schweren Abwehrkämpfen.

## 140 von 250 angreifenden Panzern vernichtet

## Voller deutscher Abwehrerfolg im Kampfraum Saporoshje

### Die schweren Verluste der feindlichen Kriegs- und Handelsflotten im Monat September

Aus dem Führerhauptquartier, 1. Oktober.

Das Oberkommando der Wehrmacht gibt bekannt:

An der Landfront des Kubanbrückenkopfes wiesen unsere Truppen mehrere starke Angriffe der Sowjets ab. Feindliche Kampfgruppen, die erneut zu landen versuchten, wurden vernichtet.

Im Kampfraum südöstlich Saporoshje brachten die gestrigen Kämpfe einen vollen Abwehrerfolg. Die mit stärksten Infanterie- und Panzerkräften unternommenen Durchbruchsversuche des Feindes wurden abgeschlagen. Die Sowjets erlitten hohe blutige Verluste, von 250 angreifenden Panzern wurden 140 vernichtet.

Am mittleren Dnjepr sind noch erbitterte Kämpfe um einzelne feindliche Brückenköpfe im Gange.

In verschiedenen Abschnitten der Mitte und im Norden der Ostfront wurden örtliche Angriffe der Sowjets abgewiesen.

Die Luftwaffe griff mit zusammengefaßten Kampf-, Sturzkampf- und Schlachtfliegerverbänden wirkungsvoll in die Kämpfe südostwärts Saporoshje und am mittleren Dnjepr ein.

Ein Unterseeboot versenkte im Schwarzen Meer einen feindlichen Dampfer von 800 BRT.

An der süditalienischen Front kam es gestern nur südlich des Vesuvs zu nennenswerten Kämpfen. Vorstöße britischer Panzerkräfte wurden dort abgewiesen.

Im Mittelmeer erzielte die Luftwaffe Bombentreffer auf zwei feindliche Kriegsfahrzeuge und beschädigte sie schwer. Begleitende Jäger schossen hierbei drei feindliche Flugzeuge ab.

Bei den feindlichen Luftangriffen am 29. September und in der Nacht zum 30. September wurden trotz ungünstiger Witterung über Westdeutschland und dem niederländischen Küstengebiet 14 feindliche Flugzeuge abgeschossen.

Kriegsmarine und Luftwaffe versenkten im Monat September: ein Schlachtschiff, drei Kreuzer, zwanzig Zerstörer, drei Torpedoboote, dreizehn Schnellboote, ein Unterseeboot und mehrere Kleinst-Unterseeboote, zwei Minensuchboote, zwei Bewacher und zwanzig Landungsboote; beschädigt wurden: ein Schlachtschiff, achtzehn Kreuzer, siebzehn Zerstörer, ein Torpedoboot, acht Schnellboote, fünfzehn Landungsboote und fünf andere Kriegsfahrzeuge.

Ferner wurden 55 Handelsschiffe mit zusammen 315 700 BRT und ein Transportsegler versenkt oder vernichtet und 133 weitere Schiffe mit über 600 000 BRT beschädigt.

Die Beschädigungen zahlreicher getroffener Kriegs- und Handelsschiffe sind so schwer, daß auch mit der Vernichtung eines Teiles dieser Schiffe gerechnet werden kann.

From September 28 the *Gruppe* was based for a some time at the airfield at Bolskaya Kostromka, about 50 km. southeast of Krivoi Rog. The *Gruppe*'s targets lay on the great Dniepr bend, where powerful Soviet forces were attacking from the southeast in the direction of Zaporozhye. This bitterly contested sector of the front was mentioned often in *Wehrmacht* communiques. The articles above were printed in the *Völkischer Beobachter* on September 29 and October 1, 1943 and describe German defensive successes in the Zaporozhye sector.

This photograph of Rudel was taken through the closed canopy of his aircraft just before he took off on another mission. In these days his face has become serious and concerned. Many crews have failed to return, including *Oberleutnant* Mende and his gunner, who were posted missing over the area north of Krivoi Rog. On the cabin window are graduations for judging dive angles from 30 to 90 degrees.

In the autumn of 1943 the *Gruppe*'s area of operations extended from Krivoi Rog to Melitopol, from Nikopol and Zaporozhye on the Dniepr to Kremenchug in the north of the great bend of the river. Effective attacks were made on the bridges across the Dniepr but the Russians had usually thrown a pontoon bridge across the river by the next day. The photograph shows Rudel's aircraft just before the attack on the bridge near Romankovo. The photograph was taken by *Leutnant* Fickel's gunner. *Gruppe* Adjutant, Fickel was awarded the Knight's Cross on 6/6/1944.

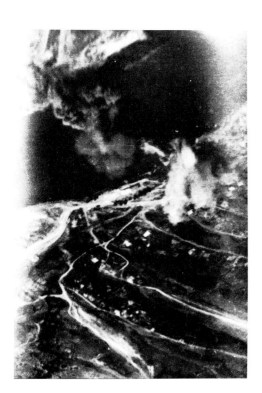

Right: The bombs strike the center of the target. Several vehicles loaded with fuel and munitions were destroyed with the bridge.

Left: The commander of *III. Gruppe* reports on his last mission. Left: *Major* Hans-Karl Stepp, commander of the *Immelmann Geschwader* from 9/10/43 until autumn 1944; center: *Hauptmann* Becker, who was known to his friends as "Fridolin." When the war ended he was captured by Czech partisans and murdered.

## THE 1,500th COMBAT MISSION ON 10/9/1943

One day after the attack on the bridge across the Dniepr near Romankovo, Rudel flew his 1,500th combat mission. The mission was also gunner Erwin Hentschel's 1,200th. A large crowd was waiting for them on their return: *General der Flieger* Pflugbeil (*IV. Fliegerkorps*) has arrived to offer his congratulations. With the men of the *Geschwader* assembled, newsreel cameraman film the scene, while war correspondents take still photos.

*General der Flieger* Pflugbeil expresses his thanks and appreciation to *Hauptmann* Rudel, commander of *III./St.G. 2*. Center: *Ofw.* Hentschel; behind him on the right is *Feldwebel* Günther, the commander's ground crew chief.

Rudel, with the *Gruppe*'s lucky pig mascot under his arm, and Hentschel accept the congratulations of their comrades. Center: *Leutnant* Fickel, Gruppe Adjutant.

The *Geschwader*'s CO, *Major* Stepp, celebrates Rudel's achievement and the successful surprise reception. Next to him with the camera is correspondent *Leutnant* Gervais. In the background is an *Oberfähnrich* with the traditional celebration cake.

Above left: The commander's decorated car in Kostromka.

Above right: Mascot in arm, Rudel has to face the photographers.

Center: Knowing Rudel's fondness for sweets, *General der Flieger* Pflugbeil has brought a cake. Right: *Geschwader* CO *Major* Stepp; left: *Hauptmann* Rudel with the "General's cake."

The missions must go on. First, however, the *Gruppe* celebrates the great accomplishment by its CO and his gunner *Ofw.* Hentschel. At that time Hentschel had flown more missions than any other gunner; sitting next to him: war correspondent Müller-Marein, *Fahnenjunker-Feldwebel* Beyer, *Lt.* Fickel and *Lt.* Löhrl.

# Kriegsberichter im Einsatz

## Stukaflieger und 1500 Feindflüge

**Mit Hauptmann Rudel gegen den Feind / Zahlen die von Siegen sprechen**

Hauptmann R u d e l , Träger des Eichenlaubes, Gruppenkommandeur im „Stukageschwader Immelmann", flog seinen 1500. Feindeinsatz.
PK.-Aufn.: Kriegsberichter Gervais (PBZ.)

Das ist der 1500. Feindflug des Hauptmanns Rudel. Morgens gegen 8.30 Uhr. Die Luft ist diesig. Niedrig sind die Wolken. Nur fern am Horizont flattert, umrahmt von weißen Wolkenstreifen, ein blaßblaues Himmelsband wie ein schmaler Wimpel, eine freundliche Farbe über düsterem Land, denn dort schlägt die Front.

1499 Feindflüge hat Hauptmann Rudel bestanden. Das also soll der 1500. Feindflug werden. Wahrlich, wenn diese Zahl die Summe großer Gefahren ist, so ist sie auch die Summe großer kämpferischer Verwegenheiten. Ja, diese Zahl kann ein Denkmal sein, ein Denkmal großer Siege.

Dort kommt nun Hauptmann Rudel. Das helle Weißgrau der Weste, die er über der Kombination trägt, hebt sein sonnengebräuntes Gesicht hervor. Es ist ein ebenmäßiges Gesicht von sehr männlicher, gleichwohl auch ein wenig jungenhafter Prägung. Er klettert in sein Flugzeug mit dem Elan des Sportmannes. Aber dann, nachdem er an der Spitze seiner Gruppe zum Feindflug gestartet ist, hat man Gelegenheit, ihn so zu sehen, wie man ihn, den Flieger, sehen muß: Hauptmann Rudel handhabt das Steuer mit einer Leichtigkeit und einem Fahrtgefühl, das fast vergessen lassen kann, daß schwere Bomben unter Rumpf und Tragflächen des Flugzeugs hängen. Manchmal hebt er die Karte und schaut hinein. Manchmal führt er die Hand mit nachdenklicher Gebärde zur Stirn, wendet die Augen und sucht den Raum nach feindlichen Jägern ab. Manchmal streckt er den Zeigefinger, als wolle er sich selbst und seine Männer immer wieder zur Aufmerksamkeit mahnen. Rücken an Rücken mit ihm sitzt sein Bordfunker, mit dem er seit langem fliegt, unzertrennlich wie mit einem Bruder. Er aber,

**der bei diesem gleichen Flug die Zahl von 1200 Einsätzen vollendet,**

blickt gleichmütig hinter seinem Maschinengewehr hervor. Ein Bauernsohn aus sächsischem Kernland, hat der Bordfunker des Hauptmanns auch als Flieger die Ruhe bewahrt, die seinem Blut eigen ist. Jetzt ist er Oberfeldwebel; aber er weiß noch genau, wie das war, als er, anstatt über aufgewühlten Äckern und grabendurchfurchten Feldern dahinzufliegen, langsam und bedächtig seine Furchen mit dem Pfluge zog.

Wie schön, wie kraftvoll auch heute unter dem diesigen Himmel der brausende Marsch der Flugzeuge unserer Stukagruppe wirkt! Sauber abgesetzt vom grauen Hintergrund der Wolken, erscheinen die Flugzeuge mit den gewinkelten Tragflächen auch heute wie wehrhafte, gefährliche Hornissen. Und dort, wo der blaßblaue Wolkenwimpel weht, dort also ist die Front . . .

Dann erklingt eine Stimme, die dem Verband das genaue Ziel des Angriffs weist: Bereitstellungen des Feindes — Auftakt für einen feindlichen Angriff. Drunten nähern sich gelbe Rauchschwaden, Kennzeichen der vorderen Linie, auf der die deutschen Truppen stehen. Gibt es hier ein Niemandsland? Nein, unmittelbar vor den deutschen Linien sind die feindlichen Ausgangsstellungen ins zerklüftete Erdreich eingewühlt. Geschütz neben Geschütz, dann auch Panzer neben Panzer. Ja, das, was dort unten vor sich geht, das ist die knappe Pause des bedrohlichen Schweigens, das immer und überall einem Angriff voranzugehen pflegt. Dort hinein soll die Stukagruppe stürzen.

### „Wir greifen an!"

Das ist die Stimme des Hauptmanns und Kommandeurs, eine Stimme, die heute, beim 1500. Feindflug, ebenso voll überlegener Ruhe klingt wie beim ersten Angriff, den er in Polen flog. Schon beginnt der Tanz der Hornissen, jenes verwegene Schaukeln, das nichts anderes als ein Hindurchschlüpfen durch die Maschen des feindlichen Feuernetzes ist. Und dann vollzieht sich alles rasend schnell. Da ist der Sturz, der Kommandeur voran. Die übrigen Flugzeuge so exakt hinterdrein, als sei ein unsichtbares magnetisches Band von Maschine zu Maschine gezogen. Schon tauchen die kurvenden und wieder schräg nach oben steilenden Flugzeuge ihre gewinkelten Tragflächen in die Qualmmauer, die ihre Bomben entfachten. Die Bordkanonen und Maschinengewehre schleudern ihre Leuchtspurgarben in die Gräben, in denen die Sowjets geduckt, versprengt kauern. Erdfontänen wallen auf und decken sie zu. Abseits aber kriecht ein Sowjetpanzer schutzsuchend in ein ärmliches Gebüsch. Über der Vernichtung aber kurven indes die Stuka steil empor, stürzen von neuem und jagen endlich im Tiefflug heimwärts. Der 1500. Flug!

Da aber nach alledem die Stukagruppe auf ihrem vertrauten Feldflugplatz landet und Hauptmann Rudel als erster das Flugzeug verläßt, ist sein Gesicht und sind seine Bewegungen so frisch wie beim Start.

### Der Kommandierende General des Fliegerkorps ist erschienen.

In knappen, schlichten Worten werden Glückwünsche dargebracht. Und damit auch der Aberglaube seinen Zoll bekommt, schleppen Kameraden zwei quietschende Glücksschweinchen herbei. Wie aber sonst noch beschenkt man einen Kommandeur, der weder raucht noch Alkohol genießt? Mit Kuchen, mit Torten und Blumen. Diese Geschenke im Arm, lächelt Hauptmann Rudel froh.

Das ist Hauptmann Rudel: ein S t u k a f l i e g e r a u s P a s s i o n , ein Kämpfer von eiserner Unermüdlichkeit. Daher mußte ihm ein Geschenk mehr als alle anderen Geschenke gelten: Die Infanterie, zu deren Schutz und Unterstützung die Gruppe heute gestartet war, ließ durch den Feldfernsprecher sagen, daß der sowjetische Angriff, der nach Aussagen Gefangener als Unternehmen großen Stils geplant war, schon in der Bereitstellung von unseren Stukabomben zerschlagen wurde. Das Geschenk der Infanterie war Dank an die Stukaflieger.

Aus diesen Dankesworten, die in der echten Sprache der Soldaten vorgetragen wurden, nämlich knapp, kurz und in Form der Meldung, begriff man, was die Zahl 1500 bedeutet. Hohe Anerkennung sprach aus den Worten des Geschwaderkommodore. Unausgesprochen blieb das Motto der Gespräche, die sich um Hauptmann Rudels persönliches Erleben rankten. Er, der Sohn eines Pfarrers aus dem Riesengebirge, hat den Weg der Pflicht früh gesehen. Obwohl vieles, was er, der begeisterte Sportsmann, tat, eher wie Verwegenheit und Spiel aussah — er wollte nichts als Fliegen, und vom Fliegen spricht er gern. Aber daß er 60 Panzer abgeschossen, das möchte er am liebsten verschweigen. Viel lieber erinnert er sich daran, daß sein Bordfunker nach hartem Luftkampf unlängst einen Sowjetjäger in die Tiefe schickte. Aber was die Zahl seiner Feindflüge betrifft, so sagte der Kommandeur: „Die Zahl ist ein lebendiges Ding . . ."

Diese Zahl von 1500 Feindflügen, die aussagt, daß Hauptmann Rudel öfter den Motor und die Spitze seiner Bomben feindwärts gerichtet hat als irgendein anderer Flieger, die Zahl — man kann sie nicht fassen, es sei denn als Symbol erfüllter Pflicht.

Kriegsberichter M ü l l e r - M a r e i n

The action report, "Stuka Pilot and 1500 Combat Missions —With *Hauptmann* Rudel against the Enemy/Numbers which Speak of Victory", was circulated through a large part of the German press. Written by war correspondent J. Müller-Marein, the article on this page was copied from *Der Sportflieger*, issue 11, 1943. The article describes Rudel's 1,500th mission and provides a brief account of his career and background. Today Müller-Marein's comments appear under J.M.-M. in the Hamburg weekly *Die Zeit*.

## DISCUS AND JAVELIN IN HIS KIT

Throughout the entire war, Rudel spent every free minute at sports. The enthusiastic sportsman and decathlete — here with medical officer Dr. Gadermann in October 1943 — needed physical training as much as his "daily bread." He thus kept his body in good physical condition which better enabled him to cope with the stresses which every Stuka mission placed on him. In the photos: First some loosening-up exercises . . . and then javelin throwing.

. . . next is discus throwing. Medical officer Dr. Gadermann in the starting position; he intends to race the flying discus.

154

To conclude, Rudel and Dr. Gadermann run the traditional 10,000 metres. After the war, Dr. Gadermann became a professor at the University Clinic in Hamburg-Eppendorf and was later an "Olympic physician" at the Munich Olympics.

After the usual workout it's back to his quarters and then to the command post. Naturally, Rudel and his comrades of *Ill. Gruppe* only had time for sports when there was bad weather over the target area or there were shortages of fuel.

# LATE
# AUTUMN
# 1943

The CO points out the target to *Ofw.* Hentschel on a grid-map.

Above right: En route to attack troop and tank assembly areas near Kirovograd, late autumn 1943.

A bomb exploded close beside this T-34. The explosion has tipped over the steel colossus, which now lays resting on its gun turret.

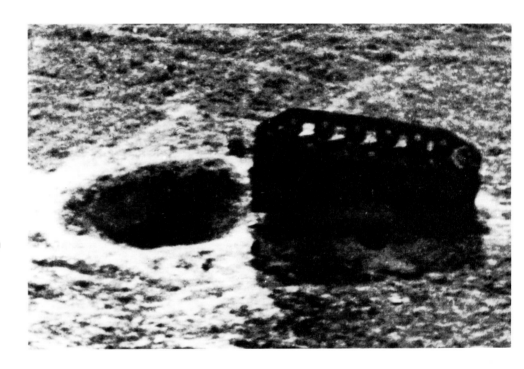

After the last mission in a strenuous day of flying, the aircraft are made ready for the early morning mission and covered with tarpaulins. The technicians in the field repair shops often worked late into the night repairing bullet damage or changing an engine.

Taken by a Stuka's automatic camera:

A diving attack on tanks, vehicles and anti-aircraft gun emplacements.

The release button on the control column is pressed: the SD 250 leaves the cradle and plunges toward the target.

The 250 kg. bomb has disappeared from the camera's view. The aircraft will now begin to pull up.

## MUD — AN OPERATIONAL PROBLEM

The "main street" of Bolskaya Kostromska, where *III. Gruppe* had its quarters. A view from the hut belonging to the photo section, showing one of the few stone buildings in which were located the offices of the *Gruppe* Staff. As vehicles often became stuck in the mud, the Stuka crews frequently rode to their aircraft on *panje* horses.

Above: As it always was on the Eastern Front in spring and fall, so it was in late 1943 at Kostromka airfield: "Comrade Mud" hampered operations by the *Immelmann Geschwader.* Supply vehicles became stuck in the morass, aircraft frequently stood on their noses on landing, and *panje* horses had to be employed to transport bombs and ammunition to the aircraft. Ground personnel have laid duckboards across the mud.

Right: The duckboards did not lead everywhere, and walking without rubber boots meant a "mud pack" for the feet.

Because the muddy conditions at Kostromka airfield were hampering operations, *III. Gruppe* flew from Kirovograd from October 27-30. The primary targets were Soviet tank units which had crossed the Dniepr and were attacking toward the west and southwest. The airfield at Kirovograd was one of the few in Russia to have concrete runways. By chance, there was a front line stage troupe in the city of Kirovograd entertaining the troops. For the Stuka crews, taking in the show was a welcome change from the routine.

A view into the overfilled hall: (from left) two Army Generals, *Hauptmann* Rudel, *Hauptmann* Becker; behind them is *Feldwebel* Partsch, *Leutnant* Fickel's gunner.

*159*

On October 28, Rudel scored several tank kills near Novo Praga, about 70 km. east of Kirovograd. This brought his total of Soviet tanks destroyed to 100. His comrades in the *Panzer-Staffel* destroyed several more of the Russian tanks, which had broken through the German lines. This T-34 explodes moments after being struck by 3.7 cm. shells from the "cannon-bird's" guns.

A photograph by a PK correspondent: the T-34 has been completely torn apart by the explosion.

## THE 100th
## TANK KILL

Moments after landing, "tank cracker" Rudel is congratulated on his 100th. Right, Dr. Gadermann; left, *Lt.* Fickel and other comrades.

The mission is discussed and, map in hand, results and observations are exchanged. From right: *Gruppe* CO, *Hauptmann* Rudel; *Lt.* Stahler; *Lt.* Fickel; Dr. Gadermann; *Oblt.* Hirsch (with back to camera).

After the day's last mission, the "100th" is suitably toasted in Kirovograd; the athlete Rudel drinks only milk as usual. Before the celebration a PK photographer took this photo of *III. Gruppe*'s officers. From left: *Lt.* Krumminga (Knight's Cross Oct. 1943, KIA 11/28/43); *Oblt.* Herling (Knight's Cross April 1943, KIA 11/28/43); medical officer Dr. Gadermann; *Gruppe* CO, *Hauptmann* Rudel; *Hauptmann* Becker; *Lt.* Dose (Knight's Cross May 1945 as *Oblt.*); *Oblt.* Rossteutscher (signals officer); *Leutnant* Fickel (Knight's Cross 6/6/1944).

# WINTER
# 1943/44

## THE KNIGHT'S CROSS WITH OAK LEAVES AND SWORDS

On November 25, 1943, *Hauptmann* Hans-Ulrich Rudel, commander of *III./SG 2*, was awarded the Knight's Cross with Oak Leaves and Swords, becoming the 42nd German soldier to receive the decoration. He was presented the decoration by the *Führer* and Supreme Commander at the *Führer* HQ in Lötzen, East Prussia (*Wolfsschanze*). Left is *Oberstleutnant* Dietrich Hrabak, at that time commander of *JG 52* with 118 victories, who was there to receive the Knight's Cross with Oak Leaves. By the war's end, Hrabak had flown 820 missions and scored 125 victories.

*Oberfeldwebel* Erwin Hentschel, Rudel's gunner, receives the Knight's cross from the Supreme Commander of the *Wehrmacht*. Hitler did not usually present the Knight's Cross personally at that time. Rudel had simply brought his gunner with him, the recommendation for the Knight's Cross having been submitted some time before. Hentschel was the most successful gunner in the *Luftwaffe* at that time, with over 1,200 combat missions and several enemy aircraft to his credit.

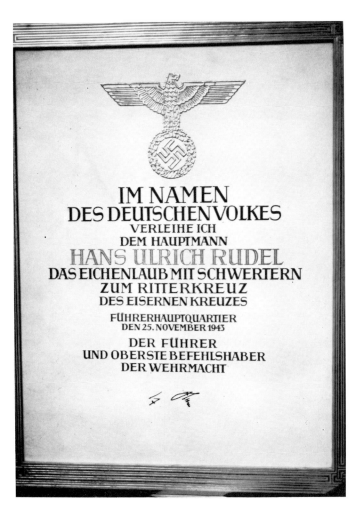

**Above left:**
The award document.

**Above right:**
Return from the FHQ in East Prussia. On the wing is Rudel's crew chief, *Feldwebel* Günther.

**Below left:**
Immediately after landing, a PK photographer takes the first "official" photo of the new wearer of the Swords.

**Below right:**
*Ofw.* Hentschel must also patiently endure the attentions of the photographer.

*I. Gruppe*, commanded by Oak Leaves wearer *Major* Alwin Boerst (Swords posthumously 4/6/44), had been flying missions from Slinka, north of Novo Ukraina (west of Kirovograd). On 1/6/1943, Rudel's *III. Gruppe* moved there as well. Once more the most frequent targets were Soviet tank assembly areas, especially those near Kirovograd, Gruskoye and Malyje Wiski. The photograph shows Slinka airfield which lay close to the Kirovograd—Pervomaysk/Bug rail line.

The aircraft are armed and loaded with bombs in the icy cold.

164

Evasive manoeuvres have failed to save these Soviet tanks: Rudel and the *10. Panzerjagdstaffel* have hunted them down in their "cannon birds."

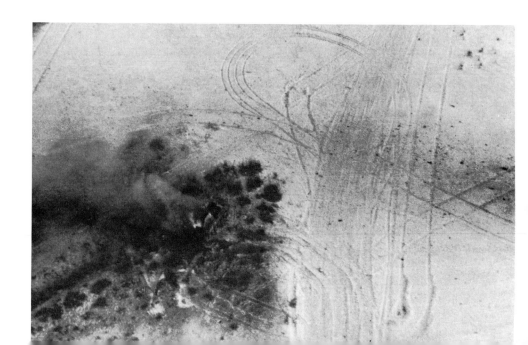

After a successful tank hunt: on the wing is the crew chief who immediately sets about making the aircraft ready for action again.

On January 9, 1944, Rudel's *Gruppe* was transferred to Pervomaysk. When poor weather or fuel shortages brought a halt to flying, the CO and his crews played hockey on the frozen river Bug. Third from the right is the *Gruppe* Technical Officer, *Leutnant* Ebersbach.

A PK correspondent photographed the CO with medical officer Dr. Gadermann, *Lt.* Schwirblat and two Rumanian officers following a hockey game on the Bug.

Above: Following an early mission over the Kirovograd area on January 25, Rudel and his adjutant were forced to make an emergency landings due to thick fog. Rudel and his gunner Hentschel taxied approximately 40 km. along a road until they came to an underpass twelve miles from Pervomaysk, where the "Stuka on foot" was forced to halt. In the photo is Rudel's aircraft parked at the side of the road; when the fog dissipated he flew back to the airfield. His adjutant also returned safe and sound after a lucky forced landing.

Below: Not all forced landings in open terrain came off as smoothly as those of *Hauptmann* Rudel and *Oberleutnant* Fickel. This Stuka overturned on landing; the crew of *Uffz.* Beneking and gunner *Gefr.* Grunewald escaped uninjured.

Zwischenspiel um Major Rudel und seinen Adjutanten

# Wer runterfällt, wird rausgeholt!

## Tiefangriff auf Panzer im Libellenflug — „Den Leutnant Fickel hat's erwischt!" — Landung zwischen Entwässerungsgräben

### Von Kriegsberichter Jupp Müller-Marein

PK im Osten.

Es sollen in diesem Bericht keine großen Worte gemacht werden, denn in dieser Zeit, da die Fronten brennen, wird so viel fürs Vaterland gestorben und gekämpft, daß es immer nur ein Intermezzo ist, wenn der einzelne dem Tod begegnet und sich wieder einmal stärker erweist als die Gefahr. Der deutsche Soldat, der deutsche Flieger haben sich oftmals stärker erwiesen. Der deutsche Soldat wird bestehen.

Was also ist in unserem Frontabschnitt und in unserer Schlachtfliegergruppe geschehen? Sie haben den Major Rudel abgeschossen, und sein Adjutant hat ihn rausgeholt. Tags darauf ging das Flugzeug des Adjutanten in die Tiefe, und Major Rudel hat ihn gerettet, da ein anderer es nicht machen konnte, sonst wäre der Adjutant verloren gewesen. Weiter ist nichts geschehen. Weiter nichts ...!

„Wer runterfällt, wird rausgeholt!" hat der Kommandeur einmal gesagt, womit er freilich nicht behaupten wollte, daß immer er es sein müsse, der sein Leben einsetzt für die Kameraden. Aber hier mußte er es eben sein! Und dabei meint er zu guter Letzt: „Mein Leben? Ich habe mein Können eingesetzt. Das war alles! Und in der Gefahr sind wir hier draußen sowieso!"

Es ist der Raum am oberen ukrainischen Bug. Ein Raum, in dem zu dieser Zeit nicht nur die Kämpfe, nein, auch die Wetterumstände ganz dramatisch sind! Regen und Gewitter in tollem Wechsel. Manchmal nur ein bißchen Sonnenschein. Wolkenberge, grau und schwarz. Ja, wenn man jetzt nicht fliegen müßte, man täte es nicht. Aber man muß fliegen, da die Sowjets nun einmal auch bei diesem Wetter durchzubrechen und die Front zu überrennen suchen; gerade bei diesem Wetter! Tag und Nacht. Sie schicken die Panzer vor und dann die Kavallerie. Und bei den Panzern rollt schon die Flak.

Also nahm der Kommandeur seine Maschine. Es war am Nachmittag, und schwere Wolken lagen über der Trostlosigkeit des ebenen Sumpflochgeländes. Er flog natürlich nicht allein. Er hatte eine Staffel mit, und natürlich war der Adjutant, Ritterkreuzträger Leutnant Hellmut Fickel, wie immer, an seiner Seite.

Um die Mittagsstunde hatte der Major bereits zwei Sowjetpanzern den Garaus gemacht, ohne daß die gegnerische Flak ihn daran hindern konnte. Deshalb flog er auch diesmal auf die gleiche Weise an: Ein Sturz aus den Wolken bis fast zur Bodennähe herunter, dann ein Heranpirschen in jener unruhigen, harten, zickzackreichen Art wie etwa die Libellen fliegen, nur wilder, viel, viel wilder. In etwa fünfzig Meter Entfernung und in denkbar geringer Höhe legte der Major sein Flugzeug blitzartig in die Waagerechte, nahm den Sowjetpanzer ins Visier, schoß, zog hoch und sah noch, wie die Stichflamme aus dem Stahlkoloß hervorzuckte. Und dann?

„Ja, dann!" erzählte der Major, als er ohne sein eigenes Flugzeug im Heimathafen ankam. „Dann tat es einen Schlag, und ich wußte sofort: Die Flak hat den Kühler getroffen. Die Kabine stand voll Rauch. Der Motor rumpelte. Ich dachte: Solange geflogen werden kann, muß geflogen werden! Aber das war nicht lange. Dicht hinter den vordersten Linien ging ich zu Boden. Ich hatte das Fahrwerk abgesprengt und rutschte mit einer Bauchlandung in eine sumpfige Wiese hinein. Was nun? Da landete Leutnant Fickel auf einer benachbarten Wiese. Wo gäbe es das auch, daß sich noch ein Adjutant seinen „Alten" im Sumpf steckenließe? Ein Volkswagen, ein Fahrzeug des Heeres, kam obendrein herangeholpert. Kurz, wir hatten es sehr bequem, zum anderen Flugzeug zu kommen. Zu viert flogen wir los, — ich am Steuerknüppel und „hinten drin" die beiden Vordschützen und Leutnant Fickel als sein eigener Fahrgast!"

Indessen, was Major Rudel nicht erzählt, ist, daß er am gleichen Tage, als die Dämmerung bereits hereingebrochen war, mit einem anderen Flugzeug noch einmal startete, um diesmal drei Sowjetpanzer abzuschießen, die dann im Schattenlicht des Abends wie eherne Fackeln brannten. Sein Adjutant flog mit.

Anderntags wurde die Schlachtfliegergruppe Rudel gegen eine sowjetische Bereitstellung am Bug eingesetzt. Die Flak schoß mörderisch, und um zu beobachten, wie das war, brauchte ich nicht erst zu fragen. Denn auch für den Berichter an Bord der Kapitänsmaschine war die Flak nicht zu übersehen. Wir flogen hinter der Kommandeurskette. Plötzlich, nachdem unser Bombensturz vollendet war, klang die Stimme meines Flugzeugführers, Freundes und Staffelkapitäns in dem Eigenverständigungsgerät: „Den Leutnant Fickel hats erwischt! Dort fliegt er! Vor uns!"

Noch in der Luft, vor der Kulisse der Wolkenwand, aus der wir gekommen waren, schlugen deutsche Jäger sich mit sowjetischen Jagdmaschinen herum. Die Maschine des Adjutanten aber zog schräg nach unten weg. Noch flog sie. Minutenlang. Zehn Kilometer, fünfzehn Kilometer, dann setzte sie in ein Kornfeld hinein, rollte in wilder Fahrt vorwärts und hätte sich eigentlich überschlagen müssen, denn die Wiese, die auf den Getreideacker folgte, war von tiefen Entwässerungsgräben durchzogen, und alte Stukaflieger wissen nicht zu sagen, wann eine Ju 87, die nach der Notlandung ausrollte, solchem Hindernis je gewachsen wäre. Diesmal war sie es. Wie durch ein Wunder. Fliegerglück! Das Flugzeug rollte durch die Gräben und stand. Das alles sah so harmlos aus wie manches im Krieg, das man aus der Höhe sieht. In Wirklichkeit war eine Flakgranate im Innern der Kabine explodiert. Der Kraftstoffbehälter war getroffen. Der Sprit floß in breiten Strömen aus. Die rechte Tragfläche hatte ein Loch, so breit, daß man es mit beiden Armen gerade noch hätte abmessen können. Das Flugzeug war total zerzaust, der Vordschütze verwundet, der Flugzeugführer heil. Er stand neben dem Flugzeug, der Leutnant Fickel, als sei nichts Besonderes geschehen. In Wirklichkeit pirschten sowjetische Kavalleristen auf der nahen Straße dahin, zügelten die Pferde, saßen schon ab und packten ihre Karabiner.

Wir von der Kapitänsmaschine der siebenten Staffel wollten neben ihm landen. Wir kurvten schon im Tiefflug über der Wiese, um zwischen den Gräben eine Landebahn auszumachen. Aber die sowjetischen Jäger ließen uns keine Ruhe. Wir mußten ein wenig hochziehen, um auf eine Aira Cobra zu schießen, während die übrigen Flugzeuge der Gruppe im Tiefflug tanzten und dann auch höher hinauf Staffeln schwirrten, denn dieser Kampf ist Abwehr und Angriff zugleich, ein Kreisen und Rundenziehen, ein Flimmern und Funkeln, das Rudels Vordschütze mit seinem handfesten Humor immer „Zirkus Velli" nennt.

Drunten stand Leutnant Fickel, dies eine Mal nicht an Rudels Seite. Er wäre verloren, wenn keiner half. Sicher stand dies eine Mal auch kein Lächeln auf seinen frischen, jungenhaften Zügen. Und gewiß konnte er nicht damit rechnen, jemals seine Heimatstadt Naumburg an der Saale wiederzusehen. Jetzt kauerte er neben seinem Vordschützen, dem er den Notverband anlegt, in einem Entwässerungsgraben und nahm Deckung, denn die bolschewistischen Jagdmaschinen stießen herunter. Noch waren die Flugzeuge der Gruppe bei ihm. Aber noch waren sie mit sich selbst beschäftigt. „Zirkus Velli ..." Wer sollte da helfen, wenn nicht der Kommandeur? Sie haben so manche Gefahr gemeinsam bestanden, er und sein Adjutant. Nun mußte es auch diese sein. Noch hielt der Kommandeur im Tiefflug die sowjetischen feuerbereiten Kavalleristen in Schach. Da setzt er zur Landung an. Zwischen den Entwässerungsgräben! Wir hörten die Stimme Rudels im FT-Gerät: „Sammeln zum Heimflug!" Wir gingen auf Höhe und zogen westwärts, staffelweise aufgereiht in der schönen, wuchtigen Formation, in der Stukas am Himmel marschieren. Auf der Erde war schon Abenddämmerung, aber in den Wolken war noch Licht. Was weiter? Nein, weiter nichts!

JANUARY-FEBRUARY 1944

From the *Berliner Illustrierten Nachtausgabe* of 7/25/1944, this article described the rescues of downed crews by *Hauptmann* Rudel. Such acts demonstrated the bonds of comradeship which existed within the *Immelmann Geschwader*. By the end of the war, Rudel had retrieved six crews that had force landed between the lines or on Soviet territory. The seventh rescue attempt went awry, resulting in the dramatic escape across the Dniepr river, of which Rudel said, "I raced with death. I was faster ... "

This Ju 87 carried out an emergency landing in enemy territory with engine damage. While the remaining aircraft of the *Gruppe* forced the Soviets under cover with strafing attacks . . .

. . . Rudel set down next to the damaged aircraft, made a safe landing and took off again with the downed crew, which had squeezed into the gunners cabin.

168

This photograph was taken in the summer of 1943. The crew of this *III. Gruppe* aircraft was also snatched from under the noses of the Russians.

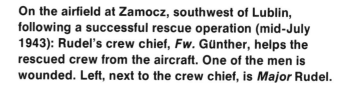

On the airfield at Zamocz, southwest of Lublin, following a successful rescue operation (mid-July 1943): Rudel's crew chief, *Fw.* Günther, helps the rescued crew from the aircraft. One of the men is wounded. Left, next to the crew chief, is *Major* Rudel.

Since 1/28/1944, ten divisions of the German Eighth Army, including the European volunteer units of the 5th SS-Panzer Division *Wiking* and the *Wallonien* Brigade had been encircled in the area of Cherkassy (Dniepr front). A demand for surrender from representatives of the so-called "National Committee for a Free Germany" was rejected. Despite heavy losses, the "Cherkassy Pocket" put up a stubborn defence, fought its way to the west and, after great sacrifices, was able to break through the Russian encirclement on February 17.

# FEBRUARY-MARCH 1944

The *Immelmann Geschwader* supported the units of the Army and *Waffen-SS* as much as weather permitted. During one such mission over the combat zone southwest of Cherkassy, this well-emplaced Soviet anti-tank position was attacked and destroyed. This photograph of the anti-tank position, protected by massed anti-aircraft guns, was taken at low altitude by war correspondent Schalber who was serving as gunner.

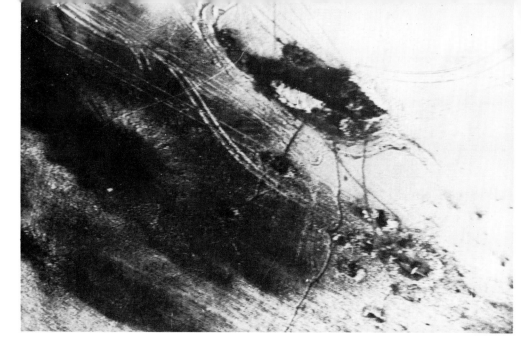

During another effective attack on 2/1/44 against gun positions northwest of Schpola (south of the Cherkassy pocket), Rudel's adjutant, *Oblt.* Fickel, flew his 500th combat mission. After landing at Pervomaysk he is congratulated by the *Gruppe* CO Rudel (right) and signals officer *Oberleutnant* Rossteutscher.

This photo was taken over the sector of the front north of Uman, approximately 50 km. west of the river Bug. After several assaults, German tanks and *Panzergrenadiere* were able to break through the Soviet lines. This photo, taken by the *Immelmann* photographer Schalber, shows the advancing German forces. The *Panzergrenadiere* have the sun at their backs, their shadows indicating the direction of the attack.

In March 1944, Rudel, who had meanwhile been promoted to *Major*, and his *Gruppe* supported the fierce defensive battles being waged by Army Group A (von Kleist) on the southern sector of the Eastern Front north of Nikolayev and about 200 km. to the south near Balta. The Soviets had succeeded in throwing bridges across the Dnestr and had established a bridgehead on Rumanian soil south of Jampol. On March 20, Rudel and his *Gruppe* flew the first seven missions of that day over the sector near Nikolayev and Balta. The eighth mission was directed at the bridges near Jampol, which were destroyed despite powerful flak and fighter defences. One of the *Gruppe*'s aircraft was hit in the motor and force-landed in enemy territory several kilometres east of the Dnestr.

# MARCH 1944: ESCAPE ACROSS THE DNESTR

"Unter keinen Umständen sollten sie mich in die Finger bekommen ...!"

von

Hans-Ulrich Rudel

MAJOR RUDEL wurde vom Führer die höchste deutsche Tapferkeitsauszeichnung, das Eichenlaub mit Schwertern und Brillanten zum Ritterkreuz des Eisernen Kreuzes, verliehen. Mit über 1800 Einsätzen ist Major Rudel der erfolgreichste deutsche Schlachtflieger. Bei einem seiner letzten Einsätze war Rudel, um notgelandete Kameraden zu retten, hinter den Stellungen des Feindes gelandet. Im folgenden berichtet er von seiner abenteuerlichen Flucht durch die sowjetischen Linien.

*Zeichnungen: Theo Matejko*

Es war ein heißer Kampftag, als ich mit meiner Gruppe zum achten Male am selben Tag startete. In aller Frühe hatte ich bereits Frühaufklärung geflogen und dann in mehreren Einsätzen meine Maschine gegen den Feind geführt. Es war nicht einmal die Möglichkeit gegeben, Mittag zu essen. Mein Magen knurrte schon bedenklich. Aber es galt ja, dem sowjetischen Vormarsch ein gebieterisches Halt entgegenzusetzen. Da konnte es keine Schonung geben. Fliegen, stürzen, angreifen, schießen, hochziehen, wieder stürzen, schießen, kurven, landen, aufmunitionieren, starten — Angriff in ununterbrochener Reihenfolge. 1800mal durchgeführt, 1800mal geklappt. Automatisch verrichtet der Körper seinen Dienst. Die Hände schieben den Gashebel rein, ziehen das Steuer an, drücken die Maschine, stellen die Verwindung ein, drücken auf die Knöpfe. Die Augen kontrollieren die Instrumente, sehen den Feind, beobachten das Gelände, erspähen die Chancen des Jägers, die Füße treten ins Seitensteuer, lassen die Maschine kurven, die angespannten Sinne erfühlen die Gefahr, bringen die Maschine immer automatisch aus dem Schußbereich der feindlichen Abwehrwaffen und Jäger, die Stimme gibt Befehle, die das Gehirn in blitzschneller Erkenntnis der Lage formt, und der Instinkt hilft über viele Gefahrenmomente hinweg.

Als ich an diesem Vorfrühlingstag startete, wußte ich nicht, daß mir die größte körperliche und seelische Belastung meines Fliegerdaseins bevorstand. Es war wie immer. Wir flogen in etwa 1200 Meter in Feindrichtung und suchten unsere Ziele auf der Erde. Plötzlich tauchen sowjetische Jäger auf. Sie fliegen amerikanische Jagdmaschinen, Aircobra. Es sind für uns Schlachtflieger gefährliche Gegner, aber wir haben zu oft die Klinge mit ihnen gekreuzt, als daß wir uns von unseren Zielen durch sie abhalten ließen. Ich gebe den Befehl, den Jägern entgegenzufliegen und sie zum Angriff zu stellen. Wir schießen aus allen Knopflöchern und kämpfen uns unseren Weg zu unseren Zielen frei. Das Ziel ist erreicht. Wir stürzen und werfen Bomben. Bordwaffen knattern, Flak schießt, Splitter durchschlagen die Flächen, kurze Abwehrbewegungen, und schon ist der Spuk zu Ende. Auf der Erde ein Knäuel von Fahrzeugen, Menschen und Pferden, dazwischen brennende Panzer. Unser Werk ist getan. Abflug nach Hause.

Ich überzähle meine Gruppe und sehe gerade, wie eine Maschine nach ihr abgeht. Doch sie schlägt nicht auf, sondern landet noch. Im Augenblick kann ich mich nicht weiter um sie kümmern, denn wieder sind die feindlichen Jäger heran, und wieder beginnt der Kampf mit unseren gefährlichen Gegnern. Doch auch diese Barriere wird übersprungen. Die Jäger sind abgeschüttelt. Dem ältesten Staffelführer übergebe ich nun den Verband für den Rückflug zum Horst. Denn ich will mich jetzt um meine notgelandete Besatzung kümmern. Also wieder nach Osten. Zum neunten Male am heutigen Tage. Mein Bordfunker, Oberfeldwebel Henschel, ruft durch die Bordverständigung: "Hoffentlich finden wir sie!" Aber ich habe mir den Platz gemerkt, und nach kurzer Zeit sehe ich sie auf einem Acker stehen. Ich drehe bei und lande neben ihnen. Freudig kommen mir die beiden Unteroffiziere entgegen. Ihr Vogel war hin. Also nehme ich nun die beiden mit in die eigene Maschine und nun starten, starten in die sichere Hut des eigenen Horstes.

Der Motor läuft auf Vollgas, aber die Maschine rührt sich nicht vom Fleck. Tief sind die Räder in den weichen Acker eingesunken. Alle Mann raus, wir versuchen, die Maschine flott zu bekommen, es ist vergeblich. Eine letzte Möglichkeit besteht. Wir müssen die Radverkleidung abschrauben, dann kommen die Räder frei. Also das Taschenmesser raus und ran an die Arbeit. Es ist vergeblich! Es brechen zwar zwei Messer ab, aber die Schrauben rühren sich nicht. Trotzdem geben wir unsere Bemühungen nicht auf. Der Start muß gelingen. Hoffentlich haben die Sowjets noch nicht gemerkt, was sich hier tut. Ich halte das Gelände ständig unter Beobachtung, denn man weiß nie, was kommt.

Wieder einmal spähe ich ringsumher, da erkenne ich plötzlich braune Gestalten. Es sind bolschewistische Soldaten, die auf uns zueilen. Nun gibt es nur noch eins. Alles liegen- und stehenlassen und weg in Richtung Westen. Irgendwo 40 oder 50 Kilometer weiter muß die Front sein. Wir traben los. Nach einiger Zeit haben wir das Ufer des Dnjestr erreicht, der hier zirka 300 Meter breit ist. Am Steilufer stehen wir und sehen 80 Meter weiter unten den Fluß. Es hilft nichts, wir müssen hinunter und hinüber. Auf dem Hosenboden treten wir die Talfahrt an. Die Ginsterbüsche geben uns zum Glück immer wieder die Möglichkeit, die rasende Abfahrt zu stoppen. Einigermaßen zerschunden, aber froh über die gelungene "Abfahrt" landen wir am Wasser. Drüben führt der Weg in die Freiheit. Die Kombination wird ausgezogen, Stiefel und Jacken müssen verschwinden, und nur mit Hemd und Hose bekleidet, den Pullover um den Bauch gewickelt, mit Koppel und Pistolentasche umgeschnallt, müssen wir durch den Fluß schwimmen.

Vorsichtig gehe ich ins Wasser. Aber sofort ziehe ich den Fuß wieder hoch. Es ist eisigkalt. Schätzungsweise 1 bis 2 Grad über Null. Aber was hilft es. Der Feind ist uns auf den Fersen. Wir müssen es wagen! Hinein in das Wasser. Beißend steigt es immer höher. Endlich schwimmen wir. Anfangs geht es ganz gut. Aber dann macht sich die Kälte doch bemerkbar. Das Blut scheint in den Adern zu erstarren. Hände und Füße werden steif. Das Gefühl geht verloren. Nur der eiserne Wille kann uns jetzt retten. Und er gibt den Befehl zum Schwimmen. Hände vor, Füße raus, Arme ran, Füße ran, Hände vor, Arme vor, Füße raus, Füße ran. Automatisch wie ein Roboter versuchen wir den Strom zu bezwingen.

Das Wasser hat hier eine starke Strömung. Die beiden geretteten Besatzungsmitglieder des notgelandeten Flugzeuges schwimmen neben mir. Aber mein Bordfunker, Oberfeldwebel Henschel, bleibt langsam zurück. Mühselig drehe ich den Kopf nach hinten. Er lächelt mir zu, und ich sehe, daß er weiterschwimmt. Noch ein paar Stöße. Ich habe Grund unter den Füßen. Ein paar Schritte weiter, und ich liege auf dem Strand, unfähig, noch eine Bewegung zu machen. Die beiden anderen kommen fast gleichzeitig mit mir an. 50 Meter zurück kämpft mein Bordfunker mit der Strömung. Plötzlich ruft er Hilfe. Die Kräfte drohen ihn zu verlassen. Sein Kopf taucht unter Wasser und kommt wieder hoch. 1400 Feindflüge sind wir zusammen geflogen, vereint auf Leben und Tod. 1400mal haben wir gemeinsam den Feind bekämpft. Da springe ich auch schon ins Wasser und schwimme Henschel entgegen. Nur noch ein paar Stöße, dann bin ich bei ihm. Das Herz klopft in rasenden Schlägen, Arme und Beine sind wie gelähmt, da sehe ich vor mir meinen alten Kameraden Henschel in den Wellen verschwinden. Fast zu gleicher Zeit, wo ich ihm greifbar nahe bin. Ich habe nicht mehr die Kraft in mir, zu tauchen, um ihn dem nassen Tod zu entreißen. Mit Aufbietung meiner letzten Kräfte komme ich wieder ans Ufer und falle, wie vom Blitz getroffen, in den Sand. Die letzten Minuten waren schwer.

Doch der Feind sitzt uns im Nacken. Wir müssen weiter. Denn lieber verrecken, als den Sowjets in die Hände fallen. Wir schleppen uns am anderen Ufer

Die Kombination wird ausgezogen, Stiefel und Jakken müssen verschwinden, und nur mit Hemd und Hose bekleidet, den Pullover um den Bauch gewickelt, Koppel und Pistolentasche umgeschnallt, müssen wir durch den Fluß schwimmen ...

Die beiden andern kommen
fast gleichzeitig mit mir an . . .

hoch und finden ein dichtes Gebüsch. Hier legen wir
uns hin, um Kräfte zu schöpfen für die vor uns liegen-
den Strapazen. Nach kurzer Zeit treibt uns die Kälte
auf. Der Ostwind fährt uns ins Gebein. Die nassen
Sachen kleben am Körper, es hilft nichts, wir müssen
uns bewegen. Nach Westen, das ist unsere Parole. Wir
stolpern los. Dörfer tauchen vor uns auf. Wir lassen
sie links und rechts liegen. Die Sonne neigt sich dem
Horizont entgegen. Noch einige Stunden, dann ist es
Nacht. Die Nacht, die uns vielleicht die Rettung
bringen kann.

Nach unseren Berechnungen müssen wir bald auf
rumänische Truppen stoßen. Denn hier im Zickzack
der beweglichen Südfront liegen oft Freund und Feind
in umgekehrter Front. Wieder steigen wir eine flache
Anhöhe hinauf. Die Füße sind wundgelaufen und
schmerzen bei jedem Schritt. Aber wir müssen weiter.
Meine beiden Kameraden sind stark erschöpft. Doch ich
kann ihnen keine Schonung gewähren. Hinter uns ist
der Feind und vor uns die Hoffnung auf Rettung.
Plötzlich stutze ich, aus der Sonne kommen vier be-
waffnete Soldaten; sie müssen uns schon eine Weile
gesehen haben, da sie selbst die Sonne im Rücken
haben. Beim näheren Hinsehen glaube ich die typischen
hohen Pelzmützen der Rumänen zu erkennen. Das muß
die Rettung sein. Wir gehen auf die vier zu, und ich
sage zu meinen Kameraden, steckt die Pistolen weg,
damit die Rumänen nicht schießen, denn als deutsche

Flieger sind wir für sie bestimmt nicht erkennbar. Inzwischen haben wir uns
auf etwa 10 Meter genähert, und ich sehe, die vier vor mir tragen keine
Pelzmützen. Wir sind den Feinden in die Hände gelaufen. Einer von den vieren trägt
eine Maschinenpistole feuerbereit im Arm, die drei anderen haben ihre Karabiner
halb im Anschlag. Zeit gewinnen, und seien es auch nur Sekunden! Ich trete unbeirrt
an den ersten heran und schlage ihn freundlich auf die Schulter. „Gott sei Dank,
Rumänen!" Doch der so Angeredete scheint nicht erfreut zu sein. „Nix Rumanski",
schreit er mich an und tritt auf mich zu. Ich weiß nur, daß ich mich nicht
gefangengebe und überlege blitzschnell, daß ich, wenn ich jetzt weglaufe, geduckt
Haken schlagen muß wie ein Hase. Da renne ich schon davon. Meine Taktik war
richtig. Die Kugeln pfiffen mir über den Kopf hinweg. Die vier rufen „Stoi"! Aber
ich renne weiter, immer im Zickzack. Plötzlich ein stechender Schmerz in der linken
Schulter. Ich bin getroffen! Ich sehe, wie das Blut aus der Wunde läuft, doch ich
laufe weiter, laufe, wie ich nie in meinem Leben bei allen Wettkämpfen, die ich als
alter Zehnkämpfer mitgemacht habe, gelaufen bin. Die vier sind hinterher. Von Zeit
zu Zeit gehen sie in Anschlag und schießen auf mich. Vergeblich. Die Schüsse gehen
vorbei. Die Flucht geht im Zickzackkurs eine flache Anhöhe hinan. Nach etwa
1500 Metern habe ich meine Verfolger 800 Meter zurückgelassen. Noch einige hundert
Meter, und ich bin jenseits des Hügels und ihren Blicken entschwunden. Aber ich bin
allein. Meine beiden Begleiter fielen bei dieser unglückseligen Verwechslung in sowjetische Gefangenschaft.

Ich stoppe etwas ab und atme tief auf. Ich sehe mich nach allen Seiten um und
muß erkennen, daß links neben mir genau parallel eine Gruppe von etwa zwölf
Soldaten ebenfalls den Hang hinabläuft, um mir den Weg abzuschneiden. Also wieder
im Tempo 1500-Meter-Lauf los, um auch diesen Verfolgern zu entgehen. Die Wunde
blutet stark, und beim Laufen sticht und reißt es in ihr, als ob jemand mit einem
Messer darin herumwühlt. Doch das ist alles belanglos, nur laufen, laufen, um den
Verfolgern zu entgehen. Da sehe ich plötzlich Reiter auftauchen, die mir ebenfalls den
Fluchtweg verlegen wollen. Das ist das Ende. Den Menschen kann ich weglaufen, aber
den Pferden nicht. Ich werde etwas langsamer und lasse mich hinfallen. Mit Händen
und Füßen scharre ich mir eine flache Mulde und lege mich hinein. Nun noch Erde
draufschmeißen, damit sie mich nicht finden. Auch das Gesicht bewerfe ich mit etwas
Erde. Ich will ihnen nicht in die Hände fallen.

Jetzt hält die links von mir laufende Verfolgergruppe an. Mein plötzliches Verschwinden ist ihnen aufgefallen. Sie warten, bis die mit Pferden ausgerüstete Gruppe
vorbeikommt, dann suchen sie systematisch das Gelände ab. Unmittelbar an mir gehen
sie vorüber. Ich habe den Eindruck, jetzt müssen sie dich gesehen haben, jetzt ist
Schluß. Aber immer wieder gehen sie an mir vorüber. Ich wage kaum zu atmen. Die
Kälte kriecht wieder hoch. Ich muß die Zähne zusammenbeißen, um nicht zu stöhnen.
Die Wunde schmerzt rasend. Arme und Beine werden steif, aber ich darf mich nicht
bewegen. Ganz still muß ich liegen. Jede Bewegung, der geringste Husten, ein
Stöhnen oder Seufzen, würde mich den Verfolgern ausliefern. Endlich scheint die

173

Jetzt hält die Verfolger-
gruppe an, dann suchen
sie systematisch das Ge-
lände ab. Unmittelbar an
mir gehen sie vorüber . . .

Qual zu Ende zu sein. Langsam hebe ich den Kopf, um mich sofort wieder hinfallen
zu lassen. Auf dem etwa 50 Meter neben mir vorbeiführenden Wege kommt eine
ganze Kompanie anmarschiert mit Pferden und Hunden. Ihnen kann ich nicht mehr
entgehen. Sie müssen mich finden. Immer näher kommt der Zug. Jetzt sind sie auf
gleicher Höhe mit mir. Mein Herz klopft so laut, daß ich glaube, sie müssen es hören.
Mit Scheppern und Klappern marschieren sie an mir vorbei. Knapp 50 Meter weiter
läßt der bolschewistische Offizier halten und ausschwärmen. Ihr Marschweg ist nach
Westen. Sie sind bereits an meinem Versteck vorbei und werden mich nicht finden.
Plötzlich ein tiefes Brummen in der Luft. Das können nur Schlachtflieger sein.
Da kommen sie auch schon an, meine ganze Gruppe, sie kreisen um zwei Fieseler-
Störche, die im Tiefstflug das Gelände absuchen. Ich sehe sie über mir hinwegfliegen
und kann nicht den Arm heben zu jenem Wink, der meine Rettung bedeuten würde.
Ganz still muß ich liegen, denn dicht bei mir sind noch immer die Sowjets. Es ist
zum Verzweifeln! Langsam ziehen die Störche über mich hinweg. Ich möchte schreien
vor Wut. Aber auch die Bolschewisten verlieren sich im Gelände.

Die Dämmerung bricht herein. Endlich kann ich aufstehen. Die Glieder sind steif
und kalt. Die Füße wund. Doch es hilft nichts, ich muß weitermarschieren nach
Westen. Ich habe einen Heißhunger, denn seit morgens früh um 5 Uhr bin ich
auf den Beinen, und außer dem Frühstück habe ich nichts mehr essen können. Die
schweren Einsätze des heutigen Tages erlaubten keine Pause. Es dunkelt schon sehr
stark, als ich wieder ein Dorf erreiche. Hier muß ich etwas zu essen finden, sonst
kann ich den Marsch nicht durchhalten. Vorsichtig umschleiche ich das Dorf, bis
ich endlich etwas abseits ein Haus finde. Hier muß ich etwas essen, und hier muß
ich mich aufwärmen. Behutsam klopfe ich ans Fenster. Niemand rührt sich. Auch auf
stärkeres Klopfen kommt niemand. Soldaten sind also nicht hier, denn sie würden

Die vier Bolschewisten rufen
„Stoi!", aber ich renne weiter,
immer im Zickzack . . .

bereits fragen, was los ist. Ich donnere also mit aller Gewalt gegen das Fenster, und als sich noch immer niemand rührt, schlage ich es mit der Faust ein. Da kommt endlich ein altes Weiblein angeschlürft. Sie öffnet nur einen kleinen Spalt die Tür und ruft mir unverständliche Worte zu. Ich drücke also die Tür ganz auf, und trotz des Gezeters der Alten gehe ich in ihre Stube. Beim Schein einer alten Petroleumlampe sehe ich einen alten Mann auf einem Brett liegen, das den beiden wohl als Lagerstatt dient. Mit der Zeichensprache versuche ich dem alten Weiblein klarzumachen, daß ich etwas zu essen brauche, aber sie reagiert nicht, sondern legt sich wieder auf das Brett, um weiterzuschlafen. Kurz entschlossen lege ich mich dazu. Wärme durchrieselt meinen Körper. Ein Gefühl tiefer Geborgenheit umfängt mich, und nach kurzen Augenblicken bin ich eingeschlafen.

Der Hunger treibt mich nach einer Stunde wieder hoch. Wieder versuche ich der Alten klarzumachen, daß ich etwas zu essen haben muß, und jetzt versteht sie mich. Sie bringt ein altes vertrocknetes Maisbrot und eingemachte große Kohlblätter an. Selten hat mir der beste deutsche Sauerkohl und Eisbein so gemundet wie dieses frugale Mahl. Neue Lebensimpulse durchströmen mich. Ich beschließe, noch ein paar Stunden zu schlafen, um dann weiterzumarschieren. Ich nehme mir beim Einschlafen vor, um eins Uhr nachts wieder aufzustehen.

Wieder liegen wir drei friedlich auf dem Brett. Ich schlafe den tiefen Schlaf der Erschöpfung. Punkt eins wache ich auf.

Mit unverständlichen Worten entläßt mich die alte Frau aus dem Haus in die inzwischen stockdunkel gewordene Nacht. Wohin muß ich mich nun wenden? Mein Kompaß ist nicht mehr zu erkennen. Es ist so finster, daß ich nicht die Hand vor den Augen erkennen kann. Da fällt mir ein, der Wind kam vom Osten, mit ihm im Rücken muß ich nach Westen kommen. Wie ein altes Segelboot stelle ich mich in den Wind und marschiere los. Hoffentlich hat der Wind nicht gedreht? Nach einiger Zeit sehe ich links und rechts von mir das Aufblitzen der Geschütze und das Leuchten der Leuchtspurmunition. Auf dieses Feuerwerk darf ich nicht zugehen, sondern ich muß mitten hindurch. Das Gehen ohne Schuhe und Strümpfe ist äußerst beschwerlich. Die Fußsohlen müssen ohne jede Haut sein, so schmerzt mich jeder Schritt. Immer

wieder muß ich stehenbleiben. Der Weg führt bergauf und bergab. In den Taleinschnitten sind Flüsse und Sümpfe. Oft stecke ich bis zur Brust im Wasser, wenn ich sie durchwaten muß. Wer den Schlamm des Ostens kennt, weiß, was ein nächtlicher Marsch, quer durchs Gelände, bedeutet. Hier bewährt sich mein ständiges sportliches Training, das ich auch im Einsatz nicht aufgegeben habe.

Wieder dämmert es im Osten. Im fahlen Licht des anbrechenden Morgens sehe ich ein Dorf vor mir. Hier muß ich wieder etwas zu essen finden, denn der Magen knurrt fürchterlich. Doch bald stelle ich fest, daß es Niemandsland ist. Das Dorf ist leer. Haus um Haus suche ich ab, umsonst, nichts Eßbares ist aufzutreiben. Weiter geht der Marsch mit der aufgehenden Sonne im Rücken.

Nach zwei Stunden etwa finde ich eine Kolonne der Rumänen. Ich schließe mich ihr an und bekomme endlich wieder etwas zu essen. Wir marschieren nun gemeinsam nach Westen. Am Horizont erscheint eine Stadt. Auf meine Frage sagen mir die rumänischen Kameraden, daß dort noch deutsche Truppen sind. Mühselig marschiere ich auf die Stadt zu. Zwei deutsche Soldaten stehen am Stadtrand. Endlich wieder deutsche Soldaten. Sie sind nicht schlecht erstaunt, als sie ein barfüßiger und zerlumpter Mann deutsch anredet und sie nach der Kommandantur fragt.

Ich nenne meinen Namen und Dienstgrad, worauf einer antwortet, „das kann jeder sagen, bei uns sehen die Majore anders aus". Ich ziehe mein Ritterkreuz aus der Tasche, als das einzige, womit ich mich ausweisen kann, denn meine Papiere habe ich natürlich beim Feindflug nicht bei mir gehabt. Bei der Kommandantur ist alles in vollem Aufbruch. Trotzdem ist die Begrüßung herzlich, meine Wunde wird verbunden, eine Decke findet sich, in die man mich hüllt, so fahre ich zum Flugplatz. Und als ob es so sein müßte, treffe ich auf eine Transportmaschine meiner Gruppe, die bald zu meinem Horst startet.

Der Stabsarzt nimmt mich unter seine Fuchtel, liebende Hände umsorgen mich, treue Augen leuchten auf, und das Händeschütteln nimmt kein Ende. Meine Freude an der Heimkehr trübt der Gedanke an das tragische Schicksal meines Bordfunkers Henschel, der in 1400 Feindflügen in treuer Kameradschaft mit mir vereint war. Und mein einziger Wunsch ist, sobald wie möglich wieder gegen den Feind zu fliegen.

Zwei Tage später ist es soweit. Ich klettere mühsam in die Maschine. Meine Füße wollen noch nicht so recht wieder mittun, der Motor läuft auf Hochtouren, dann rollt der neue Vogel über die Bahn, und in die aufgehende Sonne fliege ich wieder nach Osten, dem Feinde entgegen.

(Nachdruck verboten)

---

In an attempt to rescue the crew — this would have been the seventh he had rescued — Rudel landed near the downed aircraft. This time, however, the rescue attempt misfired; he could not take off again. How he escaped wounded from the Russians and reached the German lines on foot was described in the May 31, 1944 issue of the magazine *Wehrmacht*. The article isreproduced on pages 172-174; for a transcript of the account, see section one.

Reports on Rudel's escape from the *Völkischer Beobachter* (center) and *Der Adler* (bottom).

# Schwerterträger Rudel schlug sich durch

**Berlin, 24. März**

Der bekannte deutsche Sturzkampfflieger Rudel, Träger des Ritterkreuzes mit Eichenlaub und Schwertern, war am 20. März von einem Flug gegen den Feind nicht zurückgekehrt. Inzwischen ist er jedoch — nach geradezu abenteuerlichen Ereignissen hinter den sowjetischen Linien — wieder bei seiner Gruppe eingetroffen.

Beim Einsatz im Südabschnitt der Ostfront stießen die Flugzeuge des Majors Rudel und seines Rottenkameraden auf stärkere feindliche Gegenwehr. Der Rottenkamerad mußte sich zur Notlandung entschließen, und Major Rudel landete kurz entschlossen neben ihm, um die Besatzung dieser Maschine aufzunehmen. Auf dem schlammigen Boden vermochte er jedoch nicht wieder zu starten. Bald tauchte eine Anzahl bolschewistischer Soldaten auf, so daß die deutschen Flieger beschlossen, sich nach Westen zu unseren Linien durchzuschlagen.

Sie konnten ihre Verfolger abschütteln. Aber der breite Fluß, dessen eiskalte Fluten sie auf ihrem Weg nach Westen durchschwimmen mußten, bot ein neues, schwer zu nehmendes Hindernis. Dabei verließen Major Rudels Bordfunker, den Ritterkreuzträger Oberfeldwebel Henschel, die Kräfte, so daß er in dem eisigen Wasser ertrank. Als Major Rudel bemerkte, daß sein treuer Bordfunker, mit dem er

die Mehrzahl seiner weit über 1700 Feindflüge gemeinsam geflogen hatte, im Fluß unterging, schwamm er, der inzwischen bereits das andere Ufer erreicht hatte, noch einmal zurück, um ihn zu retten. Der Versuch blieb aber leider vergeblich. Beim Durchschwimmen des Flusses hatten die beiden anderen Kameraden ihre Kräfte derart erschöpft, daß sie die weitere Flucht vor einem plötzlich auftauchenden sowjetischen Spähtrupp nicht mehr durchhielten und dem Feind in die Hände fielen.

Nur Major Rudel, dessen sportlich gestähltem Körper die Strapazen nichts anhaben konnten, entkam den Verfolgern, die in der Dunkelheit mit Maschinenpistolen hinter ihm herfeuerten. Im Zickzacklauf, mit einem Pistolenschuß durch die Schulter, setzte Major Rudel seinen Marsch — barfuß und nur noch mit Hemd und Hose bekleidet — in westlicher Richtung weiter fort. Gegen 22.30 Uhr kam er in ein von den Sowjets besetztes Dorf, mußte aber, da er bemerkt worden war, weiterfliehen. Während Reiterpatrouillen und Spürhunde die ganze Gegend absuchten, hatte er sich seitlich der Straße mitten auf das freie Feld hingeworfen. Man fand ihn glücklicherweise nicht, und gegen 1 Uhr nachts konnte er endlich seinen Marsch nach Westen fortsetzen. Nachdem er bis morgens gegen 8.30 Uhr noch 15 bis 20 km barfuß marschiert war, traf er auf rumänische Soldaten und war gerettet.

---

## „Prima! Rumänen!"--doch es waren Sowjets

Auf Du und Du mit dem Tod — Von Spürhunden gehetzt — Flucht durch die eiskalten Fluten des Dnjestr — Major Rudel: „Es war meine größte sportliche Leistung!" / Von Kriegsberichter Josef Ollig

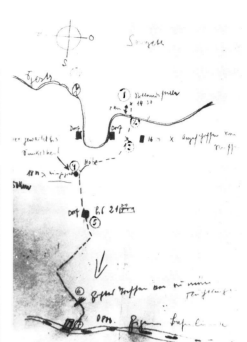

Medical officer Dr. Breisendanz poses for the photographer with his "short time" patient . . .

. . . then Rudel is interviewed by a *Luftwaffe* correspondent for German radio.

Rudel had to cover approximately 50 km. of Russian-occupied territory before reaching the German rearguards. This is his hand-drawn sketch of the dangerous and rigorous escape route.
(1) landing site on the far side of the Dnestr
(2) swimming the icy Dnestr
(3) taken prisoner, escaped and wounded in the shoulder
(4) searching Red Army men pass only a few metres away
(5) brief rest in village and search for something to eat
(6) encounters Rumanian refugees
(7) two German soldiers on the rail embankment: "you don't look like a Major to us!"

175

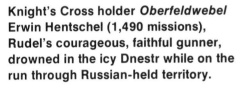

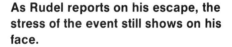

Knight's Cross holder *Oberfeldwebel* Erwin Hentschel (1,490 missions), Rudel's courageous, faithful gunner, drowned in the icy Dnestr while on the run through Russian-held territory.

As Rudel reports on his escape, the stress of the event still shows on his face.

176

# Abwehrerfolg zwischen Mogilew und Dnjepr

## Vergebliche Sowjetangriffe im Raum Tarnopol-Kowel
## USA-Kommandotrupp bei Landungsversuch niedergemacht

Aus dem Führerhauptquartier, 27. März

Das Oberkommando der Wehrmacht gibt bekannt:

Am unteren ukrainischen B u g scheiterten erneute Angriffe und Übersetzversuche der Sowjets.

Zwischen P e r w o m a i s k und B a l t a wehrten Truppen des Heeres und der Waffen-SS starke feindliche Angriffe ab. Am mittleren Dnjestr verstärkte sich der feindliche Druck. Schlachtfliegergeschwader fügten den vordringenden Sowjets schwere Verluste zu. Besonders südlich P r o s k u r o w stehen unsere Divisionen im schweren Abwehrkampf. Im Raum T a r n o p o l - K o w e l griffen die Bolschewisten vergeblich an. Nordwestlich Kowel gewannen unsere Gegenangriffe gegen zähen feindlichen Widerstand Boden.

Im Gebiet der P r i p j e t s ü m p f e brachen wiederholte Angriffe des Feindes zwischen S t y r und G o r y zusammen. Zwischen D n j e p r und T s c h a u s s y setzten die Bolschewisten mit starken Kräften ihre Durchbruchsversuche fort. Sie wurden durch unsere tapferen Grenadiere in erfolgreichem Zusammenwirken mit der Luftwaffe in harten Kämpfen zurückgeschlagen. Dabei hat sich die erste Kompanie des Grenadierregiments mot. 51 unter Führung von Oberleutnant H u n c k e durch besondere Tapferkeit ausgezeichnet. In den Kämpfen der beiden letzten Tage verlor der Feind hier über 3500 Tote, 39 Panzer, 42 Geschütze und zahlreiche andere Waffen.

Im Raum südöstlich O s t r o w wehrten lettische SS-Freiwilligenverbände zusammen mit deutschen Truppen den Ansturm mehrerer feindlicher Divisionen ab. Örtlicher Einbruch wurde abgeriegelt. An der N a r w a - F r o n t durchbrachen unsere Grenadiere, von Artillerie, Panzern, Nebelwerfern und Schlachtfliegern hervorragend unterstützt, stark ausgebaute Stellungen des Feindes und bereinigten eine Einbruchstelle.

Major R u d e l, Gruppenkommandeur in einem Schlachtgeschwader, vernichtete im Süden der Ostfront an einem Tage 17 feindliche Panzer.

Aus Italien wird nur beiderseitige Späh- und Stoßtrupptätigkeit gemeldet.

An der Ostküste des Golfes von G e n u a wurde ein nordwestlich La S p e z i a gelandeter nordamerikanischer Kommandotrupp in Stärke von zwei Offizieren und 13 Mann im Kampf niedergemacht.

Nach Tagesvorstößen nordamerikanischer Bomber gegen Südostdeutschland griffen britische Terrorflieger in der vergangenen Nacht bei geschlossener Bewölkung mehrere Städte im R u h r g e b i e t an. Durch Abwurf zahlreicher Spreng- und Brandbomben entstanden besonders in Wohnvierteln von E s s e n und O b e r h a u s e n Schäden und Verluste unter der Bevölkerung. Luftverteidigungskräfte vernichteten bei diesen Angriffen über den besetzten Westgebieten unter schwierigen Abwehrbedingungen 17 viermotorige Bomber.

# Neue Träger des Eichenlaubes

Berlin, 27. März

Der Führer verlieh das E i c h e n l a u b zum Ritterkreuz des Eisernen Kreuzes an:

Hauptmann J a b s, Gruppenkommandeur in einem Nachtjagdgeschwader, als 430. Soldaten der deutschen Wehrmacht;

Major J o p e, Kommodore eines Kampfgeschwaders, als 431. Soldaten der deutschen Wehrmacht;

Major S c h m i t t e r, Kommandeur in einem Kampfgeschwader, als 432. Soldaten der deutschen Wehrmacht;

Major Dr. O t t e, Kommandeur in einem Schlachtfliegergeschwader, als 433. Soldaten der deutschen Wehrmacht;

Oberleutnant Herbert H e i n r i c h, Batteriechef in einem niedersächsischen Artillerieregiment, geboren am 24. September 1918 in Altona als Sohn des Regierungs- und Baurats Georg Heinrich;

Sanitätsfeldwebel Karl N o w o t n i k, in einem bayerischen Füsilierbataillon, geboren am 6. Dezember 1914 in Kreutz (Kreis Grünberg, Gau Niederschlesien) als Sohn des Fabrikarbeiters N., von Beruf ist er Maurer;

Unteroffizier Fritz K r o p p, Gruppenführer in einem Neustrelitzer Grenadierregiment, geboren am 1. August 1916 in Schloppe als Sohn des Landwirts K., von Beruf ist er Landwirt.

## Arbeitsstäbe Stalingrad und Tunis werden aufgelöst

With strong tank forces the Soviets tried to push forward from the Dniestr bridgehead near Jampol in a southwesterly direction to the Rumanian border on the Pruth. Massed anti-aircraft and fighter escort protection (for the most part with American "Airacobras") were to protect the advance against Stuka attack. Major Rudel, with his group and the Panzer unit ("Cannon Birds") were transferred to Jassy, 20 km west of the Pruth. Despite his shoulder and foot injuries (he had to be carried to the plane for every mission), he led his Stuka unit in ceaseless attacks against the masses of tanks, which had a long-range operational target and generally carried gasoline cans of spare fuel on their hulls. Of the more than 30 tanks that were destroyed by his group near Falsty, about 40 kilometers north of Jassy, Rudel alone destroyed seventeen with his 20mm guns (MG 151). The Russian move forward toward Jassy and on to the Carpathian passes was thwarted for the time being.

# 17 TANKS IN ONE DAY

Masses of Soviet tanks attacking in the direction of Jassy. The first Stuka bomb bursts are visible on the right in this aerial photograph.

Tank assembly areas northeast of Jassy under a hail of bombs from Rudel's *Gruppe*.

178

Dark clouds from exploding bombs and swaths of smoke mark the destruction of several Soviet tanks.

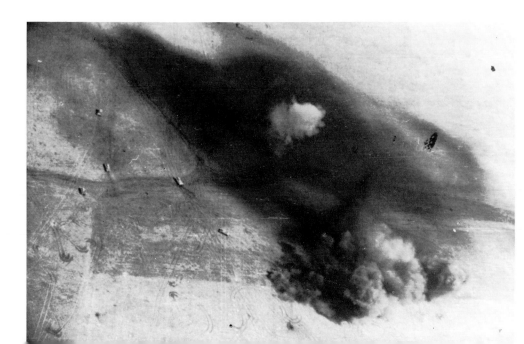

This Soviet heavy tank blew up; the explosion threw the gun turret, which weighed several tons, well to the side.

Approach to the Dnestr near Doubusari: a steel monster type JS I ("Josef Stalin", ca. 45 tons in weight, 4 man crew), knocked out by *Major* Rudel. The vehicle burned out without exploding.

Soviet tanks destroyed "Rudel style" mark the location where attacks by *III. Gruppe* and the *Panzerjagdstaffel* halted the Russian advance on 3/26/1944. Rudel and his gunner, *Ofw.* Rothmann, returned from one sortie with a "sieved" aircraft: after landing they counted eight hits from the 3 cm. cannon of American-built "Airacobra" fighters as well as several from 20 mm. guns. It was a wonder that Rudel's "cannon bird" did not go down . . .

Above: During a tank hunt in the area of Jassy, Rumania on 3/30/1944, the commander of *I. Gruppe*, *Major* Alwin Boerst, and his gunner, *Ofw.* Ernst Filius, were killed when their Ju 87G-1 was brought down. Boerst had been a wearer of the Oak Leaves since 11/30/42 and was awarded the Swords posthumously; *Ofw.* Filius received a posthumous Knight's Cross. He managed to get out of the stricken aircraft, but his parachute hung up on the airframe. Both men were buried with honours in a common grave.

# Schwerer deutscher Luftangriff auf Bristol

## Voller Abwehrerfolg zwischen Dnjepr und Tschaussy

Aus dem Führerhauptquartier, 28. März

Das Oberkommando der Wehrmacht gibt bekannt:

Bei N i k o l a j e w wurden Angriffe der Sowjets in erbitterten Nahkämpfen abgewiesen. Nordwestlich davon vereitelten Jäger und Gebirgsjäger in schneidigen Gegenangriffen den Versuch der Bolschewisten, einen Brückenkopf über den Bug zu erweitern. Im Raum von B a l t a sind weiter schwere Kämpfe im Gange. Zwischen D n j e s t r und P r u t h griffen starke deutsche Schlachtfliegerkräfte in die Kämpfe ein. Sie zerstörten zahlreiche feindliche Panzer und eine große Zahl motorisierter und bespannter Fahrzeuge. Dabei vernichtete Major Rudel wiederum neun feindliche Panzer. Er hat damit in mehr als 1800 Einsätzen allein 202 feindliche Panzer vernichtet.

Südlich P r o s k u r o w, nordwestlich T s c h e r n o w i t z, bei T a r n o p o l und im Raum von B r o d y nimmt die Abwehrschlacht mit unverminderter, Heftigkeit ihren Fortgang. Unsere Truppen leisten den sowjetischen Angriffskräften erbitterten Widerstand.

Die Besatzung von K o w e l wies erneut feindliche Angriffe ab. Nördlich Kowel gewannen unsere Divisionen im Angriff weiter Boden und zerschlugen feindliche Gegenangriffe. Bei den Kämpfen im Raum von Kowel hat sich der Leutnant K l a p p e r s t ü c k, Zugführer in einer Sturmgeschützbrigade, durch besondere Tapferkeit ausgezeichnet. Zwischen D n j e p r und T s c h a u s s y errangen unsere Truppen gegen die mit Unterstützung durch zahlreiche Panzer und Schlachtflieger angreifenden Bolschewisten erneut einen vollen Abwehrerfolg. Der Feind verlor wiederum mehrere tausend Tote und zahlreiche schwere und leichte Waffen.

Im Raum südöstlich O s t r o w kam es zu wechselvollen örtlichen Kämpfen.

Im Nordabschnitt der Ostfront hat sich das Grenadierregiment 162 unter Führung von Major H a s e zusammen mit unterstellten Infanterie- und Pioniereinheiten besonders ausgezeichnet.

Im hohen Norden an der L i z a - F r o n t nahmen ostmärkische Gebirgsjäger mehrere feindliche Höhenstellungen und vernichteten Kampfanlagen mit deren Besatzungen.

In Italien kam es gestern zu keinen Kampfhandlungen von Bedeutung.

Deutsche Schlachtflugzeuge bekämpften feindliche Schiffsziele vor A n z i o mit gutem Erfolg. Ein Frachter wurde versenkt drei weitere beschädigt.

Bei der Abwehr feindlicher Luftangriffe auf deutsche Flugplätze in S ü d w e s t f r a n k r e i c h wurden am gestrigen Tage zwanzig nordamerikanische Flugzeuge abgeschossen.

Einige feindliche Störflugzeuge drangen in der letzten Nacht in das r h e i n i s c h westfälische Industriegebiet vor.

Starke deutsche Kampfgeschwader führten in der Nacht zum 28. März einen schweren Angriff gegen B r i s t o l. Durch den Abwurf einer großen Zahl von Spreng- und Brandbomben entstanden bereits während des zusammengefaßten Angriffs umfangreiche Zerstörungen und Großbrände im Zielgebiet.

Photocopy of the *Wehrmacht* communique of March 26, 1944. Among other things, the bulletin states: ". . . Powerful German close support air forces intervened in the battles between the Dnestr and Pruth rivers. They destroyed numerous enemy tanks and a large number of motorized and horse-drawn vehicles. In the fighting *Major* Rudel destroyed nine more enemy tanks. He has now destroyed 202 enemy tanks in more than 1,800 combat missions."

# THE DIAMONDS

The highest German decoration for bravery until 12/31/1944.

The slip-case for the award certificate, with the national emblem in gold, inlaid diamond chips and gold border on a blue background.

IM NAMEN
DES DEUTSCHEN VOLKES
VERLEIHE ICH
DEM MAJOR
HANS ULRICH RUDEL
DAS EICHENLAUB MIT
SCHWERTERN UND BRILLANTEN
ZUM RITTERKREUZ
DES EISERNEN KREUZES
FÜHRERHAUPTQUARTIER
DEN 29. MÄRZ 1944
DER FÜHRER
UND OBERSTE BEFEHLSHABER
DER WEHRMACHT

The award certificate with inlaid gold lettering and the national eagle of the German Reich.

On March 29, 1944, *Major* Rudel was awarded the Oak Leaves with Swords and Diamonds to the Knight's Cross. He was the 10th soldier of the German armed forces to receive what was, at that time, still the highest decoration for bravery. He received the decoration from Hitler at the *Berghof* on the Obersalzburg near Berchtesgaden.

Above right: After the awarding of the Diamonds, Major Rudel spoke with representatives of the domestic and foreign press in Berlin.

At the beginning of April, Rudel spent several days on home leave in Alt-Kohlfurt near Görlitz. He still wears his fleece-lined flying boots, as the injuries to his feet sustained in his flight across the Dnestr have not yet healed.

With wife and "son and heir" in the rectory garden in Alt-Kohlfurt. When Rudel heard radio reports from the Eastern front, he cut short his leave and flew back with *Ofw.* Rothmann, who had been visiting family in Zittau, via Vienna and Bucharest to his *Gruppe* at Husi, east of Jassy.

Following the evacuation of Odessa on April 10, the southern sector of the Eastern Front, where *I.* and *III. Gruppen* of the *Immelmann Geschwader* were supporting the Army, stretched from the Dnestr estuary on the Black Sea to the Russian bridgehead near Tiraspol, from there to Dubossary, then ran in a westerly direction past Jassy to the north, through Targut-Frumos and west of Pascani, where it veered to the northwest.

A short time later: pre-mission briefing with officers of *II./JG 52*, which was providing the fighter escort. CO of the fighter *Gruppe* was *Major* Barkhorn, since 3/2/44 a wearer of the Knight's Cross with Oak Leaves and Swords with 250 victories (in photo on the right).

Back "at home" with *III. Gruppe* in Husi, Rumania following the presentation of the Diamonds. From left: *Lt.* Ebersbach (*Gruppe* TO); *Hauptmann* Katzschner (*Geschwader* Technical Officer); *Major* Rudel and an unidentified *Unteroffizier*.

This time the mission is to the Soviet bridgehead near Grigoriopol, east of Kishinev. Fighter escort was provided by *II./JG 52*. The Stukas attacked assembly areas and bridges.

This PK photo report appeared in the *Luftwaffe* front-line magazine *Flieger, Funker, Flak* on 5/9/1944, describing the missions against the Dnestr bridges. (Original text and photos)

Left: *Major* Rudel is with us again. One of his first missions after his return to the front was to destroy a bridge which was vital to the enemy. The photos illustrate the changes in the face of Rudel the man, the soldier and comrade before and after this mission.

Right: Several moments later comes a call from *Fliegerkorps*. Assignment: Destruction of a bridge. Already, the *Gruppe* commander's full concentration is on the important new assignment.

*185*

Left: "The bridge must go!" Uncompromising in his will to get the job done and without regard for himself — that is Rudel as his men know him in combat.

Right: The mission was difficult: Flak as seldom seen before. One crew has failed to return. . . but the bridge is no longer standing!

Like an "stairway in the air" or a "sky ladder": the Stukas have joined formation close to home on the return flight, escorted by two Bf 109s (above).

186

"The day the *Immelmann Schlachtgeschwader* reported its 100,000th combat mission marked the end of four-and-a-half years of combat flying with our Air Fleet by this particularly successful *Schlachtgeschwader*. Before the weather- and storm-torn banners of the *Geschwader*, the Chief of our Air Fleet addressed his *Schlachtflieger*. The *Geschwader* has long since returned to the hard struggle at the front, but the proud day of the 100,000th lives clearly in our memories."

**APRIL 1944: THE GESCHWADER'S 100,000TH COMBAT MISSION**

A photocopy from the Air Fleet's illustrated *Flieger, Funker, Flak* from 5/9/1944 which carried an article on the *Immelmann Geschwader*'s 100,000th mission which was flown at the beginning of April.

Schlachtgeschwader Immelmann am Tage des 100.000 Feindfluges

The airfield at Husi, Rumania, April 1944: the *Geschwader* in parade formation. The Chief of *Luftflotte 3, Generaloberst* Otto Dessloch, lauds the accomplishments of the *Geschwader* in his address.

Wearer of the Knight's Cross *Generaloberst* Dessloch (left), the Air Fleet Chief, and *Geschwader* commander *Oberstleutnant* Stepp review the *Geschwader*.

188

*III. Gruppe* with *Major* Rudel (left). Next to the commander are *Lt.* Weissbach, *Oblt.* Siekerka and *Prüfmeister* Brunnemann.

**Major** Rudel and the officers of the **Gruppe** staff.

The Air Fleet Chief presents the Knight's Cross to *Staffelkapitän* Kurt Lau and pilot *Feldwebel* Meyerling, who has been wounded in the face. On the right are two war correspondents.

*189*

*Generaloberst* Dessloch in conversation with *Major* Rudel following the festivities.

*III. Gruppe* poses for a
group photograph with its
Commanding Officer
*Hauptmann* Bauer
(Knight's Cross 12/31/43,
Oak Leaves 9/30/1944) at
Husi on 4/6/1944.

*Hauptmann* Bauer (in
March 1944 while still
leader of *3. Staffel*) at Husi,
Rumania after landing from
his 1,000th mission on
5/3/1944. He is
congratulated by "chimney
sweep" *Uffz.* Hageböcker
and his crew chief
(partially hidden).

*Hauptmann* Herbert Bauer:
Knight's cross
12/31/1943, Oak Leaves
on 9/30/44, from June
1943 until 5/4/44 leader of
*3. Staffel*, from 5/15 until
11/6/1944 commander of
*II./SG 103*, from 11/7/44
until the end of the war
commander of *I./SG 2*.

# MAY-JUNE 1944: "THE MERRY VALUABLES" IN HUSI

Left: May 12, 1944: With a most serious face, an Army *Gefreiter* reports to the CO, "The merry valuables are present!." The name of the *Gefreiter* was Alfred Rossmann of Stargard in Pomerania, who was a stage manager and actor and led the front-line review, "Merry Valuables." After a wild sea voyage to Constantia and a bus trip to the Husi airfield, he hoped to put on a guest performance with his troupe.

Right: After the war, Alfred Rossmann, now a stage manager and actor in Vienna, described his experiences in Husi with the *Immelmänner* in this article in the *Pommerschen Zeitung*, Hamburg.

**Aus der Presse:**

**Die Pommersche Zeitung**

Hamburg 1. Mai 1971

DIE POMMERSCHE ZEITUNG ist das alleinige Organ der Pommerschen Landsmannschaft auf Bundesebene und für West-Berlin; sie erscheint wöchentlich. — Herausgeber: Pommerscher Zentralverband e. V. 2000 Hamburg 13, Johnsallee 18.

(Teilausschnitt:) Frühlingsbrief aus Wien:

Lassen Sie mich, liebe Landsleute, schließlich noch über eine wenig erfreuliche österliche Episode berichten, die mir ewig in Erinnerung bleiben wird. Dabei handelt es sich wahrlich nicht um etwas süßes Osterei, sondern um ein sehr bitteres, und das Osterwasser bestand aus dem Schwarzen Meer:

Es war in der Osternacht des Jahres 1944. Unsere „KDF-Truppe", der unter anderen Kollegen auch die Hamburger Pianistin und jetzige Klavierlehrerin Anna Riepenhausen angehörte (die mir späterhin freundlicherweise die Fotos schickte), fuhr mit dem letzten Schiff von Odessa über das Schwarze Meer nach Constantia/Rumänien.

Dieses Gewässer sollte seinem Namen alle Ehre machen! Wir kamen nämlich in ein Unwetter, wie es weiland der „Fliegende Holländer" nicht dramatischer erlebte! Stundenlang dauerte der schreckliche Sturm! Der böse Poseidon scheint dort zu Hause zu sein . . .

Leider hatte die Angelegenheit auch eine sehr betrübliche Seite, denn es befanden sich 600 Verwundete an Bord! Trotz unseres tüchtigen Kapitäns, einem erfahrenen, Hamburger Seebär, verloren wir das Geleitboot und hatten so alle Aussicht, auf Minen zu laufen. Wohl besaßen wir Korkwesten. Wir erfuhren, was Windstärke 10 ist . . .

Dabei hatten wir so große Pläne und Aufträge: Wir sollten monatelang zur Truppenbetreuung in Rumänien spielen, u. a. auch 14 Tage beim Stukegeschwader des damaligen Majors und „Ersten Helden" Rudel. Ein Wunder, sagte der alte Käpt'n, als wir dennoch gegen Morgengrauen in Constanza landeten. Als ich Mamaia sah, war es wie eine Rettung aus der Hölle.

Als erstes halfen wir bei der Bergung der 600 Schwerverwundeten, die im Bauch des Schiffes hin- und hergeschleudert wurden. Viele dieser Armen erlebten den Ostersonntag nicht mehr. Für uns aber gab es eine Auferstehung im Sinne des Wortes.

Ein paar Tage später meldeten wir uns bei dem berühmten Kampfflieger auf dem Gefechtsstand in Husy/Rumänien. Er hatte uns schon aufgegeben. Umso größer war die Freude. Es folgten interessante Tage und ebensolche Diskussionen.

Ich war mit dem inzwischen zum Oberst avancierten Brillantenträger Rudel noch wochenlang in Verbindung und habe ihn seither nicht mehr gesehen. Die Erinnerung an einen ungemein sympathischen, bescheidenen und klugen Menschen bleibt. Die Kapitulation in Rumänien beendete unsere freundschaftliche Verbindung.

Das letzte Mal sahen wir uns in Bistritz/Siebenbürgen. Nach einem Stadtbummel gingen wir in den schönen Kurgarten. Kaum hatte es sich herumgesprochen, daß der berühmte Rudel im Kurpark sitzt, fand sich auch schon eine große Gruppe von Siebenbürger Sachsen ein, die ihm Ovationen brachte. Ja, man bereitete extra einen „Kaiserschmarren", und Oberst Rudel mußte unentwegt Autogramme geben und das mit etwas erzwungener Freundlichkeit, nach alledem, was sich dort unten ereignet hatte. Er erzählte mir u. a., daß ihm Hitler das Angebot gemacht hatte, mit seinen Leuten einen der Gebirgspässe zu halten.

Beim „Kaiserschmarren" meinte er plötzlich: „Die Siebenbürger sind hier die längste Zeit gewesen und wir werden unsere Heimat (Rudel war Schlesier) wohl auch nicht mehr zu sehen bekommen, wenn das alles so weiter geht . . ."

Womit er leider recht hatte.

Herzliche Grüße von der Donau

Ihr Alfred Roßmann, A 1210 Wien
Schöpfleutnergasse 27.

10

192

*Gefreiter* Rossmann and pianist Anna Riepenhausen wait in front of *III./SG 2*'s command post tent for the commander's decision as to when the presentation can take place.

*May-June 1944*: the front on the lower and central Dnestr and in the area of Jassy (Army Group South Ukraine under *Generaloberst* Schörner) had stabilized — not least due to the effective support of the Stukas. However, the Army units there, including some of the *Waffen-SS*, were still engaged in heavy defensive fighting. The focal points of the fighting were the Dnestr bridgeheads at Tiraspol-Tighina, Grigoriopol-Taschlyk and the territory west of the Pruth in the Jassy area. There the Soviets were attacking southwards with over-whelming forces in the direction of the Carpathian passes. The Stuka crews were in action from dawn until dark. There was scarcely a mission that was not intercepted by Russian fighters or a target without heavy flak defences! A tough job for Rudel and his comrades. He and his *Gruppe* usually took off from Husi to attack the Dnestr bridgeheads to the east. When the target was on the Jassy front to the north, the airfield at Bacau, 90 km. west of Husi, was frequently used as a staging base.

# MAY-JUNE 1944 STUKA TARGET DNESTR BRIDGEHEAD AND THE JASSY FRONT

June 1944, at the command post of *III. Gruppe* in Husi: fighter escort is arranged by telephone with *II./JG 52* and the rendezvous point is pinpointed on the map. From right: *Major* Rudel, *Lt.* Stahler (chief of *7. Staffel*), *Leutnant* Weissbach (*Gruppe Ia*), Staff Clerk *Uffz.* Rimkus (partially hidden), *Lt.* Kainz (*7. Staffel*).

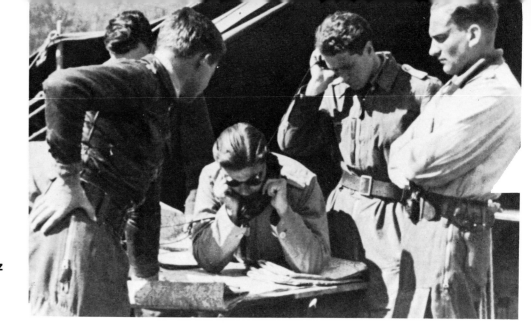

The technicians have made this Ju 87-D ready to start and are replacing the cowling. *Major* Rudel waits impatiently in the cockpit of his bomber. He will first "run up" the engine (test run at max. RPM) and then, with medical officer Dr. Gadermann as gunner, will take off at the head of his *Gruppe*.

194

This time the target for *III. Gruppe* is the Tiraspol bridgehead on the Dnestr. This photo was taken by a gunner forward through the cabin.

Soviet positions near Tighina-Bendery, west of Tiraspol (Dnestr bridgehead), under a hail of bombs from *III. Gruppe*.

Bomb strikes as seen by *Flievo* (air-ground liaison officer) Janacek, who often worked with the crews of *Immelmann Geschwader* from the front lines in the southern sector and later in Courland.

195

The Stuka liason officer has made *Major* Rudel aware of a well-camouflaged Soviet tank by radio. Moments later an explosion indicates a direct hit on the target by Rudel.

Standing in the turret of his *Panzer III, Flievo Oblt.* Rudolf Janacek observes the fall of the bombs with the 14th Panzer Division. Using his throat-type microphone, he reports the results to *Major* Rudel and suggests additional targets. (This PK photograph appeared on the cover of the *Luftwaffe* magazine *Der Adler*).

Back from the mission against the Dnestr bridgehead: the commander's face betrays the tension of the mission, which was successful in spite of heavy fire from flak and infantry weapons. As he so often did, Rudel changed aircraft prior to the next mission as his Ju 87 looked somewhat the worse for wear.

196

# Erbitterte Kämpfe um die Albaner Berge

## Vergebliche Versuche der Sowjets, das bei Jassy verlorene Gelände zurückzugewinnen

Aus dem Führerhauptquartier, 3. Juni

Das Oberkommando der Wehrmacht gibt bekannt:

Um die A l b a n e r B e r g e wurde auch gestern erbittert gekämpft. Bei und westlich L a n u v i o schlugen unsere Truppen in harten Kämpfen alle feindlichen Angriffe zurück. An den Südosthängen der Albaner Berge und beiderseits der V i a C a s i l i n a griff der Feind mit überlegenen Kräften während des ganzen Tages an. Unseren erbittert Widerstand leistenden Truppen gelang es, die feindlichen Angriffsspitzen in den Abendstunden östlich R o c c a d i P a p a und südlich P a l e s t r i n a - C a v e zum Stehen zu bringen.

Kampf- und Nachtschlachtflugzeuge griffen feindliche Kolonnen und Bereitstellungen im Raum von V a l m o n t o n e mit gutem Erfolg an.

Sicherungsfahrzeuge eines deutschen Geleits und Bordflak schossen vor K r e t a bei der Abwehr eines schweren Luftangriffes sechs feindliche Bomber ab.

An der O s t f r o n t versuchten die Sowjets vergeblich, das nördlich J a s s y in den letzten Tagen verlorene Gelände zurückzugewinnen. Bei der Abwehr ihrer Angriffe wurde eine aus 23 Panzern bestehende feindliche Kampfgruppe restlos vernichtet. Nordwestlich Jassy brachen deutsche und rumänische Truppen in harten Kämpfen in die stark ausgebauten feindlichen Stellungen ein und nahmen ein beherrschendes Höhengelände.

Starke Kampf- und Schlachtfliegerverbände griffen wiederholt wirksam in die Erdkämpfe ein und unterstützten die verbündeten Truppen in Angriff und Abwehr. 22 sowjetische Flugzeuge wurden über diesem Raum abgeschossen.

Major R u d e l, mit dem höchsten deutschen Tapferkeitsorden ausgezeichnet, flog an der Ostfront zum 2000. Male gegen den Feind.

Nordamerikanische Bomberverbände griffen gestern mehrere Orte in U n g a r n und R u m ä n i e n an. Fünf feindliche Flugzeuge wurden dabei vernichtet.

Einzelne britische Flugzeuge warfen in der vergangenen Nacht Bomben auf Orte im r h e i n i s c h - w e s t f ä l i s c h e n G e b i e t.

Über den besetzten W e s t g e b i e t e n und dem R e i c h s g e b i e t wurden bei Tage und in der Nacht 33 feindliche Flugzeuge, darunter 20 viermotorige Bomber, zum Absturz gebracht.

Photocopy of the
*Wehrmacht* communique
in the *Völkischer
Beobachter* from
6/3/1944, which reported
Rudel's 2,000th mission.

# JUNE 1944: THE 2,000TH COMBAT MISSION DURING THE COUNTER—ATTACK IN THE JASSY AREA

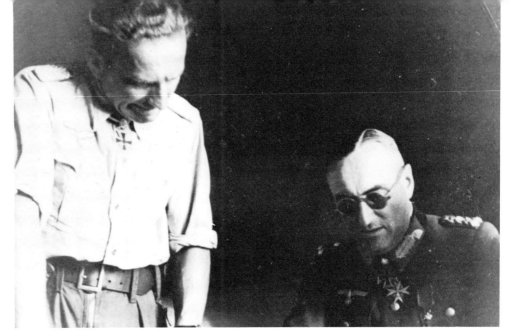

**Above: Attack operations have been going on in the Jassy area for several days. The crews of *III. Gruppe* flew their first mission against Russian field and artillery positions near Stanca at 04.20 on June 1, 1944. The airfield at Husi: The commander climbs aboard his aircraft. This will be his 2,000th mission. Target: Soviet positions southwest of Stanca.**

198

**Above right: In the command post at Husi, *Generaloberst* Ferdinand Schörner (Army Group South Ukraine) uses a map to give *Major* Rudel a summary of the attack operations planned northwest of Jassy. During the briefing they will discuss Stuka support for the attack.**

**Center: Another discussion with the commanding general, *General der Infanterie* Buschenhagen (right), and the unit commanders takes place in the presence of the commanding general of *I. Fliegerkorps*, *Generalleutnant* Deichmann (left).**

**Right: German Panzer assembly area for the attack in the direction of Stanca, northwest of Jassy.**

The 2,000th
Combat Mission
Because of the
significance of this unique
event in the history of air
warfare, two rifle-armed
honour guards were
posted next to the
*Immelmann* banner at the
edge of the airfield. The
aircraft of Rudel and his
*Gruppe* taxi past the color
party prior to takeoff.

Meanwhile, Stuka liaison
officer *Oberleutnant* Rudolf
Janacek of the 14th
Panzer-Division moves
forward in his radio-
equipped *Panzer III* to take
position in sight of the
Russian positions. From
there he will direct the
Stuka attacks on the area
of Stanca Castle. He is an
"old hand" as *Flievo* for
Rudel and his crews, and
the airmen have learned to
trust his selection of
targets.

*III. Gruppe* during a dive-
bombing attack on Soviet
positions southwest of
Stanca which were
subsequently taken by
German ground forces. A
successful Stuka attack
despite strong fighter and
Flak defences. In the photo
lower left, two diving
Stukas; on the right, one
has pulled up and is
climbing away.

Rudel landed from his 2,000th mission at Husi at 14.10. His crew chief, *Fw.* Günther, congratulates him with a bunch of flowers.

Above right: After the attack Rudel crosses the German front lines at low altitude — only several metres above the ground.

Center: One of *III. Gruppe*'s aircraft crash-landed as a result of flak damage and was immediately towed from the runway.

The commander is covered in flowers and can scarcely be seen. Left: Rudel's crew chief celebrates; right, Dr. Gadermann, who flew as Rudel's gunner on the historic mission.

Crews and ground personnel are assembled for the "congratulation parade." Left: *Oblt.* Hendrik Stahl (Knight's Cross on 12/23/42, 506th soldier of the *Wehrmacht* to receive the decoration).

Wearing a self-conscious expression, *Major* Rudel listens to the appreciative congratulatory speeches of *Generalleutnant* Deichmann (Chief of *I. Fliegerkorps*) and the *Geschwaderkommodore.* Rudel expressed his gratitude with typical military brevity, "I have only done my duty! My thanks go out to the ground crews; their efforts create the conditions necessary for success." Behind the commander on the right: *Hptm.* Hirsch, *Geschwader Ia*; far right: Knight's Cross wearer and leader of *9. Staffel, Oblt.* Dose, and the ground personnel of *III. Gruppe.*

The commander's car, decorated with oak leaves.

The members of the
headquarters staff set up
this scoreboard for their
commander's reception.

*Oberfeldwebel* Fuchs
presents a gift from the
field workshop platoon: a
scale model of the Ju 87G-
2 ''cannon-bird'', complete
with electric motor, which
he made in his spare time.
*Ofw.* Fuchs was killed
several days before the
end of the war.

202

After the final mission of
the day there was a
celebration in honour of
the great event: the
commander of *I.
Fliegerkorps* (right) next to
*Major* Rudel at the coffee
table. *Major* Becker (left), a
Staff Major with *SG 2601*,
serves the traditional
celebration cake.

To Rudel's right at the coffee table is his gunner, Dr. Gadermann; on the left, standing, is *Major* Becker who is serving the rare treat of freshly-baked cake. *Generalleutnant* Becker also appears to be looking forward to a helping of the sweet pastry which is so out of the ordinary at the front.

Part of the large group assembled for the congratulatory coffee party. From left: *Lt.* Weissbach (Ia of *III. Gruppe*), war correspondent J. Müller-Marein; from right: *Lt.* Kosslowski (Technical Officer *8. Staffel*), *Oblt.* Stahl (Leader of *8. Staffel*), *Hptm.* Kresken (Leader of Staff Flight), *Hptm.* Hirsch, medical officer Dr. Gadermann, the commander of *I. Fliegerkorps* and, at the head of the table, *Major* Rudel.

203

A photograph taken at Husi to commemorate the "2,000th": *Major* Rudel with his faithful gunner, Dr. Gadermann, and the technicians of the *Gruppe* Staff in front of the famous aircraft.

On the occasion of the 2,000th mission, Hermann Göring, Commander-in-Chief of the *Luftwaffe*, awarded Rudel the Golden Mission Clasp for *Schlachtflieger* with 2,000 pendant and diamonds. Until the end of the war, Rudel remained the sole recipient of this decoration, which was made of gold with platinum wreath and small inlaid diamonds, which were also featured on the number 2,000.

204

The Golden Pilot Badge, likewise awarded to Rudel after following his 2,000th mission by the *Reichsmarschall*. The *Luftwaffe* eagle and the symbol of the German Reich were inlaid with small diamonds.

The *Gruppe* commander's "cannon bird" is rearmed by the armorers.

"Chocks away!" *Major* Rudel and gunner Dr. Gadermann taxi out for takeoff.

While the bombers dive-bomb flak and field positions north of Targut-Frumos (here a Ju 87-D of the Staff Flight), Rudel and his *Panzer-Staffel* with their "cannon birds" see to it that several Russian tanks which have broken through get no farther.

This T-34 attempted to escape on down a dirt road. After the first shot it caught fire at once.

Below left: Rudel's shot went right through the cannon barrel of this Russian tank, putting it out of action. The tank's crew bailed out and fled. The photograph was taken by war correspondent Rothkopf, who photographed *Oberfähnrich* Heinz Meyer (Knight's Cross on 4/17/45) inspecting the tank. Meyer accompanied Rudel on many successful missions.

206

Right: June 9, 1944 — the day's flying over, the *Gruppe* is assembled. The CO presents the Knight's Cross to his adjutant, *Leutnant* Helmut Fickel.

On July 13, Rudel and his *III. Gruppe* were ordered from Husi in Rumania to the central sector of the front approximately 500 km. to the northwest, where the Soviets were attacking toward the Vistula with superior forces. For eight days the *Gruppe* supported the Army in its costly defensive battles, operating from the airfield at Cholm. The *Immelmänner* attacked targets near Horokov, Stoyanov, Kamienka, Rava-Ruska and Tomazov. On July 22, the *Gruppe* was transferred to Milec in the Vistula-San triangle. Its primary targets there were motor transport columns and tank, field and artillery positions near Jaroslav, Zapatoska, Sokolov and Rzeszov on the Wislok river. Beginning July 31, Rudel's Stuka "fire brigade" flew missions 400 km. north of Milec from Insterburg and the FHQ airfield at Lötzen, East Prussia. Sorties were flown over the combat zone southwest of Kovno, near Suvalki (Rominten Heath) and east of Rasseinen, north of Memel, where the Soviets had achieved a breakthrough which was sealed off with the help of Stuka attacks. In mid-August it once again left East Prussia. Rudel's Stuka "travelling circus", as the crews called it, supported the heroic defence by Army Group North in Courland, where units of the Army and *Waffen-SS* had succeeded in stabilizing the front. Meanwhile, *Flievo Oblt.* Janacek had also transferred to Courland, where he successfully took on the job of directing the Stuka attacks.

# FIRE BRIGADE AT THE FRONT DURING THE HOT SUMMER OF 1944

Zwischen Weichsel und Memel setzte der Feind seine Angriffe an den bisherigen Schwerpunkten fort. Er wurde bis auf örtliche Einbrüche in harten Kämpfen abgewiesen. Nördlich der Memel stehen unsere Truppen in erbittertem Kampf mit eingebrochenen stärkeren sowjetischen Kräften. Im Bereich einer Panzerarmee wurden gestern erneut 62 sowjetische Panzer abgeschossen. 27 weitere Panzer wurden durch Schlachtflieger vernichtet. Hiervon schoß Major **Rudel** allein elf Panzer ab und erzielte damit seinen 300. Panzerabschuß durch Bordwaffen.

Im Karpatenvorland und im großen Weichselbogen wurden zahlreiche Angriffe des Feindes in sofortigen Gegenstößen zerschlagen. Nur im Raum von Milec und südöstlich Warka konnten die Sowjets Boden gewinnen. Gegenangriffe sind hier im Gange.

Excerpt from the *Wehrmacht* communiques of August 5-6, 1944, describing the German defensive successes between the Vistula and Memel rivers, including the destruction of 11 Soviet tanks by *Major* Rudel, which raised his total to 300.

Fifty km. west of Jaroslav, on the San river east of Rzeszow, a Soviet tank burns following Rudel's attack.

A Stuka bombing attack meant ''end of the line'' for two more Soviet T-34s east of Rzeszow on the Jaroslav—Krakau road.

Several tanks and trucks had driven into the cover of a small ravine 60 km. southeast of Milec near Reichshof, where they were knocked out by *Major* Rudel.

After landing in Milec: Rudel's 2,100th combat mission has been a successful one. *Feldwebel* Günther, his ground crew chief, offers congratulations from the wing of the aircraft. Right: Gunner medical officer Dr. Gadermann.

The Courland campaign badge (inset) featured the coat-of-arms of the Order of the Teutonic Knights, which also served as the unit emblem of the *Immelmann Geschwader*. The badge was worn as a cuff band. Two "cannon birds" from "Rudel's travelling circus" on a frontline airfield — a harvested cornfield — at Wenden in Latvia. Also stationed there was the Fw 190-equipped *III./SG 4*. At Rudel's request, this *Gruppe* provided fighter cover for his *III. Gruppe* in addition to its close support duties.

The Russians are attempting to break through between Lake Peipus and Wirz in the direction of Dorpat, Estonia. *III./SG 2* en route to the target; armor and vehicle columns near Dorpat.

The Focke-Wulf Fw 190s of *III./SG 4* (CO *Major* Weyert) made bombing attacks in same area and then flew escort for the *Immelmann* Stukas. Here a *Kette* of Fw 190s in flight carrying SD 250 bombs. After their bombs had been dropped, they and the remaining Fw 190s successfully assumed the "fighter" role, providing escort for the Stukas. (*Lt.* Just, the author, was flying the aircraft on the right.)

East of Dorpat large columns of tanks and supply trucks were attacked and destroyed by Rudel and his *Immelmänner*, preventing a Russian breakthrough for the time being. While the Fw 190s of *III./SG 4* battled with superior numbers of Russian fighters, primarily American supplied "Airacobras", the Stukas dived one after the other on the enemy. This photograph was taken by an Army war correspondent.

Center right: Much feared by the Soviets, the "long rods" are rearmed. Then *Major* Rudel and Dr. Gadermann take off for Ergli, where forty Soviet tanks have broken through. The "cannon-bird" was accompanied by the remaining aircraft of the *Panzerjagdstaffel* and *7. Staffel*, which was assigned the bombing role.

While flying at low altitude, approximately three metres above the ground, Rudel's "cannon bird" was hit several times in the motor by anti-aircraft fire. With his aircraft on fire, he succeeded in reaching the German lines, where he carried out a forced landing at the edge of a wood. Rudel was wounded in one leg and suffered a concussion, while Dr. Gadermann sustained several broken ribs. The pair were brought back by German infantry. The photo shows Rudel back at Wenden with smoke-blackened face already discussing the next mission. Despite their injuries, he and Dr. Gadermann took off again for Ergli where they took their revenge on the Russian Flak. As well, Rudel and his comrades were able to destroy the Russian tanks which had broken through. The accompanying infantry was overcome by German ground forces. Rudel had now destroyed 320 Russian tanks. Knowing his weakness for pastries, *Generaloberst* Schörner sent a cake to Wenden with the number 320 in icing. In the photo on the left is *Oblt.* Herbert Eissele, adjutant of *III./SG 4*, who was killed in action in 1945.

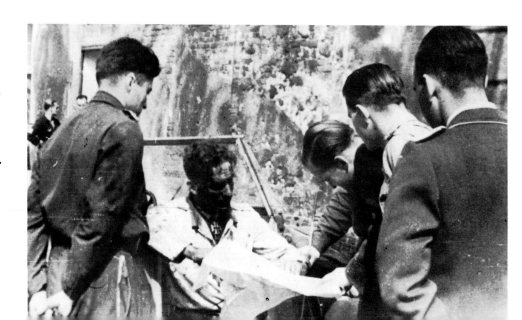

Orders reached Rudel's "fire brigade" in Kurland instructing it to transfer back to Rumania where things were heating up in the Carpathian passes. Bases from August 28 included Buzau, 70 km. northeast of the Rumanian oil center of Ploesti; Sachsisch Regen; Tasnad, near Tokai, Hungary; Miskolc on the Sajo; Sajokaza, 25 km. NE of Lake Balaton; Farmos, near Szolnok; Vecses/Budapest; Borgond, near Stuhlweissenburg, 30 km. NE of Lake Balaton; Varpalota, west of Stuhlweissenburg; and Kemenitz St. Peter, near Papa on a tributary of the Raab. The three *Gruppen* of the *Immelmann Geschwader*, the *Geschwader* Staff Flight and *10. Panzer-Staffel* with its "cannon birds" supported the costly defensive battles of the Army and *Waffen-SS*, whose situation had taken a catastrophic turn for the worse with the traitorous change of sides by the Rumanians and Hungarians. On December 24, the Soviets encircled the city of Budapest. German and Hungarian troops fought bravely in a lost cause until February 14, 1945. All relief attempts by the *Waffen-SS* under *General* Herbert Gille failed in the face of Soviet numerical superiority.

Promoted to *Oberstleutnant* on 9/1/1944, Rudel took over command of the *Geschwader* at the beginning of October. His *III. Gruppe* was now led by Knight's Cross wearer *Hauptmann* Kurt Lau. On November 7, Oak Leaves wearer *Hauptmann* Bauer took command of *I. Gruppe* while *II. Gruppe*, now equipped with Fw 190s, was commanded by *Hauptmann* Karl Kennel, also a wearer of the Oak Leaves (from 1/1/45 a *Major*, by war's end 34 air victories as a *Schlachtflieger*). CO of *10. Panzer-Staffel* was *Leutnant* Korol, an expert with the "cannon bird" who destroyed 99 Russian tanks by the end of the war and was awarded Knight's Cross on 3/12/1945. On 23 December, Rudel flew his 2,400th combat mission, destroying four Soviet tanks and raising his total to 463.

# AUTUMN AND WINTER 1944 - THE RUMANIA-HUNGARY THEATRE

Return from a successful tank hunt in Hungary. Rudel's much feared "Stuka with the long rods" is escorted by *Leutnant* Korol's "cannon-bird."

A Stuka bomber tipped on its nose while taxiing. With a rope around the tail-wheel and a "heave ho!", the so-called "flier's monument" is brought down.

212

At the beginning of November, the airfield at Sajokaza, not far from Mislolc in Hungary, was flooded in many places. An aircraft of *7. Staffel* has become stuck. By applying full power while ground crew hoist the right wing, the pilot succeeds in fighting his way out of the morass.

November 8, 1944. "Just push!" — this time it's an aircraft of *9. Staffel*. Stuka crewmen (from left) *Fw.* Freyer, *Uffz.* Gothe and *Uffz.* Langbein take a foot bath in the process.

Finally, all of *III. Gruppe*'s aircraft are on dry ground. There they were prepared for takeoff to a drier airfield.

Takeoff from the six-metre-wide road on the outskirts of Sajoskaza demanded a delicate touch on the control column and rudder pedals. First to take off from *III. Gruppe* was *Uffz.* Gothe. Ground crews watch with crossed fingers as he begins his takeoff roll. He and all of the remaining Stuka pilots managed to get off safely from the narrow surface.

# DER BESTE FLIEGER

*Das Beispiel des Oberstleutnants Rudel / Von Kriegsberichter Erwin Kirchhof*

Selbst alten Frontfliegern ist Rudel ein Rätsel. Die ihn zum erstenmal erleben, können es meist nicht fassen, daß der frische, energiegeladene, mittelgroße Pfarrerssohn mit den tiefbraunen besinnlichen Augen „der Rudel" ist. Müde und gezeichnet von den unzähligen harten Kämpfen hat man ihn sich vorgestellt, ja vielleicht verbraucht, ablösungsbedürftig, zumindest jedoch mit der Nervosität von Fliegern belastet, die ein hohes Maß harter Feindflüge hinter sich brachten. Geht bei ihm alles spurlos vorüber, die ungeheure Anspannung der Organe und der Nerven durch einen Sturzangriff, bei dessen Abfangen selbst gehärtete Schlachtflieger noch einen Schleier bekommen, Sekunden die Sehkraft verlieren? Und schleppt er sich nicht nach acht bis zehn Angriffsflügen, bei denen nicht selten mehr als fünfzigmal gestürzt wird, körperlich und geistig zerschlagen zur Ruhe? Seine über zweitausenddreihundert Einsätze waren keine Bombenflüge im üblichen Sinne. Weit über zwölftausend Hammerschläge in das Herz glühender Schlachten sind es gewesen! Von diesem Mann, der in über 600 000 Frontflugkilometern allein die Panzerkolosse von mehr als 11 vollständigen sowjetischen Panzerbrigaden vernichtete, die Kanonen zahlreicher feindlicher Pak-, Artillerie- und Flakabteilungen, den Wagenpark von zwei Sowjetdivisionen mit Bomben und Bordwaffen zerfetzte, der das Sowjetschlachtschiff „Marat" auseinanderspaltete, einen Kreuzer und siebzig Landungsboote versenkte, von diesem Mann strömt eine solche Vitalität aus, daß man sagen möchte, seine größte Stunde stehe ihm noch bevor. Wo liegt der Schlüssel des Rudelschen Rätsels?

❖

Ein Dorfteich im schlesischen Konradswaldau weist den Weg. Wieder auf der Suche nach Objekten, an denen er seinen Mut erproben konnte, kam der 15jährige Hans Ulrich Rudel eines Wintermorgens an den Teich, in dem er noch bis in den Spätherbst vor Schulbeginn gebadet hatte, und wollte ihn überspringen. Es war die schmalste Stelle, nach seiner Ansicht mußte er es schaffen. Sein erster Sprung war zu kurz. Er fiel aufs Eis, brach ein und mußte sich mühsam wieder ans Ufer arbeiten. Rudel lief nicht nach Hause. Schlotternd vor Kälte, nahm er einen noch größeren Anlauf und fiel wieder in das Eiswasser. Er kümmerte sich nicht um die Zurufe der Bauersfrauen, die dem „verrückten Pfarrerssohn" galten. Zum erstenmal hatte er gespürt, daß nicht alles im ersten Sprung zu nehmen war. Viermal sprang er — dann hatte er es geschafft. Als er in den Pfarrhof zurückging, war er entschlossen, die daraus gewonnene Erkenntnis in die Tat umzusetzen und hart gegen sich selbst zu werden. Tage später stürzte er mit dem Motorrad und brach sich ein Bein. Schon am nächsten Morgen humpelte er mit dem Gipsbein zu seinem Motorrad, ließ es sich von einem Kameraden in Gang bringen und fuhr zur Schule. Zwei Jahre später werden die Wirkungen seines täglichen und zielbewußten körperlichen Trainings weithin sichtbar. Bei den Zehnkampf-Meisterschaften seines Heimatgaues siegt seine Zähigkeit im

10 000-Meter-Lauf. Mit seinen Gesamtleistungen rückt er auf einen Schlag in die Spitzenklasse. Rudel beherrscht bald seinen Körper so, daß er mit Kunstsprüngen vom 10-Meter-Turm seine Kameraden in Bewunderung versetzt und bei Schiwettbewerben Harro Kranz und Lantschner hohe Anerkennung abnötigt. Er zählt zu den wenigen, die im Schilauf einen Salto ausführen. Wochen vor dem Abschluß seines Abiturs (1932) legt ihm der Direktor der Schule nahe, seine aktive Betätigung im NS.-Schülerbund aufzugeben, andernfalls er ihm das Abitur verweigern müßte. Rudel bleibt HJ.-Führer. „Ich kann mich doch nicht selbst aufgeben." Man weist ihn von der Schule. Er macht sein Abitur trotzdem. Als Fahnenjunker der Luftwaffe betreibt er weiterhin systematisch Sport. Es ist kein Rekordwahnsinn, der ihn in der Frühe, wenn andere noch schlafen, in jeder freien Minute auf den Sportplatz treibt und dort so lange üben läßt, bis er Hochleistungen vollbringt. Es sind auch keine „Pfarrerssohnallüren", wenn er sich des Alkohol- und Nikotingenusses enthält. Sein wacher Geist sieht die Möglichkeiten eines kommenden Krieges. Er will sich hart machen für ihn. Rudel wird zwar Offizier, aber sein großer Wunsch, Stukaflieger zu werden, geht nicht in Erfüllung. Er wird als zum Flugzeugführer untauglich abgelehnt und als Beobachter zu einer Fernaufklärer-Staffel versetzt. Mit ihr erlebt er den Polenfeldzug und dort seine ersten soldatischen Erfolge. Was er von weiten einsamen Aufklärungsflügen mit nach Hause bringt, versetzt die Führungsstäbe in Staunen. Selbst die bestgetarnten Trümpfe des Gegners entdeckt er, skizziert sie mit dem Blick des Generalstäblers und liefert damit rechtzeitig der Führung Unterlagen zu durchschlagenden Gegenoperationen. Generale sprechen von „Rudelschen Wunderkolonnen". Durch ein Versehen wird der Leutnant Rudel als fliegeruntauglich abgelöst. In einem Ausbildungshafen der Heimat verbringt er quälende Wochen und Monate. Der Frankreichfeldzug geht seinem Ende zu, all die vielfachen regulären und „kriminellen" Versuche, wieder an die Front zu kommen, waren vergeblich geblieben. Plötzlich ist der Versetzungsbefehl da. Rudel darf in einer der erfolgreichsten deutschen Sturzkampfgruppen fliegen. Der neue Fronteinsatz packt auch seinen sportgestählten Körper hart. Er ist lange nicht mehr geflogen, und die Kameraden sind die Besten der Besten.

❖

Mit dem Krieg im Osten schlägt auch seine Stunde. Sie schleudert ihn erst an die Pforte des Todes und läßt ihm wenig Hoffnung. Bei einem massierten Stukaschlag auf einen Bahnhof deutet er, im Verbandsangriff noch nicht genügend erfahren, ein Sammelzeichen seines Kommandeurs als Signal zum Sturzangriff und kippt zu früh ab. Rudel stürzt durch eine bis tief auf die Erde herabhängende Wolke, in der sein Flugzeug vereist. Wie sich sein energieloser Vogel wieder gefangen hatte, wußte er nicht zu sagen, als er mit zwei baumdicken Löchern in beiden Tragflächen auf dem Feldflughafen

landete. Er muß in die Kronen einer Birkenallee gefallen sein; denn von diesem Birkenflug brachte er noch zwei abgesplitterte dicke Äste mit, die in den Tragflächen steckten. Rudel hatte eine ruhelose Nacht. Bei einem Nebelflug in Frankreich hatte er dicht über den Baumspitzen abfangen können, nun war er hineingeschlagen, würde er das nächste Mal am Boden zerschellen? Er setzte in den folgenden Wochen alle Energien ein, um sein Sturzkampfflugzeug und den Verbandsangriff beherrschen zu lernen. In vielen freien Stunden und langen Nächten studierte er Moral und Kampftechnik der sowjetischen Erdtruppen und Flieger und entwickelte immer wirkungsvollere und überlegenere Angriffsverfahren. Auf Stalingrad flog er mit seiner Staffel mehr als 150 Angriffe, Tag für Tag, bei allen Wetterlagen. In der ersten Stunde der Not holte er aus sich und seinen Männern Hochleistungen heraus.

Seine Frau, die Mutter seines Buben, lebt seit Jahren wie viele deutsche Soldatenfrauen: zwischen Warten, Entsagung und Hingabe und in der ständigen Erwartung eines dauerhaften Glückes. Rudel kommt selten auf Urlaub, wohl nur einmal im Jahr, um in den Bergen beim Wintersport Erholung zu suchen. Aber auch hier hält ihn die Front in Atem. Täglich über den Einsatz seiner Schlachtfliegergruppe unterrichtet, wägt er ab, wann er vorn gebraucht wird. Eine Schlechtwetterperiode über dem Reich vereitelte einmal den Flug zur Front. Hauptmann Rudel fuhr mit der Bahn zum Osten, trampte auf Lokomotiv-Tendern, Kraftkrädern, Munitionsfahrzeugen und bespannten Wagen ruhelos nach vorn, dabei oft mit der Maschinenpistole den Weg freikämpfend gegen Banden. In der Frühe des Morgens, bei fast allen Wetterlagen, fliegt Major Rudel die Fronten ab und verschafft seiner Gruppe, wohl auch den Heeresverbänden, einen genauen Ueberblick über die jeweilige Kampfsituation. Es gibt fast keinen Einsatz, den er nicht an der Spitze seiner Männer fliegt und in dem er nicht immer selbst das gefährlichste Angriffsobjekt bekämpft. Sein körperliches Training, das er auch an der Front planvoll betreibt, das frühzeitige Zur-Ruhe-Gehen und die weitere Enthaltsamkeit von Alkohol und Nikotin geben ihm eine erstaunlich geistige Frische, die ihn im Kampf unterstützt. Vor jedem geschlossenen und verteilten Angriff stößt er allein im Tiefflug herunter. Er will den Feind an der entscheidensten Stelle treffen. Im Angriffsflug müssen seine Besatzungen in höchster Konzentration folgen. Nach der Zerstörung einer Brücke fliegt er in Zimmerhöhe ab und auf eine Bodenerhebung zu, die hundert Meter über dem Ufer liegt. Kurz bevor er sie überspringen will, überhöht von sich, überhöht von rechts vor sich, überhöht die Leuchtspurgeschosse leichter Flak. Gefahr für seine gesamte Gruppe erkennend, macht Rudel eine scharfe Linksschwenkung und zieht in Bodennähe um die Ausläufer des Hügels herum. Im Gänsemarsch folgt die Gruppe. Alle Geschosse der Sowjetflak ziehen über sie hinweg. Zur Bekämpfung des Hauptfeindes des Grenadiers, des Panzers, hat er sich und seine Gruppe spezialisiert. In kaum fünf Meter Höhe jagt er oft, Strauchwerk und Hügel überreitend, jede Senke ausnützend, auf die Feindpanzer, die vergebens in wilder Zickzackfahrt zu entkommen suchen. Sein Anflug gleicht dabei den Bewegungen eines Weberschiffchens. Zwei, drei Kanonenschüsse haben die meisten der von ihm abgeschossenen über 447 Sowjetpanzer zur Strecke gebracht. 24 Stunden nach seiner winterlichen Flucht durch den 300 Meter breiten Dnjepr, in dem sein alter Bordschütze vor seinen Augen ertrank, und der Bewältigung des 65 km langen Fluchtweges mit Schulterschuß und wunden Füßen ist er wieder geflogen.

„Wer abgeschossen wird und hinter den feindlichen Linien notlanden muß, wird herausgeholt." Das ist sein Grundsatz, auch in scheinbar aussichtslosen Situationen. Mehr als zehn Besatzungen hat er allein vor dem Tod oder der Gefangenschaft bewahrt

Bei einem der letzten Angriffsflüge wurde Rudel wieder einmal über den feindlichen Stellungen abgeschossen. Sein Adjutant holte ihn heraus. 1½ Stunde später vernichtete er die Sowjetflakbatterie, die ihn heruntergeholt hatte. Zwei Tage später wurde sein Adjutant abgeschossen. Rudel konnte ihn noch gerade vor der Gefangenschaft retten.

Die sowjetische Luftwaffenführung hat schon bedeutende Anstrengungen gemacht, den erfolgreichsten Schlachtflieger der Welt, wie der OKW.-Bericht Rudel nannte, und seine Gruppe zu vernichten, mindestens ihre Aktivität zu schwächen. Ganze Jagdgruppen wurden zu ihrer Bekämpfung angesetzt.

Nach einem verlustreichen Angriffstag trat der Stabsarzt zu ihm ins Zelt. Er traf ihn beim Schreiben von Briefen an die Angehörigen der Gefallenen. Als der Freund später mit ihm zum erstenmal über den Tod sprach, der gerade in den letzten Tagen oft an Rudels Maschine geklopft hatte, beendete der 28jährige schnell die Unterhaltung: „Wenn es mit mir einmal soweit sein sollte, kann ich nur mit Goethe sprechen: Macht nicht soviel Federlesen, laßt mich in den Himmel rein, denn ich bin ein Mensch gewesen, und das heißt ein Kämpfer sein."

Als Rudel vor kurzem von neuem verwundet wurde und der Stabsarzt ihm dringend riet, nun endgültig einmal längere Zeit auszuspannen, sagte er: „Ich werde Urlaub nehmen, aber Urlaub an die Front."

# WINTER 1944 HUNGARIAN THEATRE

**Photocopy of an article from *Das Reich* by correspondent Erwin Kirchhof entitled, "The Best Pilot - The Example of *Oberstleutnant* Rudel." The article outlined Rudel's career up to that time.**

Left: Since Autumn of 1944, Rudel had been flying the fast Fw 190 in action as well as the Ju 87. Here his crew chief helps him on with his parachute. The Ju 87 was flown wearing a seat-type parachute.

Right: In the cockpit of his Fw 190 prior to takeoff. This PK photograph appeared a short time later in the weekly newspaper *Das Reich*.

216

On the return flight following a joint close support operation, escorted by Fw 190s. The photograph was taken by war correspondent *Oberleutnant* Niermann, who flew the final missions with Rudel as his gunner in early 1945.

An unusually successful trio: Three war correspondent wearing the German Cross in Gold, earned while flying as gunners on missions with the *Immelmann Geschwader*. From the left: *Leutnant* Schalber, *Oberleutnant* Niermann, *Leutnant* Jung.

# WINTER 1944/45

At the *Geschwader*
command post at Borgond,
near Stuhlweissenburg on
November 17, 1944: the
CO has received a report
that Russian tanks have
broken through heading in
the direction of the Matra
mountains and are close to
Gyongyos, 60 km.
northeast of Budapest. In
the photo from the left:
*Geschwader* Adjutant
*Major* Becker listens in,
*Oberstleutnant* Rudel,
*Leutnant* Weissbach (*III.
Gruppe* command post
officer), Chief Medical
Officer Dr. Gadermann
(Knight's Cross on
8/19/44) looks for the
target on the map, and
*Hauptmann* Mrkva.

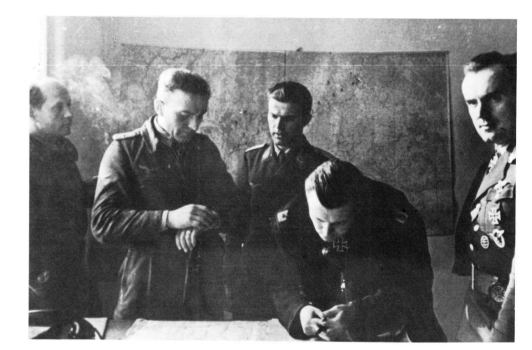

A look at his watch:
"Operations briefing at
once! Then quickest
possible takeoff, including
the *Panzer-Staffel*!"

The
*Geschwaderkommodore*
discusses the mission with
*Hauptmann* Kennel, CO of
*II. Gruppe*.

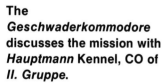

*Oberstleutnant* Rudel briefs the pilots who will be flying escort in their Focke-Wulf Fw 190s. From the left: the *Kommodore, Uffz.* Maldinger, *Fw.* Bolling. Behind, partially concealed: armorer *Fw.* Kluge and *Ofw.* Rudi Wendt, who received the Knight's Cross on 4/17/1945.

*Major* Dr. Gadermann, Rudel's gunner, before takeoff in the "cannon-bird."

*Oberstleutnant* Rudel and gunner *Major* Dr. Gadermann in the "cannon-bird" en route to attack the Russian tanks which have broken through. During this mission Rudel was wounded in the thigh by two bullets from a 13 mm. anti-aircraft gun while in low-level flight. With one bullet still embedded in his leg, he succeeded in making a smooth landing at a fighter base near Budapest. He was placed in a military hospital on Lake Balaton but was flying again only eight days later with his leg in a cast. Once again Rudel had escaped from a hospital.

With the *Geschwader* again in Stuhlweissenburg: a photo with the *Geschwader* staff to commemorate the "flier's birthday" of November 17. From right: *Lt.* Weissbach, *Hptm.* Katzschner (*Geschwader* TO), *Major* Dr. Gadermann, Rudel, *Major* Becker, *Major* Müller, *Lt.* Klinger and *Lt.* Haufe.

During the fighting in Hungary in the winter of 1944/45 the missions became harder from day to day and losses increased. In the Budapest area, Rudel and his comrades usually had to contend with superior numbers of faster Soviet fighters before they could dive on their targets through the curtain of defending flak. Also supporting the Red Army were American "Mustang" long-range fighters. Every mission became "an order to heaven." Nevertheless, Rudel and his comrades continued to attack without regard to losses. They knew that if Budapest fell the way to Pressburg (Bratislava) and Vienna would be open for the Red Army. Following the example of *II. Gruppe*, *III. Gruppe* now began to reequip with the Focke-Wulf Fw 190.

*Hauptmann* Kennel, commander of 602II. Gruppe, discusses the next mission with his wingman, *Oberfeldwebel* Liemen. They will be flying escort for Rudel's "cannon bird" and the *Panzer-Staffel*.

*II. Gruppe*'s aircraft, close support versions of the Fw 190 in winter camouflage finish, are made ready for takeoff.

Just before takeoff. The aircraft each carry a 250 kg. bomb beneath the fuselage; they will attack targets on ground and then provide fighter cover.

222

Six shining "domes" at an airfield not far from Lake Balaton (Plattensee): despite the difficult missions and strenuous combats with Soviet fighters which outnumber them ten or fifteen to one, the pilots haven't lose their sense of humour. As a joke, the officers of *II. Gruppe* got themselves haircuts like the one *Oblt.* Biermann was forced to get after suffering a head wound(left). The CO, *Hptm.* Kennel (center) is surrounded by the shaven heads of *Oblt.* Biermann, *Oblt.* Hannemann, an *Oberfähnrich* (behind), *Oblt.* Zielke, *Oblt.* Ambos and *Oblt.* Kinader.

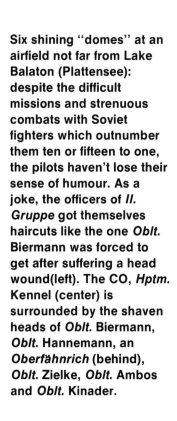

**The Sole German Soldier to Receive the Highest Decoration for Bravery**

By the end of December 1944, Rudel, much feared by the Soviets as a "tank cracker", had destroyed a total of 450 Russian tanks, the equivalent of approximately five Soviet tank corps. In the photo are the CO of the *Immelmann Schlachtgeschwader*, *Geschwader* medical officer Dr. Gadermann and *Ofw.* Rothmann, senior foreman and proven maintenance specialist on the "cannon-bird."

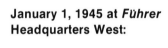

January 1, 1945 at *Führer* Headquarters West:

*Oberstleutnant* Rudel receives the supreme German decoration for bravery and is promoted to *Oberst*. Present at the ceremony are *Generaloberst* Jodl, *Generalfeldmarschall* Keitel, *Reichsmarschall* Göring and *Grossadmiral* Dönitz.

In the situation room of *Führer* Headquarters West, Rudel describes his operational experiences over the Budapest area. Second from left: *Gruppenführer* Fegelein of the *Waffen-SS*. Center: *Generaloberst* Jodl and *Generalfeldmarschall* Keitel.

The original decoration worn by Rudel. He was the sole recipient of the Knight's Cross of the Iron Cross with Golden Oak Leaves, Swords and Diamonds.

Rudel's decorations: Top center the Golden Oak Leaves, left the Oak Leaves with Swords and Diamonds, right a second copy; second row right: Oak Leaves with Swords, left Oak Leaves; bottom row from left: Golden Pilot Badge with Diamonds, Golden Mission Clasp with Diamonds and 2,000 Pendant, The German Cross in Gold. The highest Hungarian decoration, the Golden Medal of Bravery, is not in the photograph.

*Oberst* Rudel wearing the highest German decoration for bravery. The ban on flying which was imposed with the award was withdrawn by the Supreme Commander (Hitler) after a protest by Rudel.

The German News Agency (DNB) issued this press release on the day the award was presented:

## "Golden Oak Leaves with Swords and Diamonds Oberst Rudel the First Wearer

FUHRER HEADQUARTERS, 2 January (DNB) — In a decree on 12/29/1944, the Führer created the Golden Oak Leaves with Swords and Diamonds as the highest German decoration for bravery. It will be awarded twelve times at the most.

On 1 January, *Oberstleutnant* Rudel, commander of the *Immelmann Schlachtgeschwader*, became the first soldier of the German *Wehrmacht* to be awarded the decoration, receiving it from the hand of the *Führer*. At the same time, the *Führer* promoted *Oberleutnant* Rudel to *Oberst* in recognition of his proven heroism and his unique success as a pilot and fighter.''

# JANUARY — FEBRUARY 1945

## OBERST RUDEL CLEARS OUT A NEST OF TANKS

**Die fliegenden Panzerjäger sind gestartet.**
Vorn fliegt Oberst Rudel in seiner Ju 87.

Reproductions of pages one (left) and two (right) from an illustrated report in the *Illustrierte Beobachter*, issue 7, February 1945. The photo report was created by war correspondent *Hauptmann Ernst Niermann, Oberst Rudel's last gunner. The title on page one reads, "Oberst Rudel clears out a nest of tanks."*

**Der geehrteste Flieger aller Luftwaffen der Welt:
Oberst Hans Ulrich Rudel.**

Die vom Führer am 29. Dezember 1944 gestiftete höchste deutsche Tapferkeitsauszeichnung, das goldene Eichenlaub mit Schwertern und Brillanten zum Ritterkreuz des Eisernen Kreuzes, erhielt als erster Soldat der deutschen Wehrmacht, der jetzt zum Oberst beförderte Kommodore des Schlachtgeschwaders „Immelmann", Hans Ulrich Rudel aus Konradswaldau in Schlesien.

Oberst Hans Ulrich Rudel trägt als erster deutscher Soldat die höchste Tapferkeitsauszeichnung. Das goldene Eichenlaub mit Schwertern und Brillanten. Seine Heldentaten in über 2400 Feindeinsätzen gegen die Sowjets brachten ihn im Laufe des Krieges ins sagenhafte. Zuletzt war er mit dem Stab des Flieger-verbandes daran beteiligt, schon vor dem Rande zur Schulter-fahren ein Beitrag darauf... Als Soldat im Osten durchschwamm er ungeachtet eines Schulter-

**Der Bordschütze des Kommodore:**
Ritterkreuzträger Stabsarzt Dr. Gadermann
PK-Aufnahmen: Kriegsber. Niermann.

# ÖBERST RUDEL
## räumt ein Panzernest aus

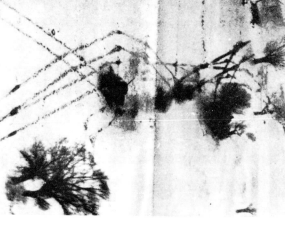

**Vier schwere Brocken eng beieinander.**
In dem dünnen Waldsaum haben sich die Sowjetpanzer einen kärglichen Tarnschutz gesucht, werden aber schon beim ersten Überflug entdeckt.

**Da ist er wieder im Visier.**
Die Garbe liegt genau im Ziel! Auch dieser T 34 haucht sein Leben aus.

**Zur Strecke gebracht.**
Ein schwarzer, fettiger Qualm steigt gen Himmel.
Der T 34 brennt aus.

**Der „unheimliche Adler" stößt.**
Schon beim zweiten Anflug treffen die Kanonen des Obersten. Kurz danach brennt der Panzer und fliegt wenig später auseinander.

**Der Feind kennt seinen Überwinder.**
Aus dem letzten der vier Panzer steigt in größter Hast die Besatzung aus und versucht Deckung zu nehmen.

**Bedeutsame Spuren im Schnee.**
Da hat ein Sowjetpanzer Haare gelassen. Aber obwohl ihn die Kanonen von Oberst Rudel erwischten, ist er noch weitergerollt.

schusses den eiskalten Dnjestr, marschierte über 60 km und bestieg kurz darauf mit wunden Füßen wieder sein Flugzeug. Diese beiden Episoden aus Frieden und Krieg kennzeichnen wohl am besten den Verdacht aller Schwierigkeiten. Wir geben den Wortlaut des Feindurteile, doch den Ausspruch eines sowjetischen Fliegers als stärkste Anerkennung: Rudel wollen wir in diesem Falle wiedergeben. Dieser Mann ist so wertvoll wie eine schlagkräftige Division.

226

On January 12-13, 1945, the Soviets launched their great offensive from the Baranov, Pulavy and Magnuszew bridge-heads on the Vistula with a massive superiority in artillery and tanks. On January 17, Soviet tanks broke into Upper Silesia, reaching the Neisse river between Görlitz and Guben five weeks later. On 31 January, the 1st White Russian Front (Zhukov) advanced to the Oder near Zehden. A short time later Soviet tanks stood on both sides of Küstrin and Frankfurt an der Oder on the east bank of the Oder. The Reich capital of Berlin, only 80 km. away, was threatened. With an immense superiority in men and material, the 2nd White Russian Front had also broken through the weak German defences and had pushed from the south into East Prussia and Pomerania.

*Oberst* Rudel, with *II.* and *III. Gruppen* and the *Panzerjagdstaffel* (*I. Gruppe* was operating independently in Hungary), supported the desperate defensive battles being waged by the German units in Upper and Lower Silesia, and then in Lower Pomerania and on the Oder front. He ignored the reinstated ban on flying. Rudel's tank kills were credited to the *Geschwader 601*'s "account" so that his disobedience would go unnoticed. "I knew that I had to act contrary to the order", Rudel told *Hauptmann* Niermann, his operations officer, gunner and war correspondent, "They can't forbid me to fly when Russian tanks are driving around on German soil!"

# FEBRUARY 1945 BATTLE ZONE SILESIA, POMERANIA, THE ODER FRONT

*Oberst* Rudel, the "flying tank death", in his "cannon-bird" over Silesia. Rudel's and his crews also dealt with Russian tanks that had broken into Silesian villages and cities. In such cases the *Immelmänner* did not attack with bombs, so as not to endanger the inhabitants.

The last of five T-34 has been destroyed by Rudel. The tank's trail ends in a cloud of smoke. As he flew over the tank it exploded, damaging the aircraft's undercarriage, which collapsed on landing. This photo was taken by war correspondent Niermann.

Ignoring the heavy defensive fire, "tank cracker" Rudel and the *Panzerjagdstaffel* attack. The Soviet tank on the left is hit and explodes; fragments damage Rudel's aircraft. A Stuka goes down in the background. At this low altitude the crew has no chance to bail out. *Ofw.* Ludwig (Knight's Cross wearer) and his gunner *Leutnant* Weissbach were killed in such an action. This realistic portrayal of an anti-tank mission was drawn by a war correspondent.

In the second half of January, Rudel's "front fire brigade" transferred to Märkisch-Friedland in eastern Pomerania, about 30 km. south of Falkenburg, where the headquarters of Army Group Vistula were located. Icy cold and deep snow on the airfield hindered operations. Anti-tank missions often misfired due to ice accumulation on the 3.7 cm cannon. Nevertheless, Rudel and his *Immelmänner* succeeded in destroying numerous Soviet tanks and motor vehicle columns and were able to provide effective support to the X. Waffen-SS Corps, III. (Germanic) Waffen-SS Pz.-Corps and Army units. Especially successful were attacks east of Deutsch-Krone and south of Schloppe. The *Kommodore*'s aircraft in winter camouflage over Pomerania.

229

1/29/1945, 14.25 hours, south of Schloppe, 30 km. south of Märkisch-Friedland: as *Uffz.* Gothe of *9. Staffel* climbs away following a low-level attack on tanks and vehicles near a farm, his gunner, *Uffz.* Peter, takes this photograph; part of the aircraft's horizontal stabiliser is visible at the bottom.

Following the mission the photograph is evaluated and the attack results reported as in this photocopy of a photograph evaluation.

| Auswertung | | | Filmkennung | Aufnahme- | | Beobachter | |
|---|---|---|---|---|---|---|---|
| | | | | Tag | Zeit | (Truppenteil) | |
| Auswerter | Tag | Uhrzeit | III./S.G. 2 | 29.1. | 14.25 | Pf. Uffz. Gothe | |
| Fw. Weggen | 5.2. 45. | 11.00 | F 5/45 | 45. | | Bf. Uffz. Peter 9./S.G. 2 | |
| Bildnummer Aufnahmeart | Bildmaßstab etwa 1: | | (in Bildmitte) | | Kartenblatt: | 1 : 300 000 | |
| | | | | | Feststellungen (wann? — wo? — wer? — was? — wie?) | | |
| 84 | Angriff auf L.k.w., Pakgeschütze und Panzer | | | | | | |
| 8 | südlich S c h l o p p e ( 3 77 ) | | | | | | |
| h = 150 m | 1.) Fahrzeug durch Bordwaffen in Brand geschossen | | | | | | |
| | | | | | | Weggen, Fw. | |

Lager-Nr. 23 N.   Heß, Braunschweig-München

The order to transfer to Fürstenwalde, between Berlin and Frankfurt on the Oder, reached Rudel in Pomerania. The missions on the Oder front went on from early in the morning until late in the evening. Attempting to escape, this T-34 became stuck in a canal between Trettin and Kunersdorf, where it was destroyed by Rudel.

Again and again, Rudel, with *II.* and *III. Gruppen* and the *Panzerjagdstaffel* (*Staffelkapitän* Korol), attacked Soviet forces between Küstrin and Frankfurt. Several missions were flown into the Trettin area, northeast of Frankfurt. On February 4, the *Gruppen* made effective attacks on tank and supply vehicle concentrations. This attack assessment photograph shows burning tanks and supply vehicles on a farm near Trettin. These hits were scored by *Leutnant* Katona of *9. Staffel*; the photograph was taken by his gunner, *Uffz.* Neumann.

*Generaloberst* Ritter von Greim, Chief of *Luftflotte 6*, with the *Immelmann Geschwader* in Fürstenwalde, about 40 km. east of Berlin, on February 5. Rudel (left) gives the *Generaloberst* an exact situation report. On April 26, Ritter von Greim was promoted to *Generalfeldmarschall* and named Commander-in-Chief of the *Luftwaffe*.

*Leutnant* Anton Korol, leader of the *Panzerjagd-Staffel* (right), was decorated with the Knight's Cross on March 12, 1945. By the end of the war Korol had flown 704 combat missions and destroyed 99 Russian tanks. On the left is *Major*, Becker who was murdered as a prisoner by Czech partisans on May 8, 1945.

230

"The German soldier, true to his oath, has made the greatest efforts on behalf his people in a matter which will never be forgotten. To the end he has been supported by all the strength of the homeland at great sacrifice. The unique accomplishments of the front and homeland will later realize their ultimate worth in the fair judgement of history."

(From the last *Wehrmacht* communique, issued May 9, 1945 by the OKW from the headquarters of the *Reichspresident*, Supreme Commander of the *Wehrmacht* and Head of Government, Grand Admiral Dönitz in Flensburg-Mürwik.)

# FEBRUARY TO THE END OF THE WAR

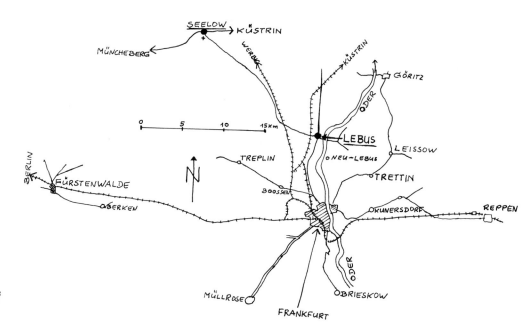

Near Lebus, north of Frankfurt, the Soviets succeeded in crossing the Oder over a pontoon bridge. On February 8, massed defensive fire met Rudel and his *Immelmänner* as they attacked the makeshift bridges and tanks. *Oberst* Rudel destroyed twelve tanks on the west bank of the Oder. As he attacked the thirteenth, a "Stalin", his aircraft was hit by a 4 cm. shell and he was severely wounded in the right leg. Summoning all of his willpower, he made a successful forced landing in the German lines. His gunner, Dr. Gadermann, administered first-aid and stopped the bleeding. Soldiers of the *Waffen-SS* took the badly-wounded pilot to their main dressing station at Seelow, between Küstrin and Müncheberg. There his shattered right leg was amputated. The doctor was amazed to see the plaster cast on Rudel's left leg.

On February 10, the *Wehrmacht* communique reported: "In recent days Oberst Rudel has knocked out eleven more Soviet tanks and raised his total to 516." (Apparently an error was made in reporting. As confirmed by witnesses, Rudel destroyed thirteen tanks in four missions on February 8. The official total, therefore, is 518 tanks destroyed.)

# Der Wehrmachtbericht vom Samstag

Aus dem Führerhauptquartier 10. Februar

Das Oberkommando der Wehrmacht gibt bekannt:

Die Verteidiger von Budapest setzen in der Burg und in der Zitadelle ihren heldenhaften Kampf fort.

Östlich des Plattensees wurden feindliche Angriffe bis auf einen inzwischen abgeriegelten Einbruch vor unseren Stellungen zerschlagen.

Nördlich der Westbeskiden wird bei Saybusch und Bielitz in Angriff und Abwehr heftig gekämpft. Im Brückenkopf von Brieg blieben Angriffe des Gegners erfolglos. Im Kampfraum von Breslau—Liegnitz—Glogau warfen die Sowjets starke Kräfte in die Schlacht und konnten trotz zäher Gegenwehr unserer Truppen nach Westen Raum gewinnen. Zwischen Fürstenberg und Küstrin wurde der Feind aus seinen Brückenköpfen weiter auf die Oder zurückgeworfen.

Im Südteil von Pommern hielt der feindliche Druck bei Arnswalde und Deutsch-Krone an, während in den übrigen Frontabschnitten unsere Abwehrerfolge ein Abflauen der feindlichen Angriffe bewirkten. Im südlichen Westpreußen nahmen die Bolschewisten nach starker Feuervorbereitung mit mehreren Schützendivisionen ihre Angriffe nordwestlich Schwetz und südwestlich Graudenz wieder auf. Sie wurden in harten Kämpfen aufgefangen. Von Osten gegen Graudenz geführte Angriffe scheiterten. Die Besatzungen von Schneidemühl und Elbin erfüllen in schweren Kämpfen und vorbildlicher Tapferkeit die ihnen übertragenen Aufgaben.

Eine aus dem Panzerschiff „Admiral Scheer" und drei Torpedobooten bestehende Kampfgruppe der Kriegsmarine griff wirkungsvoll in die Kämpfe um Elbing und Frauenburg ein.

In Ostpreußen versuchten die Bolschewisten, mit starken Infanterie- und Panzerkräften bei Landsberg und Kreuzburg unsere Front zu durchbrechen. Nach anfänglichem Geländegewinn wurde die Wucht der Angriffe durch den hartnäckigen Widerstand und die Gegenangriffe unserer Divisionen gebrochen. In erbitterten Kämpfen wurden über

hundert sowjetische Panzer vernichtet, davon 80 im Bereich des Fallschirm-Panzerkorps „Hermann Göring". Auch im Samland scheiterten heftige Angriffe der Bolschewisten.

Jagd- und Schlachtfliegerverbände griffen auch gestern in den Schwerpunkten in die Erdkämpfe ein und vernichteten außer Hunderten von Fahrzeugen 37 Panzer und 28 Geschütze. Oberst Rudel schoß in den letzten Tagen elf sowjetische Panzer ab und erhöhte damit seine Abschußerfolge auf 516 Panzer.

Aus einem durch Jäger geschützten britischen Kampffliegerverband schossen deutsche Jäger an der norwegischen Westküste elf Torpedoflugzeuge und drei Jäger ab. Leichte deutsche Seestreitkräfte und Sicherungsfahrzeuge der Kriegsmarine brachten weitere neun der erfolglos angreifenden britischen Bomber zum Absturz.

Im Westen sind zwischen dem Niederrhein östlich Nimwegen und der Maas bei Gennep heftige Abwehrkämpfe im Gange. Im Verlaufe starker Angriffe konnte der Feind im Reichswald Boden gewinnen.

An der Roer scheiterten zahlreiche Aufklärungsvorstöße und Übersetzversuche des Gegners. Am Oberlauf des Flusses riegelten Panzergrenadiere in heftigen Kämpfen den angreifenden Gegner ab, bevor er das Ostufer gewinnen konnte. Südwestlich Schleiden warf ein Gegenstoß die Amerikaner aus einer Einbruchstelle. In der Schnee-Eifel blieben die angreifenden Verbände der 3. amerikanischen Armee im zusammengefaßten Feuer aller Waffen vor oder in unserem Hauptkampffeld liegen. An der oberen Oure wurden feindliche Bereitstellungen durch unsere Artillerie zerschlagen.

Heftige Kämpfe sind um Brückenköpfe an der unteren Sauer entbrannt, die der Feind nach Zuführung von neuen Kräften auszuweiten versuchte. Mehrere Angriffe der Amerikaner südöstlich Vianden brachen unter hohen blutigen Verlusten für den Gegner schon vor unseren Stellungen zusammen. Südöstlich Remich an der Mosel warfen unsere Panzer den angreifenden Feind wieder auf seine Ausgangsstellungen zurück.

Im Unter-Elsaß blieben feindliche Aufklärungsvorstöße vor unseren Gefechtsvor-

posten liegen oder scheiterten in unserem Abwehrfeuer.

Nach schweren Kämpfen gegen die bei Tag und Nacht angreifenden de-Gaulle-Truppen wurden unsere noch auf dem Westufer des Oberrheins stehenden Kräfte mit allen Waffen und Versorgungsgütern auf das Ostufer übergeführt und vor dem nachdrängenden Feind die Brücken bei Neuenburg gesprengt. Die 21tägige Schlacht um den Brückenkopf im oberen Elsaß, in der unsere Truppen tapfer kämpfend eine oft zehnfache feindliche Übermacht abwehrten, ist damit abgeschlossen. Im Verlaufe dieser Kämpfe vernichteten unsere Truppen 200 Panzer sowie zahlreiche Panzerspähwagen und Kraftfahrzeuge des Feindes.

An der ligurischen Küste in Mittelitalien dauert die örtliche Kampftätigkeit an. Feindliche Aufklärungsvorstöße auf den Höhen östlich des Serchio scheiterten.

In dem Gebiet westlich Mostar in der Herzegowina dauern die feindlichen Angriffe an. An der unteren Drina haben unsere Truppen den Fluß nach Osten überschritten und dem zäh kämpfenden Feind die Uferhöhen nordwestlich Zvornik entrissen. Südlich der Drau stießen deutsche Truppen und Kosakenverbände im Zusammenwirken mit kroatischen Kampfgruppen konzentrisch von Osten und Westen vor und nahmen die Stadt Virovitica im Sturm.

Nordamerikanische Terrorverbände warfen am gestrigen Tage Bomben auf Magdeburg sowie auf Orte in Thüringen und Westfalen. Dabei entstanden Gebäudeschäden und Personenverluste, vor allem in Weimar und Jena. Weitere Angriffe richteten sich gegen Städte im südostdeutschen Raum. Tiefflieger terrorisierten im westlichen und südwestlichen Reichsgebiet durch Bordwaffenangriffe die Zivilbevölkerung.

Das Feuer unserer Vergeltungswaffen auf London dauert an.

Ergänzend zum Wehrmachtbericht wird gemeldet:

Der mit dem Ritterkreuz zum Eisernen Kreuz ausgezeichnete Hauptmann Rath schoß in der Nacht zum 8. Februar sechs feindliche Flugzeuge ab.

*Oberst* Rudel could not endure the Zoo Bunker military hospital for long. After only six weeks he was already back with his *Geschwader*. Despite the great pain — his partially-healed stump kept tearing open — he flew missions in support of the ground forces' desperate defensive battles. Here he is helped from his aircraft by his crew chief, Fw. Günther, after landing at *III. Gruppe*'s base at Radeberg, northwest of Dresden, Easter 1945.

*Major* Kennel, commander of *II./SG 2*, congratulates Rudel on his "flier's birthday."

Crews and ground personnel were happy to have their Chief back with them again. *Oberst* Rudel describes his last mission near Lebus and the forced landing.

*233*

A large reception for the CO, just arrived from Berlin. *Geschwader* and air base officers escort him to the command post.

The famous "cannon bird." Despite a ban on flying and paying little regard to his as yet unhealed leg wound, the legendary "Eagle of the Eastern Front" continued to fly combat missions. On April 17, the *Geschwader* staff and *II. Gruppe* transferred to Kummer near Niemes in northern Sudetenland. *III./SG 2* was operating out of Kletzan, north of Prague, while *II. Gruppe* was flying missions in Austria.

The U.S. Air Force smashed the important supply lines to the Eastern Front. American long-range fighters now also attacked German air bases in Army Group Schörner's combat zone. On April 16, the aircraft of *III. Gruppe* were destroyed by a U.S. low-level attack on Kletzan. The German infantry's hopes of further air support went up in smoke and flames.

*Oberst* Hans-Ulrich Rudel, with 2,530 combat missions the most successful pilot in the history of air warfare, and the members of his *Geschwader* continued to do their duty until the last day of the war. Through their missions they preserved the lives of many of their comrades on the ground and saved countless refugees from falling into the hands of the Red Army. — This sketch was done by Wolfgang Rapp in the prisoner of war hospital in Fürth in June 1945.

Released from captivity. Driven from his home like millions of others, severely wounded in the war; the chaos of bomb-destroyed Germany, the military dictatorship of the occupying powers, the political persecution and the agitation against everything soldierly made him think of his battle motto: "He is lost, only who gives up on himself!"

A burned-out Ju 87 of *III./SG 2 Immelmann*. Stalin had good reason to be satisfied with his American allies.

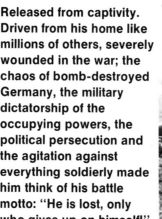

In Düsseldorf in 1946 with his young sons Siegfried and Hans-Ulrich.

Der erste
Tatsachenbe[...]
aus Argenti[...]

Görings
Männer
im Argentinien

# THE POST-WAR PERIOD: ARGENTINA

In 1950 extensive coverage was given in West German newspapers to the German flying aces and aircraft designers active with the Córdoba aircraft factory in Argentina. The Hamburg *Stern* reported: "The greatest service that men like Rudel, Baumbach and Galland could have done for the reputation of Germany, may have been the fact that they evaded the comedy of a de-nazification proceeding." The headline reads: "The first factual report from Argentina. Göring's men in Argentina."

Rudel with Galland (right) and Baumbach who, like the German test pilots Behrens and Steinkamp, was killed in a fatal crash together with Henrici. The photo was taken in May 1953.

The *Pulqui II* (Arrow II) constructed in Córdoba by the famous former chief designer of the Focke-Wulf works, Professor Tank and his design group. Tank made the first test-flight himself and later demonstrated the jet fighter to Argentine president General Peron.

236

Following the demonstration flight the *Pulqui II* was refuelled and test flown by an Argentine pilot.

Above: Rudel in front of his rented "Chalet Mary" in Carlos Paz, about 30 km. from Córdoba. In this house he wrote his war memoirs *Trotzdem* in his spare hours. On weekends he drove to the "Sierra Grande", whose mountains reached over 3,000 metres and were mastered by Rudel despite his prosthesis.

Above right: General Peron (right) in December 1954 with Rudel in Buenos Aires, where the President — an enthusiastic motorcyclist — took part in a road test.

237

Center: The engine of Rudel's second-hand American car "gave up the ghost" in the mountains and he is now driving a 1938 Mercedes 170-V, which held out for a long time on the poor mountain roads. Immediately after leaving work — he is seen here checking through Córdoba airfield security — it's off to the mountains: The peaks are calling . . .

Below: The artificial leg built for Rudel by the master Streide in Kufstein/Tirol had to endure a great deal. It even survived this jump across a crevice in the "Giants" of the Sierra Grande.

Left: Playing tennis in
Córdoba.

Right: In fine form —
despite the prosthesis —
into the mountain river.

At a water-sports meet in
the province of Córdoba.
Of this photo Rudel said, "I
couldn't extend my
wooden foot, which cost
me points."

Skiing down Monte
Cathedral at the ski resort
of Bariloche, Christmas
1951.

Above left: Downhill run at the Argentine ski championships at Bariloche, August 1949.

Above right: In San Carlos de Bariloche the war-amputee sport skier was able to prove himself against the strongest international competition. Rudel competed despite the fact that his prosthesis had been repaired by a non-professional.

Center: The international skiing championships at the Argentine sports center: climbing with the Bolivian downhill racing champion and another skiing ace.

Below: Rudel with world champion Stein Eriksen, who won the slalom. The "crazy German with the wooden leg" — as the Argentines called him, took fourth place.

The *Hamburger Abendblatt*, from 1/13/1950 reported, "Unparalleled Energy — Argentines speaking of German wartime pilot Rudel."

Below left: Before a tennis match with the legendary Otto Skorzeny. Skorzeny had been awarded the Knight's Cross for the freeing of Mussolini from Gran Sasso (9/12/1943) and later received the Oak Leaves for further exploits.

Below right: A reunion with his friend soon afterwards in the Spanish capital, where Skorzeny was active as an industrial sales representative. Skorzeny died suddenly in Madrid at age 67 on 7/5/1975. The remains of the great German soldier were brought home in an urn on July 16, 1975 and placed in the family grave site at Döblinger cemetery in Vienna. Present at the funeral were more than 1,000 citizens of Vienna, many of his former *Waffen-SS* comrades and many other former members of the German armed forces. Rudel took leave of his friend and comrade with a moving eulogy and lauded his courageous life with the words, "You did much more than your duty — you made history!"

# Beispiellose Energie

## Argentinien spricht von dem deutschen Kriegsflieger Rudel

*Hans-Ulrich Rudel, als Flieger im letzten Krieg der einzige Inhaber des Goldenen Eichenlaubs mit Schwertern und Brillanten zum Eisernen Kreuz, ist 1948 schwerkriegsbeschädigt nach Argentinien ausgewandert. Im Gegensatz zu vielen falschen Gerüchten bringen wir hier auf Grund von Briefen an einen Hamburger Freund eine Schilderung, die zeigt, mit welcher Zähigkeit und Geschicklichkeit Rudel drüben sich ein neues Ansehen zu schaffen weiß.*

Bei den internationalen Skimeisterschaften, die in Argentinien im August des vorigen Jahres in Bariloch stattfanden, mußte Rudel gegen stärkste internationale Klasse antreten. Guzzi Lantschner machte den Zweiten in der Kombination. Rudel war ganz besonders vom Rennpech verfolgt, indem er, mit nicht sachgemäß reparierter Prothese, laufen mußte, so daß der letzte Krafteinsatz nicht voll gewagt werden konnte. Während des Trainings war ihm die Prothese zweimal gebrochen. Sie konnte aus Mangel an Fachleuten nur von einem Klempner repariert werden (Seine erste Prothese, bei noch offener Wunde, fertigte im Kriege sein Bordmechaniker aus drei Aluröhren und einer Ledermanschette an.)

Diese Skileistung ist aber bei weitem nicht seine Jahresbestleistung. Vor einigen Monaten (März 1949) machte er den Versuch der Besteigung des Aconcagua. Hören sie seine eigene Schilderung: „Im März war ich am Aconcagua, der 7000 m hoch ist, und nur wenige Bezwinger hat. In 6950 m Höhe mußte ich umkehren, nachdem mich mein Begleiter — ein italienischer Olympia-

springer, der schon einmal oben war — bei 6000 m im Stich gelassen hatte. In 6950 m Höhe irrte ich vier Stunden — ohne Sauerstoff — herum und fand den letzten Einstieg nicht. Dann gab ich es auf und kehrte mit den letzten Reserven um. Das Steigen in diesen Höhen ist wahnsinnig schwer, und man kann viel darüber sagen. Der Berg forderte schon viele Tote, u. a. den Bergsteiger Link, der 1936 als „erste deutsche Besteigung" die olympische Medaille dafür bekam!"

Rudels Leistungen als Tennisspieler im Einzel wie im Doppel sind auf gleicher Höhe. So gewann er im vorigen Jahr ein Tennisturnier und wurde bei den Meisterschaften seiner Fabrik (Belegschaft einige tausend Mann) im Herreneinzel sechster und war im Doppel bereits unter den letzten Vier. Auch seine ausgezeichneten Ergebnisse im Langstreckenschwimmen sind hervorragend.

Neben diesen Sportarten vernachlässigt er seine Leichtathletik keineswegs. Noch bevor er im Mai 1948 nach drüben ging (seine Familie ist heute noch hier) erreichte er im Hochsprung schon wieder 1,60 m. Rudel war vor Beginn des Krieges Olympia-Anwärter im Zehnkampf Sein sportliches und streng auf Training eingestelltes Leben fand durchaus nicht immer die Gegenliebe seiner Vorgesetzten. Im Gegenteil. Sein Sport kostete ihm einmal, wenn auch nur auf bestimmte Zeit, seine Qualifikation als Flugzeugführer. Kasino-Leben war nicht sein Metier. Er raucht und trinkt heute noch nicht.

# ON THE
# HIGHEST PEAK
# IN THE ANDES

A view of the Tronador, at 3,700 metres the mightiest peak in the San Carlos de Bariloche nature preserve. It was a tempting target for Rudel and his sporting friends in the "Club Andino" in Bariloche.

On a tour of the Andes: Rudel (left) with Dr. Morghen, the mountaineer from Innsbruck. The photo was taken by Dr. Dangl, physician at a local sulphur mining operation.

242

A sketch showing the highlights of Rudel's expedition to the "King of the Cordilleras", the Aconcagua, and to Llullay-Yacu on the Argentine frontier.

Climbing in the giants of the Sierra Grande about 60 km. from Rudel's home in Córdoba. He often trained there in preparation for the climb of the 6,920-metre-high Llullay-Yacu, the highest volcano on earth (extinct). The mountain, located in the midst of the Puna de Atacama, the worlds third largest desert, was a great challenge for Rudel. He was to scale the mountain three times.

The Aconcagua in the Argentine Andes, at 7,020 metres the highest peak in the Americas. On 12/31/1951 bad weather forced Rudel to turn back only 50 metres below the summit.

# THREE TIMES
UP THE
HIGHEST
VOLCANO
ON EARTH

Ten expeditions had tried in vain to conquer the 6920-metre-high extinct volcano Llullay-Yacu in the Argentine Andes, which stands not far from the border with Chile. The first successful attempt was made by the team of Hans-Ulrich Rudel (right), Dr. Rudolf Dangl (center), and Dr. Karl Morghen of Innsbruck. This photo was taken at the 5,800 meter level.

View from the campsite on Llullay-Yacu at about 6,000 metres. Rear left can be seen a portion of the "Salar" salt lake.

After successfully reaching the summit, the team discovered Inca ruins which at first had been mistaken for graves. The remains of walls are clearly visible in the snow.

After the first successful expedition. Back at the sulphur mine where Dr. Dangl was active as physician. From left: Rudel, Dr. Dangl, Dr. Morghen and mine engineer Deverga who was forced to turn back as a result of altitude sickness. During the descent, Rudel fell on an icy slope and slid nearly 400 metres; fortunately he landed uninjured in a large snowdrift.

In order to solve the mystery of the "Inca graves", Rudel undertook a second expedition between November 30, and December 14 of that same year. Before setting out he was received by General Peron who congratulated him on his first climb. Taking part in the second expedition were Rudel's former *Geschwader* comrade Max Dainz and photographer Erwin Neubert of the Durer Publishing Co. of Buenos Aires. The team was escorted to base camp by Argentine soldiers. View of the peak of Llulay-Yacu from the sulphur mine.

As had the first expedition, the second went via the Andes road through Salta to Caipe, and from there by truck to the mine. After arriving in Caipe: (from left) engineer Deverga (he waited with a truck), Max Dainz, expedition photographer Erwin Neubert, Rudel, Mrs. Leyerer, Lt. Villafane, two mountain soldiers.

Above left: A short rest on the way to the mine. From left: Neubert, Villafane, police lieutenant Rubart, Rudel, Dainz. In the foreground Argentine mountain soldiers; in the background the Socompa, 6,030 metres high.

Above right: Rudel attempts to uncover something with a pickaxe. It is December 10, 1953. Erwin Neubert left the signal station to take photographs and failed to return. His comrades found him 80 metres below the summit; he had been killed in a fall. It was not until the third expedition that his body was recovered. At his parents' request Neubert was buried on the mountain.

60 metres below the summit of Llulay-Yacu. These ruins were apparently a signal station from the last years of the Inca empire, from where fire signals were sent to Socomba; similar structures were discovered there. A mystery to Rudel and his party was the discovery of wood in the walls and a pile of firewood nearby. There were no trees there within a radius of 300 kilometres.

The entrance to a stone hut.

The dead friend they had left behind gave Rudel no peace. Barely five weeks after the tragic death of Erwin Neubert, Rudel made his third climb of Llulay-Yacu. It was a duty of respect that they bury their dead comrade as soon as possible — near the summit as requested by his parents. Also taking part in the climb were Rudel's wartime comrade Dainz, mine engineer Deverga and Dr. Dangl, as well as the recent immigrant Hack and the experienced climber Dr. Christmann.

# WITHIN TEN MONTHS: UP THE 6,920 METRE VOLCANO FOR THE THIRD TIME

**Above:** For Rudel it is the third time in 10 months that he has conquered the highest volcano on earth; for Dainz (right) the second. This photo was taken on January 16, 1954 at the mine before starting the difficult journey across the Atacama desert.

**Above right:** Crossing the dry salt lake on the trip from the "Casualidad" sulphur mine to the base camp at the foot of the volcano was not without difficulties. Several times the truck had to be shovelled free.

**Center:** Hans-Ulrich Rudel (right) and Max Dainz in front of their tent at the 5,500 metre level.

**Below:** Dr. Christmann and Hack were suffering from altitude sickness and remained behind at the base camp. Dr. Dangl, Dainz and Rudel fought their way upwards step by step in the thin mountain air. They made 80-100 metres per hour. The photo shows Rudel with ski pole and climbing irons on an icy slope. A frigid wind blew through the valley; temperature -15 degrees.

**Left:**
Only thirty metres to go and Rudel will have climbed the 6,920 metre mountain for the third time in ten months.

**Right:**
It took Rudel's and Dainz' last reserves of strength to carry in the heavy blocks of basalt in the oxygen-poor air to erect the stone grave. The photo shows the highest and loneliest grave in the world. Rudel attached a metal plate with the following inscription in German and Spanish:

"Here rests Erwin Neubert born 6/21/25 in Bethel, Germany, killed in a fall on 12/10/53 on Llulay-Yacu."

A short rest on the summit, which consists of volcanic basalt. The photo was taken by his former *Geschwader* comrade.

Max Dainz photographed by Rudel on the summit.

Before beginning the difficult descent, Rudel and Dainz left behind a small flag in the old Reich colours of black-white-red in a metal case. It bore the inscription in Spanish: "Germany salutes the new Argentina and its great friend and president Juan D. Peron."

On the way back to the mine a last look from the desert and a photograph of Llulay-Yacu for the parents of their dead climbing companion Erwin Neubert.

A reception by President Peron in Buenos Aires at which Rudel described the three expeditions in detail. From the left: General Jaurequi, Dainz, Rudel, President Peron, Dr. Christmann, Hack.

**Below left:**
Hermann Buhl (born in Innsbruck in 1924, killed in a fall in 1957), who, in 1953, became the first man to climb the Nanga Parbat (8,125 metres) in the Himalayas alone, sent this photo and congratulations to Rudel on becoming the first to scale Llulay-Yacu. The photo shows Buhl after returning from the peak of Nanga Parbat.

**Below right:**
The title page from the book *From Stukas to the Andes*, in which Rudel described his three Andes expeditions.

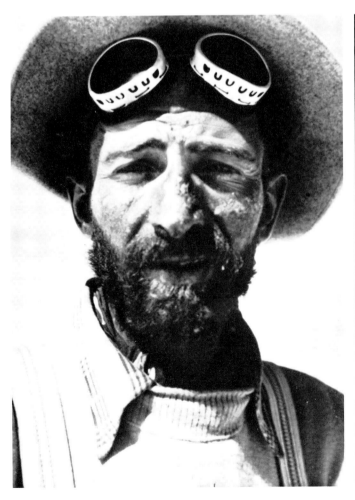

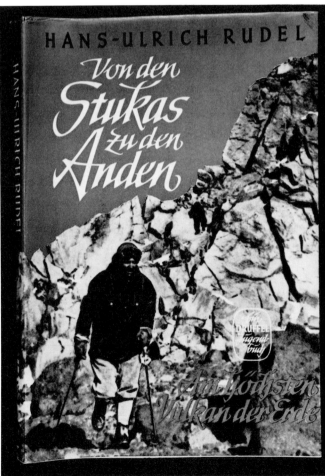

**Above:**
On the beach near Villa Gesell, Rudel no longer shows the strain of climbing the volcano.

**Above right:**
January 1954: after the third Andes expedition a brief vacation at Villa Gesell, about 400 km. south of Buenos Aires. Right: Max Dainz.

**Center:** The last photo taken with his mother, whom he had invited in 1954 to vacation in Villa Carlos Paz.

With German-Argentines on the EL DORADO sports flying field in Missiones, the northernmost province of Argentina, in April 1955. Rudel was very active in South America, speaking to German clubs and collecting for *Kameradenhilfe*, an organization which sent food parcels to German prisoners of war in the prison camps of the occupying powers and supported their families. *Kameradenhilfe* also assisted returning POWs and ex-members of the *Geschwader* who were in need. Next to Rudel are Frau Hübner, Frau Jahn and Herr Jahn.

# MEMORIES
# OF
# GENERAL PERON

**Above: Hans-Ulrich Rudel visited Argentine president Juan Peron several times during his exile in Spain. They had maintained a close friendship since Rudel's period in Córdoba. Rudel and Peron at Benidorm, a spa on Spain's southeast coast.**

**Above right: On a walk in Benidorm: Peron, his second wife Isabelita (president of Argentina following Peron's death) and Rudel.**

254

**Center: After Peron's return to the state residence in Olivos in 1974: from left: adjutant Colonel Vicente Damasco, Hans-Ulrich Rudel, General Juan Peron.**

**Below right: October 1974 in Olivos, Argentina: last farewell to the late president General Juan Peron.**

**Below left: A photo of General Peron with inscription, given by him to his close friend during a visit to Madrid in 1964.**

# REUNION WITH HIS GESCHWADER

**On May 22, 1965, a memorial to the fallen of the *Immelmann Stuka-Geschwader*, paid for by contributions from ex-members, was dedicated on Burg Staufenberg near Lollar, north of Giessen. Illustrated is the report published by the *SG 2* information newsletter. On the right is the title page of the *Immelmann* newsletter.**

Liebe "Immelmänner",

"Geschwaderchronisten" – wie ich einer bin – sind sich nicht sicher, ob dies das 17. oder 18. Geschwadertreffen ist. Trotz dieser "Ungewißheit" weiß ich, daß wir uns zweimal in Ziegenhain / Bez. Kassel (Bahnhofsrestaurant u. Rathaussaal) trafen, dann in Frankfurt/Main (Park-Hotel bzw. Rassbachs "Baracken-Pilsquelle" am Bahnhof), danach zweimal auf Burg Gleiberg, bis endlich das "Landekreuz" für uns auf der "Immelmann-Burg" in Staufenberg ausgelegt wurde. Einige örtliche kleinere Treffen gingen diesem hessischen "Rundflug" voraus.

Am 22. Mai 1965 konnten wir auf Burg Staufenberg in Anwesenheit des letzten Geschwaderkommodores, Oberst a.D. Hans-Ulrich Rudel, des Inhabers der nur einmal verliehenen höchsten deutschen Tapferkeitsauszeichnung, unser Ehrenmal zur Erinnerung an unsere gefallenen, vermißten und verstorbenen Kameraden des Stukageschwaders "Immelmann" einweihen. Dafür danken wir vor allem unserem lieben Kameraden, Ingenieur Horst Schiemann, dem Initiator und nimmermüden Ehrenmalsaktivisten, dem das Schicksal leider nicht mehr vergönnte, die Vollendung und Einweihung zu erleben. Ferner sei seinen Mitarbeitern der Ehrenmals-Arbeitsgemeinschaft, den Kameraden Günther Behling, Max Dainz, Herbert Hentrich, Hans von Herder, Wilhelm Kern, Helmut Mehlich, dem Bildhauer Gustav Nonnenmacher, Oberst a.D. Hans-Ulrich Rudel und Wilhelm Thomas gedankt. Unser aller Dank gilt vor allem auch der Gemeinde Staufenberg, Herrn Bürgermeister Fuchs, dem Gemeinderat als Vertreter aller Staufenberger, für die Unterstützung zur Errichtung des Denkmals auf Gemeindegrund. Außerdem danken wir "Immelmänner" dem Hessischen Ministerium für Wirtschaft und Verkehr in Wiesbaden für die Erteilung der Genehmigung. Dem Bildhauer, Herrn Nonnenmacher in Worms-Hochheim, danken wir für den künstlerischen Entwurf, der Firma Gebrüder Rincker (Metall- u. Kunstgießerei in Sinn/Dillkreis) für den Bronzeguß und der Firma Ernst Zecher (Baugeschäft in Staufenberg), namentlich Herrn Baumeister Winfried Zecher, für die solide Bauausführung. Nicht zuletzt 1000-Dank allen Kameraden und Firmen, die durch ihre Spenden die finanziellen Voraussetzungen zur Errichtung des Ehrenmals des Stukageschwaders "Immelmann" schufen.

25 Jahre "danach" stehen wir wieder am Ehrenmal, dem äußeren Zeichen unserer inneren Verbundenheit mit unseren Kameraden, die nicht – wie wir – vom Schicksal begünstigt wurden. Als "Kameradschaft der Überlebenden" wollen wir uns ihres Opfers für unser Vaterland bei all unserem Tun im Alltagsleben würdig erweisen.

GESCHWADERTREFFEN

23. MAI 1970
BURG STAUFENBERG

Traditionsgemeinschaft des Stukageschwaders „IMMELMANN"

Above: Rudel visited the western occupation zone several times from Argentina and took part in every annual reunion of his *Immelmann Geschwader*. The newspapers of the occupying powers in west and central Germany usually published imaginative "sensational reports" of the gatherings. As here at Frankfurt in 1955, Rudel was always greeted by war comrades and friends. From left: Kurt Eigenbrodt, Ulf Weiss-Vogtmann, former *Oberst* Rudel, Günther Just.

Above right: A reunion with old comrades in Frankfurt am Main beneath the tradition-filled emblem of the *Immelmann Geschwader*.

Center: The fate of missing comrades is explained and many memories are exchanged.

Just before departure a photo to commemorate the reunion in Frankfurt. Between Rudel and the author (right) is Hans Rassbach, who organized the meeting in his tavern at the railway station.

Left: The last commander of *SG 2 Immelmann* as he gives his address at the commemoration of the memorial at Burg Staufenburg, May 22, 1965. On the column of the Stuka memorial for the fallen, missing and still imprisoned members of the *Geschwader* are the words: "The spirit of sacrifice conquers death." The bronze Stuka *Rotte* and the linked outlines on the column are symbols of the comradeship between the crews and ground personnel during their service in the war. (The photo was taken in 1969.)

Below left: After the laying of wreaths by *Oberst* (Rtd.) Rudel, Max Dainz, Willibald Kern and Günther Behling in 1971.

Below right: *Major* (Rtd.) Hans von Herder, oldest *Geschwader* member, during his address during the honouring of the fallen in 1972. As a cadet, von Herder was a friend of *Pour le Mérite* wearer, Max Immelmann. He was a great-great grandson of poet and philosopher Johann Gottfried von Herder and was a *Major* with the headquarters staff of *SG 2*. He died on January 16, 1975 at the age of 81. At his last resting place in Stuttgart-Mohringen, Rudel laid a wreath with stripes in the black-white-red colours of the Reich flag which was used until the end of the First World War. Von Herder had been highly decorated in that conflict.

Left: After the ceremony: *Major* Hans von Herder (Rtd) and his wife in conversation with the Rev. Karl-Heinz Otte, a former pilot.

Right: The diving *Stuka-Rotte* (pair) on the memorial. The pair was the smallest operational unit.

A partial view of the assembled *Geschwader* members during the playing of *Ich hatt' einen Kameraden* by the Lollar youth band at the memorial.

258

A reunion after 27 years between former *Major* (Medical) and professor of medicine Dr. Ernst Gadermann (Knight's Cross, 850 missions as Rudel's gunner) left, and *Oberst* Rudel (Rtd); next to Rudel is Günther Behling. Prof. Dr. Gadermann, a famous heart and circulatory specialist, director of sports medicine at the Munich Olympic Games, died at age 59 in Hamburg of a heart attack.

The gable end of the Staufenburg knight's castle, where the annual *Geschwader* reunion took place. The castle is situated on a 266-metre-high cone of basalt on Highway 3, between Giessen and Marburg. It was built in the first half of the 12th century and was never the home of an earl's family by the same name as is published in foreign travel brochures.

A view through the castle gate into the small romantic half-timbered town of Staufenburg, a popular vacation spot.

The town, which generously provided the site for the memorial, has erected a signpost.

The title page of *Trotzdem* ("Nevertheless"), which Rudel wrote in South America. It has been translated into many languages and has reached a total publication in Germany and abroad of over one million copies.

The book appeared in France in 1951 with a foreword by Pierre Clostermann, France's most successful fighter pilot of the Second World War.

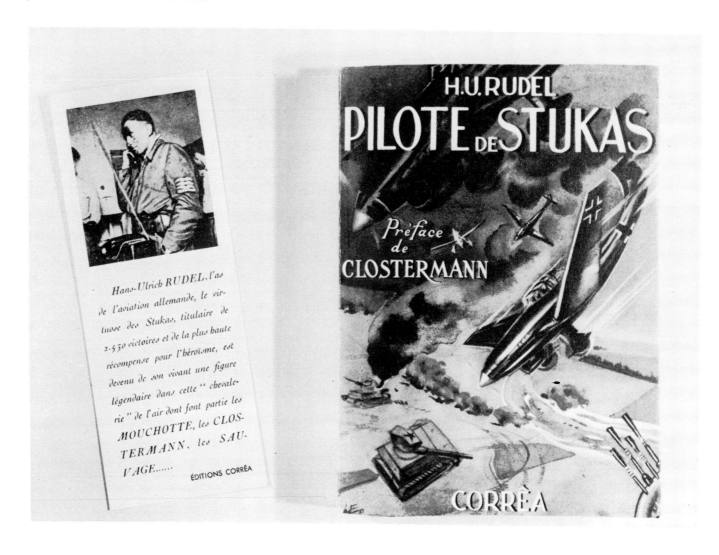

Hans-Ulrich RUDEL, l'as de l'aviation allemande, le virtuose des Stukas, titulaire de 2.530 victoires et de la plus haute récompense pour l'héroïsme, est devenu de son vivant une figure légendaire dans cette "chevalerie" de l'air dont font partie les MOUCHOTTE, les CLOSTERMANN, les SAUVAGE......

ÉDITIONS CORRÊA

H.U. RUDEL
PILOTE DE STUKAS
Préface de CLOSTERMANN
CORRÊA

# PHOTOS FROM A PRIVATE ALBUM

A youth group has invited *Oberst* Rudel into their camp. The group's flag is the coat-of-arms of the Teutonic Knights, which was also the *Geschwader* emblem of *SG 2*.

In Frankfurt am Main in February 1955 at the Ford offices. At that time Rudel was an industrial salesman on a business trip. (Left the author, right a business associate.)

Author day in August 1959 in Lippoldsberg on the Weser, in the monastery courtyard of the author Hans Grimm (born 1875, died 1959). Rudel reads from his book. Left, Hans Grimm, who died on September 27, 1959 and was buried near the monastery.

After the show in the monastery courtyard: autographs on the assembly line.

During a ceremony to inaugurate a memorial to the fallen in Dillingen, Saar.

Passport clearance at Frankfurt airport before the return flight to South America, where Rudel negotiated export contracts for German firms.

At a sports meet as guest of Paraguayan president, General Alfredo Stroessner (with hat, to Rudel's right). Rudel was in Paraguay on a business trip.

A photo, which is published here for the first time in Europe: the President of Paraguay presents his son Gustavo his officer's commission during a ceremony at the officers academy. General Stroessner's parents emigrated from Hof, Germany to Paraguay at the turn of the century.

Summer 1973: General Stroessner in the *Bundesrepublik*, (West Germany) where he visited relatives in Hof, Saale. Rudel was also invited to the family reunion, where this photo was taken.

Below:
From left: Gustavo Stroessner, Hans-Ulrich Rudel, General Stroessner, Heinz Stroessner.

"During the downhill race at the Argentine skiing champion-ships in Bariloche my prosthesis broke", remembered the disabled sportsman, smiling, "the leg flew out of my pants. Everyone cried hysterically: 'doctor! doctor!' But all I needed was a tinsmith." Similar excitement occurred on the tennis court. "The *senioritas* almost fainted when I smacked the racket against my wooden leg to rouse the ball boys." After his return from South America, Rudel scarcely missed an opportunity to prove himself in competition: not only in events for the disabled but also as a participant among non-disabled athletes.

# COMPETITIVE SPORTS

**Above: With his prosthesis: divefrom the 10 meter board into Lake Wörther.**

**Above right: Water skiing at Karnten on Lake Wörther.**

**High bridges were also enticing; here Rudel dives from the road bridge in Carlos Paz, Argentina.**

Above left: In 1960 he placed third in the mens singles event at the Tirolean tennis championships despite being the only disabled veteran to compete. Here he is photographed with three sporting friends.

Above: Despite his artificial leg, extremely quick reactions.

Center: Concentration on the ball — men's singles in Cham.

267

Below: The third Bavarian disabled tennis championships in 1963 at Cham where he took second place. After the meet in conversation with state minister Niederalt (left) and the Bavarian Minister of State, Dr. Schedl.

**Left:**
**A newspaper report on Rudel's victory at a ski meet.**

**Right:**
**An article in the "German Soldier's Times" from January 18, 1963 entitled "Rudel Again."**

**"Proper waxing is half the victory" — A photo from the West German skiing championships in the Willingen winter sports area in the Waldecker uplands.**

### Rudel gewinnt Skirennen

Der 43jährige Oberst a. D. Hans-Ulrich Rudel gewann am 10. Januar 1960 in der Altersklasse zwei den vom österreichischen Skiverband auf der Hohen Salve in Hopfgarten bei Kitzbühl veranstalteten Riesentorlauf. Rudel, der als einziger Versehrter (er ist beinamputiert) zwischen lauter gesunden und vielfach prominenten Skikanonen mitlief, fügte damit der einmaligen Serie seiner sportlichen Erfolge als Bergsteiger, Tennisspieler und Skifahrer, einen neuen hinzu.

### Immer wieder Rudel

Nachdem Oberst Rudel am vergangenen Sonntag beim Pillersee-Pokal in Fieberbrunn Tirol, im Abfahrtslauf den 2. Platz belegt hatte, gelang ihm am letzten Sonntag ein neuer Erfolg und zwar beim Plattenrain-Pokal in Arzl/Piztal, wurde er erneut Zweiter hinter dem langjährigen früheren österreichischen Meister Eberhard Kneissel. Rudel, der einzige Träger der höchsten deutschen Tapferkeitsauszeichnung, ist beinamputiert.

268

**During the nineteen-sixties Rudel was able to win numereous victory trophies in his age class at the West German ski association's championships, which were held in Willingen and Winterburg. Once he was even German and Dusseldorf city champion.**

**Left: This photo is from his thich sports album and was taken during a run at Brixen, Tirol.**

**Right: An outstanding snapshot of Rudel in the giant slalom at the Tirolian Championships in Austria.**

**Below left: During ski lessons in 1967 in the Tirol: everyone in class 3-C of the Innsbruck-Pradl secondary school definitely wanted their picture taken with the famous Stuka pilot and skier.**

269

**Below: From the "Munich Mercury", September 23, 1970: Rudel was featured in a section in which well-known figures spoke out on sports.**

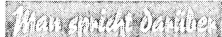

Versehrten-Skimeister Hans-Ulrich Rudel, Oberst a. D. und berühmtester Stuka-Flieger des Zweiten Weltkrieges, machte nach einem Schlaganfall („Ich rauche und ich trinke nicht – aber wir vergessen alle, daß wir keine zwanzig Jahre mehr sind, sondern schon Mitte der Fünfzig...") einen Wies'n-Bummel. Rudel, der im Winter an den Wochenenden kaum jeweils unter drei Skirennen fuhr, macht heuer mal Pause. „Aber dann komme ich wieder – und natürlich auch zum Ski-Derby der Sportprominenz in Bad Wiessee."

Rudel never missed a major post-war football event, unless called away on business. In 1954 he was in Bern, Switzerland when the German national team won the world championship. As a souvenir, the German trainer Sepp Herberger sent Rudel this photo with the inscription: "To *Oberst* Rudel with friendly greetings — Sepp Herberger." The photo shows the former trainer of the German team and team captain Fritz Walter (right) as they are carried triumphantly from the field by German fans.

270

June 8, 1958 in Malmo, Sweden: Rudel congratulates long-time friend Sepp Herberger and the German national team following their 3-1 victory over Argentina in the first round of the world championships. In the background left is goalkeeper Helmut Rahn, left trainer Gawlicek, far right partially concealed is Herkenrath and next to him between Herberger and Rudel is masseur Deuser.

# WARTIME ENEMIES BECOME FRIENDS

Left: Hans-Ulrich Rudel in 1943 during operations on the Kerch peninsula; at that time a *Hauptmann* and wearer of the Oak Leaves.

Right: Pierre Clostermann in parade uniform in 1945 wearing all of the highest French, British and Soviet decorations.

272

Former enemies in the air become friends: Pierre Clostermann, Frat successful wartime pilot, and Hans-Ulrich Rudel, the world's most successful combat pilot, have been friends for many years. The photo is from 1968 when they attended the Richard Wagner festival together in Bayreuth, where "Siegfried" from "The Ring of the Nibelungen" was presented.

ON THE
STIMMERSEE
IN KUFSTEIN

**Above: Rudel's beautifully situated "refuge" in Kufstein, Tirol on the Stimmer See. As a "special" industrial representative for German export firms in South America, Rudel was often abroad for long periods. Vacations in the Tirol were rare.**

**274**

**Above right: The early riser need only look at the neighbouring 1,565 metre mountain — the Pendling — to find out what the weather is like.**

**The Stimmer See, a favourite vacation spot. In the summertime, any local out for a walk who found a wooden leg alone on the shore, knew that Rudel was once again swimming in the lake.**

A photograph from the year 1960.

Frau Ursula Rudel, Rudel's wife, in her parents' garden.

Medals, commemorative
plates and victory cups in
the living room . . .
Below left:

. . . in the workroom, the
hall closet and everywhere
space is available —
reminders of the one-
legged athlete's many
victories in sporting events.

Below right:
Three of the most beautiful
victory cups; from left:
Mayor Schaller's Trophy,
the Tirolean Disabled
Skiing Championship
Trophy 1969 and the
"Hotel Post" Prize won in
the Fernpass giant slalom
in 1970.

An oil painting by A. Grubl and the many models built by comrades, friends and young admirers of the famous "cannon bird", remind every visitor of the unique accomplishments of the most successful pilot in the history of warfare.

277

# BIBLIOGRAPHY

| | |
|---|---|
| Hans-Ulrich Rudel | »Trotzdem« |
| | »Von den Stukas zu den Anden« |
| Günther Just | »Hans-Ulrich Rudel – Adler der Ostfront« |
| | »Die ruhmreichen Vier – Mölders, Marseille, Nowotny und Rudel erzählen« |
| Peter C. Smith | »Stuka – Die Geschichte der Ju 87« |
| Pierre Clostermann | »Die große Arena – Erinnerungen eines französischen Jagdpiloten in der R.A.F.« |
| | »Brennender Himmel« |
| R. F. Toliver/T. J. Constable | »Das waren die deutschen Jagdflieger-Asse 1939–1945« |
| | »Immelmann – Der Adler von Lille« (verfaßt von seinem Bruder 1942) |
| Curt Strohmeyer | »Stukas! – Erlebnisse eines Fliegerkorps« |
| Cajus Bekker | »Angriffshöhe 4000 – Kriegstagebuch der deutschen Luftwaffe« |
| A. Galland/K. Ries/R. Ahnert | »Die deutsche Luftwaffe 1939–1945« |
| Ernst Obermaier | »Die Ritterkreuzträger der Luftwaffe 1939–1945 – Band I Jagdflieger« |
| Kenneth Munson | »Die Weltkrieg-II-Flugzeuge – Alle Flugzeuge der kriegführenden Mächte« |
| Rudolf Lusar | »Die deutschen Waffen und Geheimwaffen des 2. Weltkrieges und ihre Weiterentwicklung« |
| John Milsom | »Die russischen Panzer – Die Geschichte der sowjetischen Panzerwaffe 1900 bis heute« |
| Paul Carell | »Unternehmen Barbarossa« |
| Erich Kern | »Opfergang eines Volkes – Der totale Krieg« |
| | »Adolf Hitler und der Krieg« |
| | »Liddel Harts Geschichte des Zweiten Weltkrieges (Band I und II)« |
| | »Der Kessel von Tscherkassy – 5. SS-Panzer-Division ›Wiking‹«<br>(Ein Dokumenten- und Kartenwerk der Truppenkameradschaft 5. SS-Pz.-Div. »Wiking«) |
| Erich Murawski | »Die Eroberung Pommerns durch die Rote Armee« |
| Herausgeber Peter Young/<br>Deutsche Bearbeitung<br>Dr. Christian Zentner | »Der große Atlas zum II. Weltkrieg« |

»dtv-Atlas zur Weltgeschichte, Band 2, 9. Aufl. Okt. 1974«

»Jäger-Blatt für Angehörige von Jagdfliegereinheiten – Offizielles Organ ›Der Gemeinschaft der Jagdflieger e. V.‹« 2322 Lütjenburg, Postfach 72

»Mitteilungsblatt der Traditionsgemeinschaft Stuka-Geschwader Immelmann«

»Mitteilungsblatt Traditionsverband 121. Inf.-Div. (ostpreuß. ›Adler-Schild-Division‹)«

»Alte Kameraden – Unabhängige Zeitschrift deutscher Soldaten – Organ der Traditionsverbände und Kameradenwerke«

»Der Freiwillige«, Zeitschrift der HIAG, Osnabrück, Postfach 3023

»Der Adler«, Herausgegeben unter Mitwirkung des Reichsluftfahrtministeriums, (1941–44)

»Der Weg«, Heft 3/1954

Kizinna-Archiv, 24 Lübeck, Korvettenstraße 98

Pressefotograf Walter Becker, Siegen

Bibliothek für Zeitgeschichte, 7 Stuttgart

Bundesarchiv/Zentralnachweisstelle, 51 Aachen-Kornelimünster

Bundesarchiv/Militärarchiv, 78 Freiburg

Bundesarchiv/Bildarchiv, 54 Koblenz

Oberst a. D. Hans-Ulrich Rudel: Privat- und Geschwaderbilder, Gespräche mit dem Autor

Zeitgeschichtl. Archiv (Abt. Luftwaffe) des Verfassers

Flugblätter und Bilder von Angehörigen der »Traditionsgemeinschaft des Stuka-Geschwaders Immelmann«

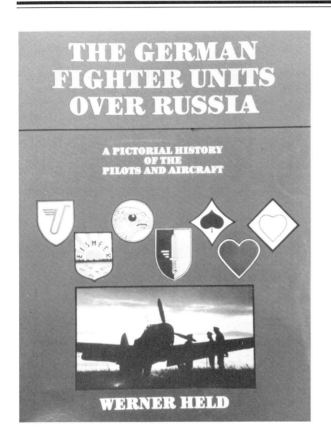
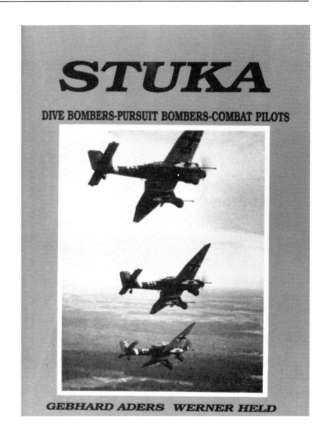

# THE HG PANZER DIVISION

by
## ALFRED OTTE

A
L
S
O

F
R
O
M

S
C
H
I
F
F
E
R

M
I
L
I
T
A
R
Y

H
I
S
T
O
R
Y

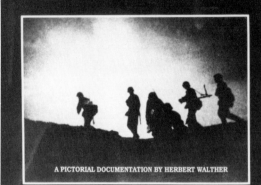

# THE WAFFEN-SS

A PICTORIAL DOCUMENTATION BY HERBERT WALTHER

# THE HEAVY FLAK GUNS

GERMAN
• 88mm • 105mm • 128mm • 150mm GUNS
AND BALLISTIC DIRECTIONAL EQUIPMENT

## 1933-1945

### Werner Müller

# PANZER

## A PICTORIAL DOCUMENTATION

### HORST SCHEIBERT

#### SCHIFFER MILITARY

## THE GERMAN NAVY AT WAR
### 1935-1945 VOLUME 1
# THE BATTLESHIPS

A HISTORY OF THE "BIG SHIPS"

•POCKET BATTLESHIPS•CRUISERS•
AIRCRAFT CARRIER "GRAF ZEPPELIN"

### SIEGFRIED BREYER    GERHARD KOOP

## THE GERMAN NAVY AT WAR
### 1935-1945 VOLUME 2
# THE U-BOAT

### SIEGFRIED BREYER    GERHARD KOOP

THE U-BOAT•LIGHT NAVAL WEAPONS•NAVAL INFANTRY DIVISIONS•NAVAL AVIATION•
HARBORS AND BASES•WARSHIP CONSTRUCTION YARDS•NAVAL CITATIONS•
UNIFORMS•INSIGNIAS OF RANK AND SERVICE FLAGS